MW00830507

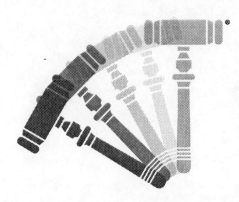

Casenote® *Legal Briefs*

BUSINESS
ORGANIZATIONS

Keyed to Courses Using

Hamilton, Macey, and Moll's
The Law of Business Organizations: Cases,
Materials, and Problems
Twelfth Edition

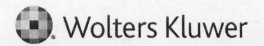

This publication is designed to provide accurate and authoritative information in regard to the subject matter covered. It is sold with the understanding that the publisher is not engaged in rendering legal, accounting, or other professional services. If legal advice or other expert assistance is required, the services of a competent professional person should be sought.

— From a Declaration of Principles adopted jointly by a Committee of the American Bar Association and a Committee of Publishers and Associates

Copyright © 2016 CCH Incorporated. All Rights Reserved.

Published by Wolters Kluwer in New York.

Wolters Kluwer Legal & Regulatory Solutions U.S. serves customers worldwide with CCH, Aspen Publishers, and Kluwer Law International products. (www.WKLegaledu.com)

No part of this publication may be reproduced or transmitted in any form or by any means, electronic or mechanical, including photocopy, recording, or utilized by any information storage and retrieval system, without written permission from the publisher. For information about permissions or to request permissions online, visit us at www.WKLegaledu.com or a written request may be faxed to our permissions department at 212-771-0803.

To contact Customer Service, e-mail customer.service@wolterskluwer.com, call 1-800-234-1660, fax 1-800-901-9075, or mail correspondence to:

Wolters Kluwer
Attn: Order Department
P.O. Box 990
Frederick, MD 21705

Printed in the United States of America.

1 2 3 4 5 6 7 8 9 0

ISBN 978-1-4548-7321-1

About Wolters Kluwer Legal & Regulatory Solutions U.S.

Wolters Kluwer Legal & Regulatory Solutions U.S. delivers expert content and solutions in the areas of law, corporate compliance, health compliance, reimbursement, and legal education. Its practical solutions help customers successfully navigate the demands of a changing environment to drive their daily activities, enhance decision quality and inspire confident outcomes.

Serving customers worldwide, its legal and regulatory solutions portfolio includes products under the Aspen Publishers, CCH Incorporated, Kluwer Law International, ftwilliam.com and MediRegs names. They are regarded as exceptional and trusted resources for general legal and practice-specific knowledge, compliance and risk management, dynamic workflow solutions, and expert commentary.

Format for the Casenote® Legal Brief

Nature of Case: This section identifies the form of action (e.g., breach of contract, negligence, battery), the type of proceeding (e.g., demurrer, appeal from trial court's jury instructions), or the relief sought (e.g., damages, injunction, criminal sanctions).

Fact Summary: This is included to refresh your memory and can be used as a quick reminder of the facts.

Rule of Law: Summarizes the general principle of law that the case illustrates. It may be used for instant recall of the court's holding and for classroom discussion or home review.

Facts: This section contains all relevant facts of the case, including the contentions of the parties and the lower court holdings. It is written in a logical order to give the student a clear understanding of the case. The plaintiff and defendant are identified by their proper names throughout and are always labeled with a (P) or (D).

Palsgraf v. Long Island R.R. Co.

Injured bystander (P) v. Railroad company (D)

N.Y. Ct. App., 248 N.Y. 339, 162 N.E. 99 (1928).

Party ID: Quick identification of the relationship between the parties.

NATURE OF CASE: Appeal from judgment affirming verdict for plaintiff seeking damages for personal injury.

FACT SUMMARY: Helen Palsgraf (P) was injured on R.R.'s (D) train platform when R.R.'s (D) guard helped a passenger aboard a moving train, causing his package to fall on the tracks. The package contained fireworks which exploded, creating a shock that tipped a scale onto Palsgraf (P).

🏛 RULE OF LAW
The risk reasonably to be perceived defines the duty to be obeyed.

FACTS: Helen Palsgraf (P) purchased a ticket to Rockaway Beach from R.R. (D) and was waiting on the train platform. As she waited, two men ran to catch a train that was pulling out from the platform. The first man jumped aboard, but the second man, who appeared as if he might fall, was helped aboard by the guard on the train who had kept the door open so they could jump aboard. A guard on the platform also helped by pushing him onto the train. The man was carrying a package wrapped in newspaper. In the process, the man dropped his package, which fell on the tracks. The package contained fireworks and exploded. The shock of the explosion was apparently of great enough strength to tip over some scales at the other end of the platform, which fell on Palsgraf (P) and injured her. A jury awarded her damages, and R.R. (D) appealed.

ISSUE: Does the risk reasonably to be perceived define the duty to be obeyed?

HOLDING AND DECISION: (Cardozo, C.J.) Yes. The risk reasonably to be perceived defines the duty to be obeyed. If there is no foreseeable hazard to the injured party as the result of a seemingly innocent act, the act does not become a tort because it happened to be a wrong as to another. If the wrong was not willful, the plaintiff must show that the act as to her had such great and apparent possibilities of danger as to entitle her to protection. Negligence in the abstract is not enough upon which to base liability. Negligence is a relative concept, evolving out of the common law doctrine of trespass on the case. To establish liability, the defendant must owe a legal duty of reasonable care to the injured party. A cause of action in tort will lie where harm,

though unintended, could have been averted or avoided by observance of such a duty. The scope of the duty is limited by the range of danger that a reasonable person could foresee. In this case, there was nothing to suggest from the appearance of the parcel or otherwise that the parcel contained fireworks. The guard could not reasonably have had any warning of a threat to Palsgraf (P), and R.R. (D) therefore cannot be held liable. Judgment is reversed in favor of R.R. (D).

DISSENT: (Andrews, J.) The concept that there is no negligence unless R.R. (D) owes a legal duty to take care as to Palsgraf (P) herself is too narrow. Everyone owes to the world at large the duty of refraining from those acts that may unreasonably threaten the safety of others. If the guard's action was negligent as to those nearby, it was also negligent as to those outside what might be termed the "danger zone." For Palsgraf (P) to recover, R.R.'s (D) negligence must have been the proximate cause of her injury, a question of fact for the jury.

Concurrence/Dissent: All concurrences and dissents are briefed whenever they are included by the casebook editor.

▶ ANALYSIS
The majority defined the limit of the defendant's liability in terms of the danger that a reasonable person in defendant's situation would have perceived. The dissent argued that the limitation should not be placed on liability, but rather on damages. Judge Andrews suggested that only injuries that would not have happened but for R.R.'s (D) negligence should be compensable. Both the majority and dissent recognized the policy-driven need to limit liability for negligent acts, seeking, in the words of Judge Andrews, to define a framework "that will be practical and in keeping with the general understanding of mankind." The Restatement (Second) of Torts has accepted Judge Cardozo's view.

Analysis: This last paragraph gives you a broad understanding of where the case "fits in" with other cases in the section of the book and with the entire course. It is a hornbook-style discussion indicating whether the case is a majority or minority opinion and comparing the principal case with other cases in the casebook. It may also provide analysis from restatements, uniform codes, and law review articles. The analysis will prove to be invaluable to classroom discussion.

Quicknotes
FORESEEABILITY A reasonable expectation that change is the probable result of certain acts or omissions.

NEGLIGENCE Conduct falling below the standard of care that a reasonable person would demonstrate under similar conditions.

PROXIMATE CAUSE The natural sequence of events without which an injury would not have been sustained.

Issue: The issue is a concise question that brings out the essence of the opinion as it relates to the section of the casebook in which the case appears. Both substantive and procedural issues are included if relevant to the decision.

Holding and Decision: This section offers a clear and in-depth discussion of the rule of the case and the court's rationale. It is written in easy-to-understand language and answers the issue presented by applying the law to the facts of the case. When relevant, it includes a thorough discussion of the exceptions to the case as listed by the court, any major cites to the other cases on point, and the names of the judges who wrote the decisions.

Quicknotes: Conveniently defines legal terms found in the case and summarizes the nature of any statutes, codes, or rules referred to in the text.

Wolters Kluwer Legal & Regulatory Solutions U.S. is proud to offer *Casenote® Legal Briefs*—continuing thirty years of publishing America's best-selling legal briefs.

Casenote® Legal Briefs are designed to help you save time when briefing assigned cases. Organized under convenient headings, they show you how to abstract the basic facts and holdings from the text of the actual opinions handed down by the courts. Used as part of a rigorous study regimen, they can help you spend more time analyzing and critiquing points of law than on copying bits and pieces of judicial opinions into your notebook or outline.

Casenote® Legal Briefs should never be used as a substitute for assigned casebook readings. They work best when read as a follow-up to reviewing the underlying opinions themselves. Students who try to avoid reading and digesting the judicial opinions in their casebooks or online sources will end up shortchanging themselves in the long run. The ability to absorb, critique, and restate the dynamic and complex elements of case law decisions is crucial to your success in law school and beyond. It cannot be developed vicariously.

Casenote® Legal Briefs represents but one of the many offerings in Legal Education's Study Aid Timeline, which includes:

- *Casenote® Legal Briefs*
- *Emanuel® Law Outlines*
- Emanuel® *Law in a Flash* Flash Cards
- Emanuel® *CrunchTime®* Series

Each of these series is designed to provide you with easy-to-understand explanations of complex points of law. Each volume offers guidance on the principles of legal analysis and, consulted regularly, will hone your ability to spot relevant issues. We have titles that will help you prepare for class, prepare for your exams, and enhance your general comprehension of the law along the way.

To find out more about our law school tools for success, visit us at *www.WKLegaledu.com* or email us at *legaledu@wolterskluwer.com*. We'll be happy to assist you.

A. Decide on a Format and Stick to It

Structure is essential to a good brief. It enables you to arrange systematically the related parts that are scattered throughout most cases, thus making manageable and understandable what might otherwise seem to be an endless and unfathomable sea of information. There are, of course, an unlimited number of formats that can be utilized. However, it is best to find one that suits your needs and stick to it. Consistency breeds both efficiency and the security that when called upon you will know where to look in your brief for the information you are asked to give.

Any format, as long as it presents the essential elements of a case in an organized fashion, can be used. Experience, however, has led *Casenote* ® *Legal Briefs* to develop and utilize the following format because of its logical flow and universal applicability.

NATURE OF CASE: This is a brief statement of the legal character and procedural status of the case (e.g., "Appeal of a burglary conviction").

There are many different alternatives open to a litigant dissatisfied with a court ruling. The key to determining which one has been used is to discover *who is asking this court for what.*

This first entry in the brief should be kept as *short as possible.* Use the court's terminology if you understand it. But since jurisdictions vary as to the titles of pleadings, the best entry is the one that addresses who wants what in this proceeding, not the one that sounds most like the court's language.

RULE OF LAW: A statement of the general principle of law that the case illustrates (e.g., "An acceptance that varies any term of the offer is considered a rejection and counteroffer").

Determining the rule of law of a case is a procedure similar to determining the issue of the case. Avoid being fooled by red herrings; there may be a few rules of law mentioned in the case excerpt, but usually only one is *the* rule with which the casebook editor is concerned. The techniques used to locate the issue, described below, may also be utilized to find the rule of law. Generally, your best guide is simply the chapter heading. It is a clue to the point the casebook editor seeks to make and should be kept in mind when reading every case in the respective section.

FACTS: A synopsis of only the essential facts of the case, i.e., those bearing upon or leading up to the issue.

The facts entry should be a short statement of the events and transactions that led one party to initiate legal proceedings against another in the first place. While some cases conveniently state the salient facts at the beginning of the decision, in other instances they will have to be culled from hiding places throughout the text, even from concurring and dissenting opinions. Some of the "facts" will often be in dispute and should be so noted. Conflicting evidence may be briefly pointed up. "Hard" facts must be included. Both must be *relevant* in order to be listed in the facts entry. It is impossible to tell what is relevant until the entire case is read, as the ultimate determination of the rights and liabilities of the parties may turn on something buried deep in the opinion.

Generally, the facts entry should not be longer than three to five *short* sentences.

It is often helpful to identify the role played by a party in a given context. For example, in a construction contract case the identification of a party as the "contractor" or "builder" alleviates the need to tell that that party was the one who was supposed to have built the house.

It is always helpful, and a good general practice, to identify the "plaintiff" and the "defendant." This may seem elementary and uncomplicated, but, especially in view of the creative editing practiced by some casebook editors, it is sometimes a difficult or even impossible task. Bear in mind that the *party presently* seeking something from this court may not be the plaintiff, and that sometimes only the cross-claim of a defendant is treated in the excerpt. Confusing or misaligning the parties can ruin your analysis and understanding of the case.

ISSUE: A statement of the general legal question answered by or illustrated in the case. For clarity, the issue is best put in the form of a question capable of a "yes" or "no" answer. In reality, the issue is simply the Rule of Law put in the form of a question (e.g., "May an offer be accepted by performance?").

The major problem presented in discerning what is *the* issue in the case is that an opinion usually purports to raise and answer several questions. However, except for rare cases, only one such question is really the issue in the case. Collateral issues not necessary to the resolution of the matter in controversy are handled by the court by language known as *"obiter dictum"* or merely *"dictum."* While dicta may be included later in the brief, they have no place under the issue heading.

To find the issue, ask *who wants what* and then go on to ask *why did that party succeed or fail in getting it.* Once this is determined, the "why" should be turned into a question.

The complexity of the issues in the cases will vary, but in all cases a single-sentence question should sum up the issue. *In a few cases,* there will be two, or even more rarely, three issues of equal importance to the resolution of the case. Each should be expressed in a single-sentence question.

Since many issues are resolved by a court in coming to a final disposition of a case, the casebook editor will reproduce the portion of the opinion containing the issue or issues most relevant to the area of law under scrutiny. A noted law professor gave this advice: "Close the book; look at the title on the cover." Chances are, if it is Property, you need not concern yourself with whether, for example, the federal government's treatment of the plaintiff's land really raises a federal question sufficient to support jurisdiction on this ground in federal court.

The same rule applies to chapter headings designating sub-areas within the subjects. They tip you off as to what the text is designed to teach. The cases are arranged in a casebook to show a progression or development of the law, so that the preceding cases may also help.

It is also most important to remember to *read the notes and questions* at the end of a case to determine what the editors wanted you to have gleaned from it.

HOLDING AND DECISION: This section should succinctly explain the rationale of the court in arriving at its decision. In capsulizing the "reasoning" of the court, it should always include an application of the general rule or rules of law to the specific facts of the case. Hidden justifications come to light in this entry: the reasons for the state of the law, the public policies, the biases and prejudices, those considerations that influence the justices' thinking and, ultimately, the outcome of the case. At the end, there should be a short indication of the disposition or procedural resolution of the case (e.g., "Decision of the trial court for Mr. Smith (P) reversed").

The foregoing format is designed to help you "digest" the reams of case material with which you will be faced in your law school career. Once mastered by practice, it will place at your fingertips the information the authors of your casebooks have sought to impart to you in case-by-case illustration and analysis.

B. Be as Economical as Possible in Briefing Cases

Once armed with a format that encourages succinctness, it is as important to be economical with regard to the time spent on the actual reading of the case as it is to be economical in the writing of the brief itself. This does not mean "skimming" a case. Rather, it means reading the case with an "eye" trained to recognize into which "section" of your brief a particular passage or line fits and having a system for quickly and precisely marking the case so that the passages fitting any one particular part of

the brief can be easily identified and brought together in a concise and accurate manner when the brief is actually written.

It is of no use to simply repeat everything in the opinion of the court; record only enough information to trigger your recollection of what the court said. Nevertheless, an accurate statement of the "law of the case," i.e., the legal principle applied to the facts, is absolutely essential to class preparation and to learning the law under the case method.

To that end, it is important to develop a "shorthand" that you can use to make marginal notations. These notations will tell you at a glance in which section of the brief you will be placing that particular passage or portion of the opinion.

Some students prefer to underline all the salient portions of the opinion (with a pencil or colored underliner marker), making marginal notations as they go along. Others prefer the color-coded method of underlining, utilizing different colors of markers to underline the salient portions of the case, each separate color being used to represent a different section of the brief. For example, blue underlining could be used for passages relating to the rule of law, yellow for those relating to the issue, and green for those relating to the holding and decision, etc. While it has its advocates, the color-coded method can be confusing and time-consuming (all that time spent on changing colored markers). Furthermore, it can interfere with the continuity and concentration many students deem essential to the reading of a case for maximum comprehension. In the end, however, it is a matter of personal preference and style. Just remember, whatever method you use, underlining must be used sparingly or its value is lost.

If you take the marginal notation route, an efficient and easy method is to go along underlining the key portions of the case and placing in the margin alongside them the following "markers" to indicate where a particular passage or line "belongs" in the brief you will write:

N   (NATURE OF CASE)
RL   (RULE OF LAW)
I   (ISSUE)
HL   (HOLDING AND DECISION, relates to the RULE OF LAW behind the decision)
HR   (HOLDING AND DECISION, gives the RATIONALE or reasoning behind the decision)
HA   (HOLDING AND DECISION, applies the general principle(s) of law to the facts of the case to arrive at the decision)

Remember that a particular passage may well contain information necessary to more than one part of your brief, in which case you simply note that in the margin. If you are using the color-coded underlining method instead of marginal notation, simply make asterisks or checks in the margin next to the passage in question in the colors that indicate the additional sections of the brief where it might be utilized.

The economy of utilizing "shorthand" in marking cases for briefing can be maintained in the actual brief writing process itself by utilizing "law student shorthand" within the brief. There are many commonly used words and phrases for which abbreviations can be substituted in your briefs (and in your class notes also). You can develop abbreviations that are personal to you and which will save you a lot of time. A reference list of briefing abbreviations can be found on page x of this book.

C. Use Both the Briefing Process and the Brief as a Learning Tool

Now that you have a format and the tools for briefing cases efficiently, the most important thing is to make the time spent in briefing profitable to you and to make the most advantageous use of the briefs you create. Of course, the briefs are invaluable for classroom reference when you are called upon to explain or analyze a particular case. However, they are also useful in reviewing for exams. A quick glance at the fact summary should bring the case to mind, and a rereading of the rule of law should enable you to go over the underlying legal concept in your mind, how it was applied in that particular case, and how it might apply in other factual settings.

As to the value to be derived from engaging in the briefing process itself, there is an immediate benefit that arises from being forced to sift through the essential facts and reasoning from the court's opinion and to succinctly express them in your own words in your brief. The process ensures that you understand the case and the point that it illustrates, and that means you will be ready to absorb further analysis and information brought forth in class. It also ensures you will have something to say when called upon in class. The briefing process helps develop a mental agility for getting to the *gist* of a case and for identifying, expounding on, and applying the legal concepts and issues found there. The briefing process is the mental process on which you must rely in taking law school examinations; it is also the mental process upon which a lawyer relies in serving his clients and in making his living.

Abbreviations for Briefs

acceptance	acp	offer	O
affirmed	aff	offeree	OE
answer	ans	offeror	OR
assumption of risk	a/r	ordinance	ord
attorney	atty	pain and suffering	p/s
beyond a reasonable doubt	b/r/d	parol evidence	p/e
bona fide purchaser	BFP	plaintiff	P
breach of contract	br/k	prima facie	p/f
cause of action	c/a	probable cause	p/c
common law	c/l	proximate cause	px/c
Constitution	Con	real property	r/p
constitutional	con	reasonable doubt	r/d
contract	K	reasonable man	r/m
contributory negligence	c/n	rebuttable presumption	rb/p
cross	x	remanded	rem
cross-complaint	x/c	res ipsa loquitur	RIL
cross-examination	x/ex	respondeat superior	r/s
cruel and unusual punishment	c/u/p	Restatement	RS
defendant	D	reversed	rev
dismissed	dis	Rule Against Perpetuities	RAP
double jeopardy	d/j	search and seizure	s/s
due process	d/p	search warrant	s/w
equal protection	e/p	self-defense	s/d
equity	eq	specific performance	s/p
evidence	ev	statute	S
exclude	exc	statute of frauds	S/F
exclusionary rule	exc/r	statute of limitations	S/L
felony	f/n	summary judgment	s/j
freedom of speech	f/s	tenancy at will	t/w
good faith	g/f	tenancy in common	t/c
habeas corpus	h/c	tenant	t
hearsay	hr	third party	TP
husband	H	third party beneficiary	TPB
injunction	inj	transferred intent	TI
in loco parentis	ILP	unconscionable	uncon
inter vivos	I/v	unconstitutional	unconst
joint tenancy	j/t	undue influence	u/e
judgment	judgt	Uniform Commercial Code	UCC
jurisdiction	jur	unilateral	uni
last clear chance	LCC	vendee	VE
long-arm statute	LAS	vendor	VR
majority view	maj	versus	v
meeting of minds	MOM	void for vagueness	VFV
minority view	min	weight of authority	w/a
Miranda rule	Mir/r	weight of the evidence	w/e
Miranda warnings	Mir/w	wife	W
negligence	neg	with	w/
notice	ntc	within	w/i
nuisance	nus	without	w/o
obligation	ob	without prejudice	w/o/p
obscene	obs	wrongful death	wr/d

Table of Cases

The General Partnership

Quick Reference Rules of Law

Martin v. Peyton

Creditor (P) v. Alleged partner (D)

N.Y. Ct. App., 158 N.E. 77 (1927).

NATURE OF CASE: Action to hold parties as partners in an existing firm.

FACT SUMMARY: Peyton (D) and others (D) loaned money to a partnership so that it could carry on its brokerage business.

🏛 RULE OF LAW
While words are not determinative, where a transaction bears all of the aspects of a loan, no partnership arrangement will be found.

FACTS: The partnership of Knauth (D), Nachod (D), and Kuhne (D) was in financial difficulty. Hall (D), one of the partners, arranged a loan from Peyton (D) and other friends (D). In exchange for the loan of $2,500,000 in liquid securities, Peyton (D) and the others (D) were to receive a percentage of the profits until the loan was repaid. The relevant loan provisions and conditions were: Peyton (D) was to have a veto over speculative investments; an insurance policy was to be taken out on Hall's (D) life; the securities could be pledged as a loan; and Peyton (D) and the others (D) were to receive dividends from the securities. Peyton (D) could not bind the partnership, nor could he initiate any action on his own. The agreement specifically stated that it was a loan and not a partnership arrangement. It stated that no liability was to accrue to Peyton (D) and the others (D) for partnership debts. Martin (P), a creditor of the partnership, brought suit against it plus Peyton (D) and the others (D). Martin (P) alleged that a partnership interest had been formed by the agreement. The court found for Peyton (D).

ISSUE: Where the only control exerted or sharing of profits occurs to protect and pay off a loan, will a partnership arrangement be found?

HOLDING AND DECISION: (Andrews, J.) No. Words alone are not determinative of a relationship. Merely declaring that no partnership is intended will not be dispositive of the issue. If the words, acts, and agreements establish the existence of a partnership arrangement, the parties will be liable as partners. Nothing in Peyton's (D) words or actions establishes a partnership. Therefore, we must look to the contract alone. Nothing in it is other than what were necessary precautions to protect the loan. Any control was negative in nature and was to prevent any misuse of the funds. Peyton (D) had no right to control or initiate policy or to bind the contract. This was a loan, and Peyton (D) and the others (D) are not liable. Judgment affirmed.

► ANALYSIS

A partnership results from either express or implied contracts. An arrangement for the sharing of profits is often an important factor in determining the existence of a partnership. Of equal importance is the right to share in the decision-making function of the partnership and/or to bind the partnership to contractual obligations.

■■■

Quicknotes

EXPRESS CONTRACT A contract the terms of which are specifically stated; may be oral or written.

IMPLIED CONTRACT An agreement between parties that may be inferred from their general course of conduct.

PARTNERSHIP A voluntary agreement entered into by two or more parties to engage in business and to share any attendant profits and losses.

UNIFORM PARTNERSHIP ACT, § 6 A contract that creates an association of two or more persons to carry on a business for profit as co-owners creates a partnership.

■■■

Smith v. Kelley

Alleged partner (P) v. Partnership (D)

Ky. Ct. App., 465 S.W.2d 39 (1971).

NATURE OF CASE: Suit seeking an accounting.

FACT SUMMARY: Kelley (D) and Galloway (D), partners in an accounting firm, hired Smith (P). Smith (P) later claimed to be a partner in the firm, with a right to share in its profits.

🏛 RULE OF LAW
Unless the rights of third parties are involved, a partnership cannot exist in the absence of an intention to create it.

FACTS: Kelley (D) and Galloway (D) were partners in an accounting firm for which Smith (P) went to work as a salaried employee. Smith (P) contributed no assets to the firm, had no authority to hire or fire personnel or to make purchases, had no managerial authority, executed no promissory notes on behalf of the firm, and was not obligated to bear any losses of the firm. Kelley (D), Galloway (D), and another employee all concurred in the fact that there had never been any agreement that Smith (P) would be a partner or would share in the firm's profits. However, Smith (P) was held out to members of the public as a partner and was designated as a partner on the firm's tax returns and a statement filed with a state agency. Smith (P) was also listed as a partner in connection with a contract entered into by the firm and in connection with a lawsuit the firm filed. Thus, after resigning from three-year tenure with the firm, Smith (P) claimed to have been a partner and argued that he was entitled to 20 percent of the firm's profits. When Kelley (D) and Galloway (D) disputed his right to share in the firm's profits, Smith (P) sued for an accounting. The Chancellor concluded that no partnership had existed and therefore dismissed the action. Smith (P) appealed.

ISSUE: Unless the rights of third parties are involved, may the existence of a partnership arrangement be established despite proof that there was never any intention to create one?

HOLDING AND DECISION: (Clay, Commr.) No. Unless the rights of third parties are involved, a partnership cannot exist in the absence of an intention to create it. A partnership is a contractual relationship, and the Chancellor, after evaluating the testimony of all the witnesses, found that there was never any agreement that Smith (P) would be a party or would share in the firm's profits. In an action by an outsider, the parties' conduct might estop them from denying that Smith (P) was a partner in the firm. But, for purposes of an action for an accounting, actual intent that a party be accorded the status of a partner must be established. Since the evidence presented justified the conclusion that Smith (P) was not intended to enjoy the status of a partner, the Chancellor properly dismissed his action. Affirmed.

▌ ANALYSIS

The rule announced by the *Smith v. Kelley* court is not applied uncompromisingly. In fact, certain factors are frequently deemed sufficient to establish a partnership even where no such arrangement was intended. For example, an agreement to share profits was, at common law, often considered sufficient to prove a partnership. Under the Uniform Partnership Act, such an agreement is deemed prima facie evidence of the existence of a partnership arrangement. Of course, as was acknowledged by the *Smith v. Kelley* court, third parties may find it easier to establish a partnership than might a would-be partner.

■══■

Quicknotes

CONTRACT An agreement pursuant to which a party agrees to act, or to forbear from acting, in exchange for performance on the part of the other party.

PARTNERSHIP A voluntary agreement entered into by two or more parties to engage in business and to share any attendant profits and losses.

PRIMA FACIE EVIDENCE Evidence presented by a party that is sufficient, in the absence of contradictory evidence, to support the fact or issue for which it is offered.

■══■

Summers v. Dooley

Partner (P) v. Partner (D)

Idaho Sup. Ct., 481 P.2d 318 (1971).

NATURE OF CASE: Claim for reimbursement of partnership funds.

FACT SUMMARY: In Summers's (P) suit against his partner Dooley (D) for reimbursement of his expenditure of $11,000 for the purpose of hiring an employee, Dooley (D) contended that because he did not approve of hiring the additional employee, the majority of partners did not consent to his hiring, and that Summers (P) should not be reimbursed for his unilateral hiring decision.

🏛 RULE OF LAW
Business differences in a partnership must be decided by a majority of the partners provided no other agreement between the partners speaks to the issues.

FACTS: Summers (P) and Dooley (D) entered into a partnership for the purpose of operating a trash collection business. The business was operated by the two men and when either of them was unable to work, the non-working partner provided a replacement at his own expense. Dooley (D) became unable to work, and Summers (P), at his own expense, hired an employee to take Dooley's (D) place. Four years later, Summers (P) approached Dooley (D) regarding the hiring of an additional employee, but Dooley (D) refused. Summers (P), on his own, then hired another person and paid him out of his own pocket. Dooley (D) objected and refused to pay for the new person out of partnership funds. Summers (P) kept the man employed, but filed an action against Dooley (D) for reimbursement of Summers's (P) expenditures of $11,000 in hiring the extra employee. Dooley (D) argued that the majority of partners had not approved of the hiring, and that Summers (P) should not be reimbursed for his unilateral hiring decision. The trial court denied Summers (P) relief, and he appealed.

ISSUE: Must business differences in a partnership be decided by a majority of the partners provided no other agreement between the partners speaks to the issues?

HOLDING AND DECISION: (Donaldson, J.) Yes. Business differences in a partnership must be decided by a majority of the partners provided no other agreement between the partners speaks to the issues. Here, the record shows that although Summers (P) requested Dooley's (D) acquiescence in the hiring of the extra employee, such requests were not honored. In fact, Dooley (D) made it clear that he was "voting no" with regard to the hiring of an additional employee. An application of Idaho law to the factual situation presented here indicates that the trial court was correct in its disposal of the issue since a majority of the partners did not consent to the hiring of the extra man. Dooley (D) continually voiced objection to the hiring. He did not sit idly by and acquiesce to Summers's (P) actions. Thus, it would be unfair to permit Summers (P) to recover for an expense that was incurred individually, not for the benefit of the partnership, but rather for the benefit of one partner. Affirmed.

▶ ANALYSIS

The rule that any difference arising as to ordinary matters connected with the partnership business may be decided by a majority of the partners is subject to any agreement between them. Partnership agreements often contain provisions vesting management in a managing partner or management committee. The same result, however, may be reached without explicit agreement on the basis of course of conduct.

■■■

National Biscuit Company v. Stroud

Bread supplier (P) v. Copartner (D)

N.C. Sup. Ct., 106 S.E.2d 692 (1959).

NATURE OF CASE: Suit to recover for goods sold.

FACT SUMMARY: Stroud (D) advised National Biscuit Company (National) (P) that he would not be responsible for any bread the company (P) sold to his partner. Nevertheless, National (P) continued to make deliveries.

🏛 RULE OF LAW
The acts of a partner, if performed on behalf of the partnership and within the scope of its business, are binding upon all copartners.

FACTS: Stroud (D) and Freeman entered into a general partnership to sell groceries under the name of Stroud's Food Center. Both partners apparently had an equal right to manage the business. The partnership periodically ordered bread from National Biscuit Company (National) (P). Eventually, however, Stroud (D) notified National (P) that he would not be responsible for any additional bread the company (D) sold to Stroud's Food Center. Nevertheless, National (P) sent, at Freeman's request, additional bread of a total value of $171.04. On the day of the last delivery, Stroud (D) and Freeman dissolved their partnership. Most of the firm's assets were assigned to Stroud (D), who agreed to liquidate the assets of the partnership and to discharge its liabilities. National (P) eventually sued Stroud (D) to recover the value of the bread which had been delivered but never paid for. Stroud (D) denied liability for the price of the bread, contending that his notice to the company (P) that he would not be responsible for further deliveries had relieved him of any obligation to pay for the bread. The trial court rendered judgment in favor of National (P), and Stroud (D) appealed.

ISSUE: May a partner escape liability for debts incurred by a copartner merely by advising the creditor, in advance, that he will not be responsible for those debts?

HOLDING AND DECISION: (Parker, J.) No. The acts of a partner, if performed on behalf of the partnership and within the scope of its business, are binding upon all copartners. According to the appropriate provisions of the Uniform Partnership Act, all partners are jointly and severally liable for all obligations incurred on behalf of the partnership. If a majority of the partners disapprove of a transaction before it is entered into, then they may escape liability for whatever obligations that transaction ultimately incurs. But Freeman and Stroud (D) were equal partners, with neither possessing the power to exercise a majority veto over the acts of the other. Freeman's acts were entered into on behalf of the partnership, were within the scope of its ordinary business, and probably conferred a benefit upon both Freeman and Stroud (D) as partners. Under these circumstances, it is proper to hold Stroud (D) liable for the price of the bread delivered by National (P) even after Stroud's (D) notice that he would not be held responsible for additional shipments. Affirmed.

▶ ANALYSIS

The rule adopted by the Uniform Partnership Act is consistent with traditional principles of agency law. In the absence of a contrary provision in the parties' partnership agreement, each partner acts as the agent of the partnership and of each other partner. Of course, only acts that are performed on behalf of the partnership and are consistent with its purposes are binding on other partners. However, even an act that was outside the scope of a partner's duties may bind his copartners if they ratify it.

■=■

Quicknotes

GENERAL PARTNERSHIP A voluntary agreement entered into by two or more parties to engage in business whereby each of the parties is to share in any profits and losses therefrom equally and each is to participate equally in the management of the enterprise.

PARTNERSHIP A voluntary agreement entered into by two or more parties to engage in business and to share any attendant profits and losses.

UNIFORM PARTNERSHIP ACT, § 15 All partners are jointly and severally liable for the acts and obligations of the partnership.

■=■

Kessler v. Antinora

Partner (P) v. Partner (D)

N.J. Super. Ct., App. Div., 653 A.2d 579 (1995).

NATURE OF CASE: Appeal from summary judgment for plaintiff in action for recovery of partnership losses.

FACT SUMMARY: Antinora (D), who contributed labor to a joint venture with Kessler (P), who contributed capital, contended that he was not liable to Kessler (P) for partnership losses where the partnership agreement did not address how losses would be apportioned among the partners.

🏛 RULE OF LAW
Where a joint venture partnership agreement is silent as to how losses will be apportioned among two partners, one who contributes capital and the other who contributes labor, neither partner is liable to the other for any loss sustained by the joint venture.

FACTS: Kessler (P) and Antinora (D) executed a seven-page agreement called "Joint Venture Partnership Agreement" for the building of a residence whereby Antinora (D) would serve as the general contractor and Kessler (P) would provide the capital. The agreement provided that upon sale of the dwelling Antinora (D) would receive 40 percent of the net profits and Kessler (P) would receive 60 percent. The agreement, however, was silent about losses. After three years, the building was built and sold, but at a loss. Kessler (P), who was repaid all but around $79,000 of the money he advanced brought suit to recover 40 percent of that amount plus claimed interest of around $85,000, from Antinora (D). No amount was presented on the value of Antinora's (D) services over the three-year period as general contractor. The trial court granted Kessler (P) summary judgment, finding that statutory partnership law governed, and awarded him close to $66,000. The state's intermediate appellate court granted review.

ISSUE: Where a joint venture partnership agreement is silent as to how losses will be apportioned among two partners, one who contributes capital and the other who contributes labor, is neither partner liable to the other for any loss sustained by the joint venture?

HOLDING AND DECISION: (King, J.) Yes. Where a joint venture partnership agreement is silent as to how losses will be apportioned among two partners, one who contributes capital and the other who contributes labor, neither partner is liable to the other for any loss sustained by the joint venture. Here, the trial court incorrectly rejected Antinora's (D) theory that the parties risked and lost their unrecovered contributions, whether in the form of money or labor. Contrary to the trial court's holding, the states applicable section of the Uniform Partnership Law does not control here because the parties had a specific agreement, which was silent on losses, and which indicated only that Kessler (P) would be repaid his investment from the sale of the house only, not by Antinora (D). The statute makes clear that it is subject to any agreement between the partners, and here the agreement did not suggest that any of Kessler's (P) risked and lost money would be repaid in part by Antinora (D) or that Antinora's (D) risked labor would be repaid in part by Kessler (P). Such an interpretation of the agreement is consistent with common law cases, which have held that where one party contributes money and the other labor, neither party is liable to the other for contribution of any loss sustained. Upon loss of both some money and labor, the loss falls upon each partner proportionately without any legal recourse. Here, Kessler's (P) loss was in determinative dollars while Antinora's (D) loss was in labor, which is difficult, if not impossible, to quantify. Any attempt by the court to reconstruct the parties' intent as to losses would be speculative. Reversed.

▶ ANALYSIS

The general common law rule of partnership law is that in the absence of an agreement, "the law presumes that partners and joint adventurers intended to participate equally in the profits and losses of the common enterprise, irrespective of any inequality in the amounts each contributed to the capital employed in the venture, with the losses being shared by them in the same proportions as they share the profits." However, some courts have held that this general rule is inapplicable, as here, where one of the partners contributes money and the other contributes labor, reasoning that each party has in essence agreed to lose his own capital—one in the form of money, the other in labor—or that the parties have implicitly agreed that their respective contributions are to be valued equally.

■■■

Quicknotes

JOINT VENTURE Venture undertaken based on an express or implied agreement among the members, with a common purpose and interest, and an equal power of control.

PARTNERSHIP A voluntary agreement entered into by two or more parties to engage in business and to share any attendant profits and losses.

■■■

Roach v. Mead

Lender (P) v. Borrower (D)

Or. Sup. Ct., 722 P.2d 1229 (1986).

NATURE OF CASE: Appeal from judgment imposing vicarious liability.

FACT SUMMARY: Berentson (D) contended he was not vicariously liable for the negligent acts of his partner, Mead (D), because such acts were outside the scope of the partnership's business.

🏛 RULE OF LAW
Each partner is responsible to third parties for the acts of the other partner when such could reasonably have been thought by the third party to fall within the purpose of the partnership.

FACTS: Mead (D) had acted as Roach's (P) attorney on several traffic violations and tax matters. Subsequently, Mead (D) became law partners with Berentson (D). Roach (P) consulted with Mead (D) concerning the investment of $20,000. Mead (D) borrowed the money from Roach (P) at a stated interest rate. Mead (D) was unable to repay the loan, and Roach (P) sued, contending the partnership owed him the money based upon a vicarious liability theory. Berentson (D) contended that such a loan was outside the scope of the partnership and, therefore, he could not be found vicariously liable. The trial court found that Roach (P) acted reasonably in believing that he was receiving legal advice from Mead (D) with regard to the investment of the money and, therefore, found Berentson (D) vicariously liable. Berentson (D) appealed, and the court of appeals affirmed. Berentson (D) then appealed to the Supreme Court of Oregon.

ISSUE: Is one partner responsible to third parties for the acts of the other partner where that third party reasonably believes that those acts were within the partnership business?

HOLDING AND DECISION: (Jones, J.) Yes. Each partner is responsible to third parties for the acts of the other partner when such could reasonably have been thought by the third party to fall within the purpose of the partnership. The liability of partners for each other is based upon the principal-agency relationship between them. The reasonable belief of a third party when dealing with a partnership that such acts fall within the purpose of the partnership must be respected. Thus, where one partner acts negligently within the scope of his partnership business, all partners are responsible for the damages resulting from those negligent acts. When a lawyer borrows money from a client, this falls within the reasonable expectations of the client, arising out of the attorney/client relationship that such acts are within the scope of the law partnership.

As a result, Berentson (D) was vicariously liable for his partner's acts. Affirmed.

▶ ANALYSIS

This case rests upon the factual determination as to whether or not particular acts fall within the business purpose of a partnership. Each case should be determined on its individual merits, and each factual situation may change the result. The court found as a matter of fact that Roach (P) acted reasonably in believing that Mead (D) was acting as his attorney when he borrowed the money. Because the stated purpose of the partnership was a law partnership, when Mead (P) acted as an attorney, Berentson (D) was fully responsible for such actions.

Quicknotes

JOINT AND SEVERAL LIABILITY Liability amongst tortfeasors allowing the injured party to bring suit against any of the defendants, individually or collectively, and to recover from each up to the total amount of damages awarded.

VICARIOUS LIABILITY The imputed liability of one party for the unlawful acts of another.

Meinhard v. Salmon

Joint adventurer (P) v. Coadventurer (D)

N.Y. Ct. App., 164 N.E. 545 (1928).

NATURE OF CASE: Award of an interest in a lease.

FACT SUMMARY: Meinhard (P) and Salmon (D) were coadventurers in a lease on a hotel, but prior to the expiration of that lease, Salmon (D) alone, without Meinhard's (P) knowledge, agreed to lease the same and adjacent property.

🏛 **RULE OF LAW**
Joint adventurers owe to one another, while their enterprise continues, the duty of finest loyalty, a standard of behavior most sensitive.

FACTS: Salmon (D) leased from Gerry a New York hotel on Fifth Avenue for a period of 20 years. Later, Salmon (D) entered into a joint venture with Meinhard (P) who contributed money while Salmon (D) was to manage the enterprise. Near the end of the lease, Gerry, who owned adjacent property as well as the hotel, desired to raze those buildings and construct one large building. Gerry, unable to find a new lessee to carry out his intentions, approached Salmon (D) with the idea when there was less than four months to run on his and Meinhard's (D) lease. The result was a 20-year lease to Midpoint Realty Company, wholly owned and controlled by Salmon (D). Meinhard (P) was never informed of the planned project or the negotiations for a new lease. After he learned of it, he made the demand on Salmon (D) that the lease be held in trust as an asset of the venture, which was refused. This suit followed with an award to Meinhard (P) of a 25 percent interest in the lease, one-half of his value in the hotel lease proportionate to the new lease, while on appeal it was increased to 50 percent. Salmon (D) appealed, arguing that he breached no duty to Meinhard (P).

ISSUE: Do joint adventurers owe to one another while their enterprise continues the duty of finest loyalty?

HOLDING AND DECISION: (Cardozo, C.J.) Yes. Joint adventurers owe to one another while their enterprise continues the duty of finest loyalty, a standard of behavior most sensitive. Many forms of conduct permissible in a workday world for those acting at arm's length are forbidden to those bound by fiduciary ties. Here, Salmon (D) excluded his co-adventurer from any chance to compete, from any chance to enjoy the opportunity for benefit that had come to him alone by virtue of his agency. It was likely that Salmon (D) thought that with the approaching end of the lease he owed no duty to Meinhard (P), but, here, the subject matter of the new lease was an extension and enlargement of the subject matter of the old

one. As for Meinhard's (P) remedy, he should have been awarded one share less than half of the shares in Midpoint Realty Company. Reversed and new trial ordered.

DISSENT: (Andrews, J.) The adventure by its express terms ended. The contract by its language and by its whole import excluded the idea that the tenant's expectancy was to subsist for the benefit of Meinhard (P).

▶ *ANALYSIS*

One of the most important aspects of the partnership relation is the broad fiduciary duty between partners. "The unique feature is their symmetry; each partner is, roughly speaking, both a principal and an agent, both a trustee and a beneficiary, for he has the property, authority and confidence of his copartners, as they do of him. He shares their profits and losses, and is bound by their actions. Without this protection of fiduciary duties, each is at the others' mercy." Judson A. Crane and Alan R. Bromberg, *Law of Partnership*, § 68, at 389 (1968).

▮═▮

Quicknotes

FIDUCIARY DUTY A legal obligation to act for the benefit of another, including subordinating one's personal interests to that of the other person.

GENERAL PARTNERSHIP A voluntary agreement entered into by two or more parties to engage in business whereby each of the parties is to share in any profits and losses therefrom equally and each is to participate equally in the management of the enterprise.

JOINT ADVENTURER An individual who combines his knowledge, skill, money and property with that of others for the purpose of forming a single business entity.

▮═▮

Enea v. Superior Court

Partner (P) v. Court (D)

Cal. Ct. App., 34 Cal. Rptr. 3d 513 (2005).

NATURE OF CASE: Petition to set aside summary judgment for defendants in action for breach of fiduciary duties.

FACT SUMMARY: Enea (P) claimed that his former partners, the Daniels (D), breached their fiduciary duty of loyalty to the partnership, the purpose of which was to hold and rent real estate, by renting partnership property to themselves at less than fair market value, notwithstanding that the partnership agreement did not expressly prohibit such conduct or require that rentals be made at fair market value.

🏛 RULE OF LAW
Partners breach their fiduciary duty by engaging in deliberate conduct that has the effect of reducing partnership profits, even though such conduct is not expressly prohibited by the partnership agreement.

FACTS: Enea (P) was a partner with the Daniels (D) in a partnership, the sole asset of which was a building in which offices were rented out. The Daniels (D) rented out office space to themselves at less than fair market value, and Enea (P) brought suit for breach of fiduciary duty based on this conduct. The Daniels (D) defended by arguing that the partnership agreement did not require that rentals be made at fair market value and that there was no agreement among the partners to maximize rental profits. Agreeing with the Daniels (D), on the basis of a statute that provides that a partner does not breach any duty merely because the partner's conduct furthers the partner's own interests, the trial court granted them summary judgment. The state's intermediate appellate court granted review.

ISSUE: Do partners breach their fiduciary duty by engaging in deliberate conduct that has the effect of reducing partnership profits, even though such conduct is not expressly prohibited by the partnership agreement?

HOLDING AND DECISION: (Rushing, J.) Yes. Partners breach their fiduciary duty by engaging in deliberate conduct that has the effect of reducing partnership profits, even though such conduct is not expressly prohibited by the partnership agreement. Partners owe each other the duty to carry out the enterprise with the highest good faith toward one another, and are the others' fiduciaries. Partners may not engage in self-dealing at the partnership's expense, but here that is exactly what the Daniels (D) did; they occupied partnership property at below-market rates, thereby causing the partnership to lose the additional rent

it could have obtained from a tenant willing to pay market-rate rent. This duty is not negated by state statute that provides that a partner does not breach any duty merely because the partner's conduct furthers the partner's own interests, since the intent of that provision is to excuse partners from accounting for incidental benefits obtained in the course of partnership activities without detriment to the partnership. Here, the Daniels' (D) conduct did not "merely" benefit them, but it benefited them at the expense of the partnership. They were not entitled in effect to convert partnership assets to their own and appropriate the value the partnership would otherwise have realized as distributable profits. Moreover, the trial court erroneously ruled that the Daniels (D) had not duty to collect market rents in the absence of a contract expressly requiring them to do so. That ruling turns partnership law on its head, since the law has never been that partners owe each other only those duties they explicitly assume by contract. On the contrary, partners' fiduciary duties are imposed by law, and their breach sounds in tort. Finally, the Daniels (D) argued—and the trial court found—that they were entitled to occupy the property at less than fair market value because the primary purpose of the partnership was to hold the building for appreciation and eventual sale. Even if that were true, the mere anticipation of eventual capital gains that might flow to the partnership in no way entitles individual partners to divert for themselves benefits that would otherwise flow to the partnership. In any event, such a premise does not justify summary adjudication. A peremptory writ of mandate shall issue directing respondent court to vacate its order granting defendants' motion for summary adjudication. Reversed and remanded.

▶ ANALYSIS

The statute at issue in this decision was modeled on section 404 of the Uniform Partnership Act (1997), also known as the Revised Uniform Partnership Act or RUPA, which contains an explicitly exclusive enumeration of a partner's duties. After noting that a partner owes fiduciary duties of loyalty and care, the uniform Act declares that those duties are "limited to" obligations listed there. RUPA § 404(b), (c). The court in this case, however, rejected the Daniels' (D) argument that the statute provided the exclusive statement of a partner's obligation to the partnership and to other partners, finding that in adopting the RUPA, the legislature left the articulation of the duty of loyalty to traditional common law processes and did not want the

Continued on next page.

duties of loyalty and care to be the exclusive fiduciary duties of partners. The court further found that even if the statutory enumeration of duties were exclusive, it would not entitle the Daniels (D) to rent partnership property to themselves at below-market rates, since the first duty listed in the statute is "[t]o account to the partnership and hold as trustee for it any property, profit, or benefit derived by the partner in the conduct . . . of the partnership business or derived from a use by the partner of partnership property . . . ."

■▬■

Quicknotes

BREACH OF FIDUCIARY DUTY The failure of a fiduciary to observe the standard of care exercised by professionals of similar education and experience.

PARTNERSHIP A voluntary agreement entered into by two or more parties to engage in business and to share any attendant profits and losses.

■▬■

Bane v. Ferguson

Retired law partner (P) v. Law firm (D)

890 F.2d 11 (7th Cir. 1989).

NATURE OF CASE: Appeal from dismissal of law partner's negligence and breach of contract claims.

FACT SUMMARY: Bane (P) claimed that Ferguson (D) and other firm managers (D) negligently breached fiduciary duties when they terminated his retirement benefits.

🏛 RULE OF LAW
If the dissolution of a corporation is motivated by good faith judgment for the benefit of the corporation, rather than the personal gain of the officers, no liability attaches to the dissolution.

FACTS: Bane (P) retired from a law firm in which he had been a partner and began receiving a pension pursuant to a noncontributory company retirement plan. The plan instrument provided that the plan, and the payments made under it, would end when and if the firm dissolved without a successor entity. Several months later, the firm merged with another large and successful Chicago firm. The merger proved to be a disaster, and the merged firm was dissolved without a successor, leading to the cessation of Bane's (P) retirement benefits. Bane (P) filed suit, alleging Ferguson (D) and the other member of the firm's managing council acted unreasonably in deciding to merge, in making certain purchases, and in leaving the firm shortly before its dissolution. Bane (P) alleged negligent mismanagement, not deliberate wrongdoing. The district court dismissed and Bane (P) appealed.

ISSUE: If the dissolution of a corporation is motivated by good faith judgment for the benefit of the corporation, rather than the personal gain of the officers, may liability attach to the dissolution?

HOLDING AND DECISION: (Posner, J.) No. If the dissolution of a corporation is motivated by good faith judgment for the benefit of the corporation, rather than the personal gain of the officers, no liability attaches to the dissolution. Here the competence, not the good faith of Ferguson (D), was complained of. Ferguson (D) owed no fiduciary duty to Bane (P) since he was no longer an active partner. Even if a fiduciary duty had existed, however, the business judgment rule would protect Ferguson (D). Affirmed.

▶ ANALYSIS

The court discussed Bane's (P) four different theories of liability. The Uniform Partnership Act did not apply since its purposes were to protect active partners. No fiduciary duty was found to exist. There was no breach of contract and no tort liability, either.

■=■

Quicknotes

BUSINESS JUDGMENT RULE Doctrine relieving corporate directors and/or officers from liability for decisions honestly and rationally made in the corporation's best interests.

CONTRACT An agreement pursuant to which a party agrees to act, or to forbear from acting, in exchange for performance on the part of the other party.

FIDUCIARY DUTY A legal obligation to act for the benefit of another, including subordinating one's personal interests to that of the other person.

PARTNERSHIP A voluntary agreement entered into by two or more parties to engage in business and to share any attendant profits and losses.

UNIFORM PARTNERSHIP ACT, § 20 Partners have an obligation to provide true and full information of all things affecting the partnership to any partner.

■=■

Singer v. Singer

Partner (P) v. Partner (D)

Okla. Ct. App., 634 P.2d 766 (1981).

NATURE OF CASE: Appeal from judgment imposing a constructive trust on property.

FACT SUMMARY: Stanley Singer (D) and Andrea Singer (D), who were partners in Josaline Production Co. (Josaline) (P), contended that a provision in Josaline's (P) partnership agreement and other partnership contracts that permitted each partner to enter into business transactions that were in competition with the partnership's interests, permitted them to take advantage of a business opportunity that Josaline (P) had failed to take for itself.

🏛 RULE OF LAW
A partnership may contract away its right to expect a noncompetitive fiduciary relationship with its partners.

FACTS: The partnership agreement of Josaline Production Co. (Josaline) (P), a family partnership, as well as other partnership contracts, provided that "Each partner shall be free to enter into business and other transactions for his or her own separate individual account, even though such business or other transaction may be in conflict with and/or competition with the business of this partnership. Neither the partnership nor any individual member of this partnership shall be entitled to claim or receive any part of or interest in such transactions, it being the intention and agreement that any partner will be free to deal on his or her own account to the same extent and with the same force and effect as if he or she were not and never had been members of this partnership." At a partnership meeting, several investment opportunities were raised, including the purchase of land that had minerals on it, but the decision of whether to purchase the land was deferred. After the meeting, siblings Stanley Singer (D) and Andrea Singer (D) formed Gemini Realty Co. (Gemini), and through Gemini purchased the land without any consultation with any of the Josaline (P) partners. Joe Singer (P), who had initially learned of the opportunity and had asked Stanley (D) to look into it, demanded to be permitted to purchase 50 percent of the property. When his demand was rebuffed he and Josaline (P) brought suit against Stanley (D) and Andrea (D), claiming that they had breached their fiduciary duties to the partnership and that Josaline (P) was entitled to participate in the investment. The trial court ruled for Josaline (P) and ordered that the property be held in constructive trust for Josaline (P). The state's intermediate appellate court granted review.

ISSUE: May a partnership contract away its right to expect a noncompetitive fiduciary relationship with its partners?

HOLDING AND DECISION: (Boydston, J.) Yes. A partnership may contract away its right to expect a noncompetitive fiduciary relationship with its partners. If it were not for the provision in the partnership agreement and other partnership contracts that permitted partners to compete with each other and the partnership, Josaline (P) would be correct in asserting that by reason of the fiduciary aspects of partnership it would be entitled to participate in Stanley (D) and Andrea's (D) investment. However, the partnership clearly and unambiguously contracted away its right to expect a noncompetitive fiduciary relationship with its partners. Therefore, Stanley (D) and Andrea (D) had a contractual right to compete with Josaline (P) and its other partners "as if there had never been a partnership." Merely because Josaline (P) had expressed interest in the property did not preclude intra-partnership competition. However, once Josaline (P) has acquired an asset or investment opportunity, the partners may not compete with the partnership for that partnership asset or investment. Reversed and remanded.

► ANALYSIS

As this case demonstrates, partners—and, similarly, members of limited liability companies—may contract away many of the fiduciary obligations imposed by law. However, some states limit the types of fiduciary duties that may be limited or omitted. For example, Delaware provides that a partnership agreement may not limit or eliminate liability for any act or omission that constitutes a bad faith violation of the implied contractual covenant of good faith and fair dealing.

▪━▪

Quicknotes

CONSTRUCTIVE TRUST A trust that arises by operation of law whereby the court imposes a trust upon property lawfully held by one party for the benefit of another, as a result of some wrongdoing by the party in possession so as to avoid unjust enrichment.

PARTNERSHIP A voluntary agreement entered into by two or more parties to engage in business and to share any attendant profits and losses.

▪━▪

Meehan v. Shaughnessy

Partner (P) v. Law firm (D)

Mass. Sup. Jud. Ct., 535 N.E.2d 1255 (1989).

NATURE OF CASE: Appeal from denial of relief on a counterclaim for breach of a partnership agreement in a partnership action.

FACT SUMMARY: After leaving Parker Coulter (D), the law firm in which they were partners, Meehan (P) and Boyle (P) filed this suit to recover amounts owed to them under the partnership agreement. Parker Coulter (D) counterclaimed, alleging violation of fiduciary duties and breach of the partnership agreement.

🏛 RULE OF LAW
Partners owe each other a fiduciary duty of the utmost good faith and loyalty.

FACTS: Meehan (P) and Boyle (P), partners in the law firm of Parker Coulter (D), planned to start their own firm. In the meantime, they continued to work full schedules and to generally maintain their usual standard of performance at Parker Coulter (D). After giving notice, Meehan (P) and Boyle (P) spoke with a majority of referring attorneys and obtained authorizations from a majority of clients whose cases they planned to take with them. The partnership agreement provided that a partner could remove a case upon payment of a "fair charge," subject to the right of the client to stay with the firm. Boyle (P) did not provide Parker Coulter (D) with the list of those cases until two weeks after it had been requested. Meehan (P) brought this action after Parker Coulter (D) refused to return the capital contributions made by Meehan (P) and Boyle (P) or to return their share of the dissolved firm's profits. Parker Coulter (D) counterclaimed that Meehan (P) and Boyle (P) violated their fiduciary duties and breached the partnership agreement when they unfairly acquired consent from client and attorneys to remove their cases from Parker Coulter (D). The trial court rejected all of Parker Coulter's (D) claims for relief. Parker Coulter (D) appealed.

ISSUE: Do partners owe each other a fiduciary duty of the utmost good faith and loyalty?

HOLDING AND DECISION: (Hennessey, C.J.) Yes. Partners owe each other a fiduciary duty of the utmost good faith and loyalty. While affirmatively denying any plans to leave the partnership, Meehan (P) and Boyle (P) made secret preparations to obtain removal authorizations from clients. Boyle (P) also delayed providing his partners with a list of clients he intended to solicit until he had obtained authorization from a majority of those clients. Finally, the content of the letter sent to the clients was unfairly prejudicial to Parker Coulter (D) because it did not clearly present to the clients the choice they had be-

tween remaining at Parker Coulter (D) and moving to the new firm. By engaging in these preemptive tactics, Meehan (P) and Boyle (P) violated the duty of utmost good faith and loyalty that they owed their partners. Thus, they have the burden of proving that the clients would have consented to removal in the absence of any breach of duty. The trial judge erred in finding that they did not unfairly acquire consent from clients and referring attorneys to withdraw cases but correctly found that they did not breach their duty by improperly handling cases for their own benefit or by secretly competing with the partnership. Reversed in part and remanded.

▶ ANALYSIS

The ABA Committee on Ethics and Professional Responsibility, in Informal Opinion 1457 (April 29, 1980), set forth ethical standards for attorneys announcing a change in professional association. The standard provides that any notice must explain to a client that he or she has the right to decide who will continue the representation. Further, the court noted that a partner has an obligation to render on the demand of any partner true and full information of all things affecting the partnership. Here, Meehan (P) and Boyle (P) continued to use their position of trust and confidence to the disadvantage of Parker Coulter (D).

■■

Quicknotes

FIDUCIARY DUTY A legal obligation to act for the benefit of another, including subordinating one's personal interests to that of the other person.

■■

Rapoport v. 55 Perry Co.

Partner (P) v. Partnership (D)

N.Y. App. Div., 376 N.Y.S.2d 147 (1975).

NATURE OF CASE: Appeal from denial of summary judgment to both parties in a declaratory judgment action interpreting a partnership agreement.

FACT SUMMARY: The Rapoports (P) contended that their partnership agreement with the Parneses (D) permitted the Rapoports (P) to assign their partnership interest to their adult children without the Parneses' (D) consent and that their adult children had become partners without such consent. The Parneses (D) took the position that that the partnership agreement did not permit the introduction of new partners without consent of all the existing partners.

🏛 RULE OF LAW

A provision in a partnership agreement that "No partner or partners shall have the authority . . . to sell, transfer, assign . . . his or their share in this firm, nor enter into any agreement as a result of which any person shall become interested with him in this firm, unless the same is agreed to in writing by a majority of the partners . . . except for members of his immediate family who have attained majority, in which case no such consent shall be required," does not permit entry into the partnership of adult children of partners without the consent of all the partners.

FACTS: The Rapoport (P) family entered into a partnership agreement with the Parnes (D) family, forming the 55 Perry Co., a partnership. One of the partnership agreement's provisions stipulated that "No partner or partners shall have the authority . . . to sell, transfer, assign . . . his or their share in this firm, nor enter into any agreement as a result of which any person shall become interested with him in this firm, unless the same is agreed to in writing by a majority of the partners . . . except for members of his immediate family who have attained majority, in which case no such consent shall be required." Members of the Rapoport (P) family assigned a 10 percent interest to their adult children. The Parneses (D) were advised of the assignment and an amended partnership certificate reflecting the assignment was filed. However, when the Rapoports (P) requested the Parneses (D) execute an amended partnership agreement to reflect this change, the Parneses (D) refused, taking the position that the partnership agreement did not permit the introduction of new partners without consent of all the existing partners. The Rapoports (P) brought suit for a judgment declaring that they had the right to assign their interest to their adult children without the Parneses' (D) consent and that the children were part-

ners of the partnership. Both parties moved for summary judgment. The trial court, finding the agreement ambiguous, and, therefore, that there was a triable issue of fact, denied the motions. The state's intermediate appellate court granted review.

ISSUE: Does a provision in a partnership agreement that "No partner or partners shall have the authority . . . to sell, transfer, assign . . . his or their share in this firm, nor enter into any agreement as a result of which any person shall become interested with him in this firm, unless the same is agreed to in writing by a majority of the partners . . . except for members of his immediate family who have attained majority, in which case no such consent shall be required," permit entry into the partnership of adult children of partners without the consent of all the partners?

HOLDING AND DECISION: (Tilzer, J.) No. A provision in a partnership agreement that "No partner or partners shall have the authority . . . to sell, transfer, assign . . . his or their share in this firm, nor enter into any agreement as a result of which any person shall become interested with him in this firm, unless the same is agreed to in writing by a majority of the partners . . . except for members of his immediate family who have attained majority, in which case no such consent shall be required," does not permit entry into the partnership of adult children of partners without the consent of all the partners. The provision poses no ambiguity, as it is clear from the entire agreement that the parties intended to observe the differences set forth in that law between a full partner and an assignee, and did not intend to give a partner the right to transfer a full partnership interest to his adult children without the consent of all the other partners, but, rather, intended to limit a partner with respect to his right to assign a partnership interest, i.e., to assign a share of the profits, to the extent of prohibiting such an assignment without consent of other partners except to his adult children. Under the Partnership Law, unless the parties have agreed otherwise, a person cannot become a member of a partnership without the consent of all the partners, whereas an assignment of a partnership interest may be made without consent, but the assignee is entitled only to receive the profits of the assigning partner and is not entitled to interfere in the partnership's management or to access partnership books and records. The provision at issue does not contain language with respect to admitting a partner to the partnership with all rights to participate in

Continued on next page.

the management of its affairs, and such an interpretation of the provision is consistent with other provisions of the partnership agreement. Accordingly, the Rapoports (P) could not transfer a full partnership interest to their children, and the children only have the rights as assignees to receive a share of the partnership income and profits of their assignors. Summary judgment for the Parneses (D) on the issue whether the Rapoport (P) children are full partners. The restated partnership certificate was improper and must be restated to eliminate the children as partners. Reversed as modified.

DISSENT: (Nunez, J.) The trial court was correct that the provision at issue was ambiguous and presented a triable issue as to intent, which should be resolved at trial.

▶ ANALYSIS

Under the New York Partnership Law invoked by the court in this case, a partner's property rights are his rights in specific partnership property; his interest in the partnership; and his right to participate in management. In contrast, under the RUPA, property acquired by the partnership is property of the partnership and not of the partners individually. Under this approach, a partner is not a co-owner of partnership property and has no interest in partnership property that can be transferred, either voluntarily or involuntarily.

■■■

Quicknotes

PARTNERSHIP A voluntary agreement entered into by two or more parties to engage in business and to share any attendant profits and losses.

■■■

Collins v. Lewis

Partner (P) v. Partner (D)

Tex. Civ. App., 283 S.W.2d 258, (1955).

NATURE OF CASE: Suit seeking dissolution of a partnership and other relief.

FACT SUMMARY: Lewis (D) persuaded Collins (P) to enter into a partnership for the operation of a cafeteria. The venture failed to make money, allegedly because of Collins's (P) lack of cooperation.

🏛 RULE OF LAW
A partner who has not fully performed the obligations imposed on him by the partnership agreement may not obtain an order dissolving the partnership.

FACTS: After entering into a long-term lease of space in a building then under construction, Collins (P) and Lewis (D) established a partnership. Collins (P) agreed to advance money to equip a cafeteria that Lewis (D) agreed to manage, Collins (P) investment to be repaid out of the profits of the business. Delays and rising costs required a larger initial investment than the parties had anticipated, and Collins (P) eventually threatened to discontinue his funding of the venture unless it began to generate a profit. Eventually, Collins (P) sued Lewis (D), seeking dissolution of the partnership, the appointment of a receiver, and foreclosure of a mortgage upon Lewis's (D) interest in the partnership's assets. Lewis (D) filed a cross-action in which he alleged that Collins (P) had breached his contractual obligation to provide funding for the enterprise. The trial court denied Collins's (P) petition for appointment of a receiver; and a jury, after finding that the partnership's lack of success was attributable to Collins's (P) conduct, returned a verdict denying the other relief sought by Collins (P). From the judgment entered pursuant to that verdict, Collins (P) appealed.

ISSUE: Does a partner always have the right to obtain dissolution of the partnership?

HOLDING AND DECISION: (Hamblen, C.J.) No. A partner who has not fully performed the obligations imposed on him by the partnership agreement may not obtain an order dissolving the partnership. In this case, the jury specifically found that Collins's (P) conduct prevented the cafeteria venture from succeeding. It was because Collins (P) withheld the funds that were needed to cover the expenses incurred by the business, thus requiring Lewis (D) to expend the cafeteria's receipts in order to meet those expenses, that the business showed no profit. In refusing to pay these costs, Collins (P) breached his contractual obligations, and he is therefore precluded from obtaining either dissolution or foreclosure. If Collins (P) is adamant in his desire to be released from the partnership, his only recourse is to take unilateral action to end the relationship, thus subjecting himself to a suit for the recovery of whatever damages Lewis (D) may sustain. Affirmed.

▶ ANALYSIS

Sometimes partnerships are created for a specific period of time, e.g., 15 years. Or, they may be established for an indefinite but determinable period of time, as is the case with partnerships that are to continue until the death of one of the partners. For good cause, partnerships may also be dissolved by judicial decree. This last method of termination is comparatively rare, however. Even partners who are locked in an irreconcilable dispute usually manage to agree to some plan which enables one or all of them to exit gracefully, because whatever settlement the feuding individuals can work out is likely to prove more economical than court-ordered dissolution, a procedure which typically results in the partnership property being disposed of for considerably less than its actual value.

■■■

Quicknotes

DISSOLUTION Annulment or termination of a formal or legal bond, tie or contract.

■■■

Dreifuerst v. Dreifuerst

Partner (P) v. Partner (D)

Wis. Ct. App., 280 N.W.2d 335 (1979).

NATURE OF CASE: Appeal from decision dissolving a partnership.

FACT SUMMARY: In the Dreifuersts' (P) case against their brother, Dreifuerst (D), to dissolve a partnership in which they were all partners, Dreifuerst (D) contended that under Wisconsin law, he had a right to force a sale of partnership assets in order to obtain his fair share of the assets in cash upon dissolution.

> ## 🏛 RULE OF LAW
> A partnership at will is a partnership that has no definite term or particular undertaking and can rightfully be dissolved by the express will of any partner.

FACTS: The Dreifuersts (P) and their brother, Dreifuerst (D), formed a partnership operating two feed mills. There were no written articles of partnership governing the partnership. The Dreifuersts (P) served Dreifuerst (D) with a notice of dissolution and wind-up of the partnership. The dissolution complaint alleged that the Dreifuersts (P) elected to dissolve the partnership and there were no allegations of fault, expulsion, or contravention of an alleged agreement as grounds for dissolution. The partners were not, however, able to agree to a winding-up of the partnership. Hearings on dissolution were held, and Dreifuerst (D) requested that the partnership be sold and that the court allow a sale, at which time the partners would bid on the entire property. By such sale, Dreifuerst (D) argued that he could obtain his fair share of the assets in cash upon dissolution while the Dreifuersts (P) could continue to run the business under a new partnership. The trial court denied Dreifuerst's (D) request and divided the partnership assets in-kind according to the valuation presented by the Dreifuersts (P). Dreifuerst (D) appealed.

ISSUE: Is a partnership at will a partnership that has no definite term or particular undertaking and can be rightfully dissolved by the express will of any partner?

HOLDING AND DECISION: (Brown, J.) Yes. A partnership at will is a partnership that has no definite term or particular undertaking and can be rightfully dissolved by the express will of any partner. In the present case, the Dreifuersts (P) wanted to dissolve the partnership. Being a partnership at will, they could rightfully dissolve it with or without the consent of Dreifuerst (D). Here, the Dreifuersts (P) never claimed that Dreifuerst (D) violated any partnership agreement and, therefore, there has been no wrongful dissolution of the partnership. Partners who have not wrongfully dissolved a partnership have a right to wind up the partnership. Lawful dissolution gives each partner the right to have the business liquidated and his share of the surplus paid in cash. Thus, the trial court erred in ordering an in-kind distribution of the assets of the partnership. A sale is the best means of determining the true fair market value of the assets. Reversed and remanded.

▶ ANALYSIS

"Dissolution" sometimes designates the completion of the winding-up of partnership affairs. This, the end of the association, should be called termination of the partnership. Again, the term is sometimes used in referring to the process of liquidation or winding up. Lastly, the term may be used to designate a change in the relation of partners caused by any partner ceasing to be associated in carrying on the business.

■=■

Quicknotes

PARTNERSHIP A voluntary agreement entered into by two or more parties to engage in business and to share any attendant profits and losses.

■=■

Bohatch v. Butler & Binion

Former law partner (P) v. Law firm (D)

Tex. Sup. Ct., 977 S.W.2d 543 (1998).

NATURE OF CASE: Appeal from damages awarded for breach of fiduciary duty and wrongful retaliatory termination.

FACT SUMMARY: Bohatch (P) claimed that she had wrongfully been dismissed as a law partner for whistle blowing.

🏛 RULE OF LAW
The fiduciary relationship between and among law partners does not create an exception to the at-will nature of partnerships.

FACTS: Bohatch (P) was a partner in the law firm of Butler and Binion (D). She alleged that another partner was overbilling a client and repeated her concerns to others. When Bohatch (P) was let go, she alleged bad faith retaliation for her allegations. Bohatch's (P) claims of breach of fiduciary duty and breach of the duty of good faith and fair dealing were tried before a jury and damages were awarded. The appeals court held that Bohatch (P) could not recover for breach of fiduciary duty but could recover for breach of the partnership agreement because her distribution for 1991 was reduced to zero without the requisite notice. All parties appealed.

ISSUE: Does the fiduciary relationship between and among law partners create an exception to the at-will nature of partnerships?

HOLDING AND DECISION: (Enoch, J.) No. The fiduciary relationship between and among law partners does not create an exception to the at-will nature of partnerships. The firm did not owe Bohatch (P) a duty not to expel her for reporting suspected overbilling by another partner. While Bohatch's (P) claims that she was expelled in an improper way were governed by the partnership agreement, her claim that she was expelled for an improper reason was not. Affirmed.

CONCURRENCE: (Hecht, J.) I cannot see how a five-partner firm can legitimately survive one partner's accusations that another is unethical. Even if expulsion of a partner for reporting unethical conduct might be a breach of fiduciary duty, expulsion for mistakenly reporting unethical conduct cannot be a breach of fiduciary duty.

DISSENT: (Spector, J.) I would hold that partners violate their fiduciary duty to one another by punishing compliance with the Disciplinary Rules of Professional Conduct.

▶ ANALYSIS

The dissent argued that the majority was sending the wrong signal to lawyers and to the public. The duty to report overbilling and other misconduct exists for the protection of the client. Even if in error, retaliation against a partner who tried in good faith to correct a perceived problem was not good precedent for others to follow, according to the dissent.

Quicknotes

AT-WILL EMPLOYMENT The rule that an employment relationship is subject to termination at any time, or for any cause, by an employee or an employer in the absence of a specific agreement otherwise.

CONTRACT An agreement pursuant to which a party agrees to act, or to forbear from acting, in exchange for performance on the part of the other party.

FIDUCIARY DUTY A legal obligation to act for the benefit of another, including subordinating one's personal interests to that of the other person.

RETALIATION The infliction of injury or penalty upon another in return for an injury or harm caused by that party.

Saint Alphonsus Diversified Care, Inc. v. MRI Associates, LLP

Dissociated former partner (P) v. Partnership (D)

Idaho Sup. Ct., 224 P.3d 1068 (2009).

NATURE OF CASE: Appeal from grant of partial summary judgment to defendant-counterclaim plaintiff asserting counterclaim for wrongful dissociation in action for a judicial determination of a partnership interest's value.

FACT SUMMARY: Saint Alphonsus Diversified Care, Inc. (Saint Alphonsus) (P), a dissociated former partner of MRI Associates, LLP (MRIA) (D), contended that it did not wrongfully dissociate from MRIA (D), as it did not breach an express provision of MRIA's (D) partnership agreement.

> ### 🏛 RULE OF LAW
> A partner does not dissociate wrongfully from a partnership where the partnership agreement can be interpreted as not containing an express provision that the partner is alleged to have violated.

FACTS: Saint Alphonsus Diversified Care, Inc. (Saint Alphonsus) (P) had been a partner of MRI Associates, LLP (MRIA) (D) for around 19 years, when it dissociated itself from MRIA (D). MRIA's (D) partnership agreement stated that a partner "may withdraw from the Partnership at any time if" the partner reasonably believed that continued participation in the partnership: "(i) jeopardizes the tax-exempt status of such Hospital Partner or its parent or their subsidiaries; or (ii) jeopardizes medicare/medicaid or insurance reimbursements or participations; (iii) if the business activities of the Partnership are contrary to the ethical principles of the Roman Catholic Church as designated from time to time; or (iv) is or may be in violation of any local, state or federal laws, rules or regulations." After giving notice of its dissociation, Saint Alphonsus (P) brought suit for a judicial determination of what it was owed for its interest. MRIA (D) counterclaimed, claiming, inter alia, that Saint Alphonsus (P) had wrongfully dissociated because it had violated an express provision of the partnership agreement; the parties cross-moved for partial summary judgment. The trial court ruled in favor of MRIA (D), concluding that the words any partner "may withdraw from the Partnership at any time if" followed by the four defined circumstances was an express provision limiting the circumstances under which St. Alphonsus (D) could rightfully dissociate. In reaching its decision, the trial court picked one definition of the word "if" ("on condition that") and concluded that the partnership agreement established the conditions that had to exist before a partner could withdraw from the partnership without breaching the agreement. The state's highest court granted review.

ISSUE: Does a partner dissociate wrongfully from a partnership where the partnership agreement can be inter-

preted as not containing an express provision that the partner is alleged to have violated?

HOLDING AND DECISION: (Eismann, C.J.) No. A partner does not dissociate wrongfully from a partnership where the partnership agreement can be interpreted as not containing an express provision that the partner is alleged to have violated. State statute provides that dissociation is wrongful if it is "in breach of an express provision of the partnership agreement." The trial court erred in concluding that St. Alphonsus (P) violated an express provision of the partnership agreement because that court rejected a different definition of "if" that means "in the event that." The trial court also limited the word "conditions" in the partnership agreement section that contained the dissociation rules to exclude its meaning "circumstances." With these alternate meanings— "if" meaning "in the event that" and "conditions" meaning "circumstances"—the section would provide that St. Alphonsus (P) could withdraw from the partnership in the event that any of four circumstances occurred. To conclude it prohibited withdrawal unless one of those four circumstances occurred, one would have to infer that these four circumstances were exclusive. Thus, the section would not constitute an express provision limiting the circumstances in which St. Alphonsus (P) could rightfully dissociate. Because the provision limiting the right to withdraw rightfully must be an express provision, any doubt as to the meaning of the provision at issue must be resolved in favor of not limiting the right to withdraw. The provision of the partnership agreement at issue did not contain any prohibitive language. Likewise, it did not state that a partner could only withdraw from the partnership under the specified circumstances. For these reasons, the provision is not an express provision limiting the right to dissociate rightfully. Accordingly, instructions the trial court gave to the jury, indicating that the court had determined, as a matter of law, that St. Alphonsus (P) wrongfully dissociated, were prejudicial to St. Alphonsus (P), as these instructions could have affected the jury's determinations on MRIA's (D) other causes of action, and damages. Reversed and remanded.

▶ ANALYSIS

Under the Revised Uniform Partnership Act (RUPA), it is clear that wrongful dissociation triggers liability for lost future profits. Section 620.8602(3) provides that "A partner who wrongfully dissociates is liable to the partnership and

Continued on next page.

to the other partners for damages caused by the dissociation. The liability is in addition to any other obligation of the partner to the partnership or to the other partners." However, RUPA does not contain a similar provision for dissolution; RUPA does not refer to the dissolutions as rightful or wrongful. The law predating RUPA allowed for recovery of lost profits upon the wrongful dissolution of a partnership. RUPA seems to have replaced the pre-RUPA concept of dissolution with the concept of dissociation. Thus, pre-RUPA cases providing for future damages upon wrongful dissolution are no longer applicable to partnership dissolution. Because a "wrongful dissolution" referred to in the pre-RUPA case law is now, under RUPA, known as "wrongful dissociation," only when a partner dissociates and the dissociation is wrongful can the remaining partners sue for damages. When a partnership is dissolved, RUPA at § 620.8806 provides the parameters of liability of the partners upon dissolution.

■═■

Quicknotes

EXPRESS CONDITION A condition that is expressly stated in the terms of a written instrument.

■═■

CHAPTER 4

The Development of Corporation Law in the United States: Jurisdictional Competition

Quick Reference Rules of Law

Louis K. Liggett Co. v. Lee

[Parties not identified.]

288 U.S. 517, 548-565 (1933).

NATURE OF CASE: [Nature of case not stated in casebook excerpt.]

FACT SUMMARY: [Facts not stated in casebook excerpt.]

 RULE OF LAW
[Rule of law not stated in casebook excerpt.]

FACTS: [Facts not stated in casebook excerpt.]

ISSUE: [Issue not stated in casebook excerpt.]

HOLDING AND DECISION: [Holding and decision not stated in casebook excerpt.]

DISSENT: (Brandeis, J.) Fear of encroachment on the liberties and opportunities of the individual, of the subjection of labor to capital, of the evils inherent in large aggregations of capital, etc., were the reasons that general incorporation laws historically embodied severe restrictions on the size and scope of corporate activity. They were, in part, an expression of the desire for equality of opportunity. Limitation on the amount of the authorized capital of business corporations was long universal, as were limitations on the scope of a business corporation's powers and activity. At first, corporations could be formed under the general laws only for a limited number of purposes—usually those which required a relatively large fixed capital, like transportation, banking and insurance, and mechanical, mining and manufacturing enterprises. Permission to incorporate for "any lawful purpose" was not common until 1875, and until that time the duration of corporate franchises was generally limited to a period of 20, 30, or 50 years. All, or a majority, of the incorporators or directors, or both, were required to be residents of the incorporating state. The powers the corporation might exercise in carrying out its purposes were sparingly conferred and strictly construed. Severe limitations were imposed on the amount of indebtedness, bonded or otherwise. The power to hold stock in other corporations was not conferred or implied. The holding company was impossible. These restrictions were not lifted because they were no longer considered necessary to protect the public interest but because they were impossible to enforce once certain states loosened their requirements to attract corporations and thus made circumvention of tough laws via foreign incorporation possible. Now, the modern corporate structure has virtually divorced company ownership from power and concentrated that power in the hands of a few so as to give rise to a feudal type system akin to rule by a plutocracy.

▶ ANALYSIS

In the early days, the legislatures exercised the power the Crown had enjoyed to issue corporate charters on a case-by-case basis and often with particularized restrictions. As the Industrial Revolution made the corporation the ideal method of business practice, charters were increasingly standardized until general incorporation laws were eventually passed.

■■■

CHAPTER 5

The Formation of a Closely Held Corporation

Quick Reference Rules of Law

711 Kings Highway Corp. v. F.I.M.'s Marine Repair Serv., Inc.

Lessor (P) v. Lessee (D)

N.Y. Sup. Ct., 273 N.Y.S.2d 299 (1966).

NATURE OF CASE: Action for declaratory relief to declare a lease invalid.

FACT SUMMARY: 711 Kings Highway Corp. (P) leased premises to F.I.M. Marine Repair Serv., Inc. (D) to use as a movie theater, but then sought to declare the lease invalid on the ground that the intended use was outside the scope of business activities allowed in the charter.

🏛 RULE OF LAW

No act of a corporation and no transfer of property to or by a corporation otherwise lawful shall be held invalid by reason that the corporation was without capacity or power to do such act except in an action brought by a shareholder or in an action by or in the right of a corporation against an incumbent or former officer or director.

FACTS: 711 Kings Highway Corp. (711) (P) leased premises to F.I.M. Marine Repair Serv., Inc. (F.I.M.) (D) for use as a movie theater for a period of 15 years. F.I.M. (D) paid a $5,000 security deposit. 711 (P) then sought a declaratory judgment declaring the lease to be invalid or, in the alternative, rescission on the ground that the intended use was outside the scope of permissible business activities under F.I.M.'s (D) charter. F.I.M. (D) moved to dismiss, arguing that only a shareholder could assert the claim brought by 711 (P).

ISSUE: Shall no act of a corporation and no transfer of property to or by a corporation, otherwise lawful, be held invalid by reason that the corporation was without capacity or power to do such act or engage in such transfer except in an action brought by a shareholder or in an action by or in the right of a corporation against an incumbent or former officer or director?

HOLDING AND DECISION: (Anfuso, J.) Yes. No act of a corporation and no transfer of property to or by a corporation, otherwise lawful, shall be held invalid by reason that the corporation was without capacity or power to do such act or engage in such transfer except in an action brought by a shareholder or in an action by or in the right of a corporation against an incumbent or former officer or director. Clearly, under this rule, there was no substance to 711's (P) argument, as 711 (P) did not fall under either exception. Further, 711 (P) could not escape application of the rule by claiming that it did not apply to executory contracts. Complaint dismissed.

▶ ANALYSIS

"Ultra vires" literally means "beyond the powers." When a corporation does an act or enters into a contract beyond the scope of its charter, it is not necessarily illegal and it is not necessarily void. Rather, it is voidable. However, under the well-known English case, *Ashbury Railway Carriage & Iron Co. v. Riche*, 33 N.S. Law Times Rep. 450 (1875), the discussion surrounded the question of a contract's being void from the beginning because the object of the contract was beyond the powers of the corporation. The corporation was allowed to repudiate a contract on the ground of ultra vires after it had partially performed. However, the doctrine of ultra vires is declining in importance and should not be applied to Purposes Clauses of Articles of Incorporation.

■══■

Quicknotes

DECLARATORY RELIEF A judgment of the court establishing the rights of the parties.

EXECUTORY CONTRACT A contract in which performance of an obligation has yet to be rendered.

ULTRA VIRES An act undertaken by a corporation that is beyond the scope of its authority pursuant to law or its articles of incorporation.

■══■

Sullivan v. Hammer

Stockholder (P) v. Corporation (D)

Del. Ch. Ct., 1990 WL 114223 (1990).

NATURE OF CASE: Stockholder derivative suit and class action challenging a publicly held corporation's proposed significant financial support of a museum affiliated with the corporation's chairman of the board.

FACT SUMMARY: A publicly held corporation informed its stockholders of a plan to give substantial financial support to a museum named after the corporation's chairman of the board. Derivatively and as proposed class representatives, stockholders sued the corporation alleging improper gift, waste of assets, and a breach of the chairman's duty of loyalty.

🏛 RULE OF LAW
Parties can resolve stockholder litigation by settlement even where the settlement agreement provides only minimal benefits to the stockholders.

FACTS: Dr. Armand Hammer (D) was chairman of the board for the Occidental Petroleum Corporation (Occidental) (D). Occidental (D) informed its stockholders (P), before the corporation's 1989 annual meeting, the corporation was going forward with a proposal to make significant financial contributions to The Armand Hammer Museum of Art and Cultural Center in Los Angeles. Specifically, Occidental's (D) Proxy Statement informed stockholders (P) that the corporation planned to provide several forms of financial support to the museum: $50 million to fund the museum's construction costs, a 30-year rent-free lease in Occidental's (D) Los Angeles headquarters, a $24 million annuity, and an option to purchase the museum facilities for $55 million at the end of the 30-year lease. The Proxy Statement provided further that Occidental (D) would contribute a lump sum to The Armand Hammer Foundation in an amount approximately seven times Dr. Hammer's (D) total compensation in the year before his death. Sullivan (P) and other stockholders (P) filed suit in the Delaware Court of Chancery two weeks after Occidental (D) issued the Proxy Statement. The complaint alleged that the corporation's planned contributions would constitute an improper gift and waste of corporate assets, and that Dr. Hammer's (D) actions constituted a breach of his duty of loyalty to Occidental's (D) stockholders (P). Three days after the suit was filed, Occidental (D) supplemented its Proxy Statement with disclosures that the stockholders (P) sought in their complaint. Settlement discussions between the stockholders (P) and defendant began two weeks later. After several months, a Special Committee appointed by Occidental's (D) board of directors formally approved the corporation's planned charitable contributions to the two entities affiliated with

Dr. Hammer (D). All parties eventually submitted an executed proposed settlement agreement for the court's approval. In their agreement, the parties proposed to settle nine issues: (1) the Museum building would bear Occidental's (D) name; (2) the Museum would treat Occidental (D) as a corporate sponsor as long as the Museum used the building; (3) the Museum would publicly acknowledge Occidental's contribution of the building; (4) three of Occidental's (D) directors would also serve on the Museum's board; (5) Dr. Hammer (D) would immediately loan almost all of his art collections to the Museum, and ownership of the loaned collections would automatically transfer to the Museum upon Dr. Hammer's (D) death; (6) Occidental (D) would limit all future contributions to charities affiliated with Dr. Hammer (D) according to the dividends paid to Occidental's (D) stockholders; (7) all Museum-construction payments beyond $50 million would apply against Occidental's (D) agreed limit for contributions to charities affiliated with Dr. Hammer (D); (8) Occidental's (D) total contributions for construction of the Museum building would be $50 million, with an extra $10 million in such contributions expended through December 31, 1990, if the Special Committee approved them, and if the contributions would not enlarge the construction project; and (9) Occidental (D) would receive half of any payments beyond the $55 million option price for the property or half of any payment received by the Museum for transferring its interest in the property to a third party.

ISSUE: Can parties resolve shareholder litigation by settlement even where the settlement agreement provides only minimal benefits to the stockholders?

HOLDING AND DECISION: (Hartnett, V. Chan.) Yes. Parties can resolve stockholder litigation by settlement even where the settlement agreement provides only minimal benefits to the stockholder. Under Delaware law, judicial review of proposed settlements in stockholders' litigation is limited. A court can only apply Delaware law to the case's record facts, and then apply the court's own business judgment to decide whether the proposed settlement is reasonable. Six factors determine the reasonableness of a proposed settlement: (1) the strength of the plaintiff's case, (2) how difficult judicial enforcement of the plaintiff's claims will be, (3) how collectable any recovered judgment will be, (4) how onerous the litigation will be for the parties, (5) the size of the settlement compared to the possible judgment, and (6) the parties' opinions. In this case, it is highly unlikely that

Continued on next page.

Sullivan (P) will prevail on the merits. In Delaware, the business judgment rule creates a strong presumption that insulates a corporate board's decisions from stockholder challenges. A stockholder can overcome that presumption only by showing that most of the directors entered the challenged transaction for personal financial gain, that they were not independent, that they were grossly negligent of information pertinent to the transaction, or that the board's decision was so irrational that it was not a reasonable exercise of business judgment. Here, the stockholders (P) have made no showings on any of the exceptions to the business judgment rule, and the board's actions in approving the challenged contributions are therefore presumptively valid. As for the alleged impropriety of the gift, the court, again under very limited review, finds that it is reasonable, and that the stockholders' (P) claim on this issue very likely will fail. Compared to the weakness of the stockholders' (P) case, the proposed settlement confers a reasonable consideration upon the stockholders (P), even though the consideration is merely speculative. The amount of benefit to the corporation from the transactions is difficult to quantify, but Occidental (D) clearly will enjoy goodwill from the planned contributions. Although this court finds the settlement only barely acceptable, the settlement is adequate compared to the weakness of the stockholders' (P) case. Settlement approved.

▶ ANALYSIS

Although the casebook excerpt does not include the purpose clause of Occidental's (D) corporate charter, it is safe to say that heavily funding art museums is probably greatly ultra vires for a company founded for petroleum-related purposes. In addition to illustrating how weak the ultra vires doctrine has become, *Sullivan* also offers a lawyerly glimpse into some of the benefits of incorporating under Delaware law. Under the cited case of *Aronson v. Lewis*, 473 A.2d 805 (1984), a stockholder plaintiff's burden in rebutting the presumption favoring a corporate board's decisions is very heavy indeed.

■══■

Quicknotes

BUSINESS JUDGMENT RULE Doctrine relieving corporate directors and/or officers from liability for decisions honestly and rationally made in the corporation's best interests.

PROXY STATEMENT A statement, containing specified information by the Securities and Exchange Commission, in order to provide shareholders with adequate information upon which to make an informed decision regarding the solicitation of their proxies.

ULTRA VIRES An act undertaken by a corporation that is beyond the scope of its authority pursuant to law or its articles of incorporation.

■══■

Stanley J. How & Assoc., Inc. v. Boss

Arbitration firm (P) v. Corporation promoter (D)

222 F. Supp. 936 (S.D. Iowa 1963).

NATURE OF CASE: Action to recover contract price from corporate promoter.

FACT SUMMARY: Boss (D) signed a contract, on behalf of a corporation not yet formed, with How & Assoc. (P) for architectural services.

🏛 RULE OF LAW
A promoter will be liable on a contract he entered into on behalf of a corporation yet-to-be-formed.

FACTS: Boss (D), a corporate promoter, entered into a contract with How & Assoc. (P) for architectural services. How & Assoc. (P) were to design a building for a corporation Boss (D) was forming. Boss (D) signed the contract as agent for the corporation to be formed, which was to be the obligor. The corporation was never formed, and the building designed by How & Assoc. (P) was never constructed. How & Assoc. (P) sued for the contract price, alleging that Boss (D) was liable as the corporate promoter.

ISSUE: Is a corporate promoter liable for contracts signed by him as an agent for a corporation yet-to-be-formed?

HOLDING AND DECISION: (Hanson, J.) Yes. The promoter is liable for contracts signed by him for the corporation to be formed. There are three exceptions to this rule: (1) the contract is treated as an option which can be accepted by the corporation when it is formed, and the promoter agrees to form the corporation and give it the opportunity to pay; (2) a novation with the corporation assuming the promoter's liability and replacing him in the contract; and (3) the promoter remains liable even after formation but only as a surety. Boss (D) argued that his signature "as agent for the corporation to be formed which is to be obligor" makes the corporation only liable for the debt. In deciding on the meaning of ambiguous phrases, it is necessary to look at them in light of the entire contract. Much of the performance due would have been completed prior to the formation of the new contract. As a general rule, where work is to be performed prior to incorporation, the promoter will be personally liable unless another person or fund is made so under the contract. Since this was not the case, no novation clause was contained in the contract, and How & Assoc. (P) stated that it thought Boss (D) was to be liable, we must follow the general presumption that the promoter will be liable. Since Boss (D) did not plead novation, his only defense is that the contract was really a continuing offer and was not valid until accepted by the new corporation. There is no showing of this. Judgment for Stanley J. How & Assoc, Inc. (P).

▶ ANALYSIS

Statutory authority aside, this decision is a matter of policy. The law normally excuses an agent from liability for contracts he entered into in an agency capacity. The principal's reputation and resources are the ones that induced the other party to enter into an agreement. When the principal is not yet in existence, the agent's reputation and assets must be assumed to have induced the other party to enter the contract.

Quicknotes

NOVATION The substitution of one party for another in a contract with the approval of the remaining party and discharging the obligations of the released party.

PROMOTER A person who initiates the formation of a corporation.

SURETY A party who guarantees payment of the debt of another party to a creditor.

Robertson v. Levy

Business owner (P) v. Incorporator (D)

D.C. Ct. App., 197 A.2d 443 (1964).

NATURE OF CASE: Action to recover note proceeds from promoter.

FACT SUMMARY: Levy (D) formed a corporation which bought Robertson's (P) business at a time when the Articles of Incorporation were being rejected by the Corporations Commissioner.

🏛 RULE OF LAW
Knowledge of the lack of corporate status plus receipt of payments from the corporation will not estop a creditor from denying corporate form.

FACTS: Levy (D) attempted to form a corporation. The Superintendent of Corporations rejected the corporation's Articles of Incorporation (Articles). Prior to the acceptance of the corrected Articles, Levy (D) entered into a contract with Robertson (P) to purchase his business for the corporation. Levy (D) signed as corporate president. The Articles were later accepted and the corporation was validly formed. One payment was made on the note to Robertson (P), and the corporation later became insolvent. Robertson (P) sued Levy (D) on the note, claiming Levy (D) was personally liable since the contract had been signed before incorporation. The trial court found that Robertson (P) was estopped from asserting proper formation because he knew that the corporation had not been validly formed at the time of the contract and he also had accepted a payment on the note from the corporation.

ISSUE: Will knowledge of the lack of corporate status plus receipt of payments from the corporation estop a creditor from denying corporate form?

HOLDING AND DECISION: (Hood, C.J.) No. Knowledge of the lack of corporate status plus receipt of payments from the corporation will not estop a creditor from denying corporate form. The pertinent statute states that the corporation's existence does not begin until the certificate of incorporation has been issued. It further states that all persons attempting to act as a corporation without authority to do so shall be jointly and severally liable for debts and liabilities resulting from these acts. The thrust of this legislation is to destroy the common-law concepts of de facto corporations and corporations by estoppel. Equity can no longer provide relief for lack of or defective formation. A creditor, even with knowledge of the defective formation, is not estopped from looking to those who incurred the liability for payment. Part payment or part performance is immaterial. Therefore, Levy (D) is liable on the contract between the corporation and Robertson (P). The decision of the trial court is reversed with instructions.

▶ ANALYSIS

Corporate form and protection is a matter of legislative grace. To qualify, certain formalities must be met. Failure to comply subjects the incorporators to personal liability. It is not a matter of protecting innocent creditors. Since the corporation was not in existence, Levy (D) was acting in his individual capacity. It is the same situation as where the promoter enters into a contract as agent for a corporation to-be-formed. Unless the creditor agrees to a novation when the corporation is formed or specifically agrees that the promoter shall not be liable, he cannot escape contractual liability, e.g., *Stanley J. How & Assoc., Inc. v. Boss*, 222 F. Supp. 936 (S.D. Iowa 1963).

■▬■

Quicknotes

DE FACTO CORPORATION A corporation arising from the good faith attempt to comply with the statutory requirements of establishing a corporation.

DE JURE CORPORATION A corporation that results from the incorporator(s)' full satisfaction of the statutory requirements of establishing a corporation.

ESTOPPEL An equitable doctrine precluding a party from asserting a right to the detriment of another whom justifiably relied on the conduct.

NOVATION The substitution of one party for another in a contract with the approval of the remaining party and discharging the obligations of the released party.

QUO WARRANTO PROCEEDINGS A proceeding brought in order to determine whether an officer legally holds office or a corporation legally holds a franchise.

■▬■

Frontier Refining Company v. Kunkel's, Inc.

Creditor (P) v. Purported-partnership (D)

Wyo. Sup. Ct., 407 P.2d 880 (1965).

NATURE OF CASE: Appeal from dismissal of action on the ground that a business entity is not a partnership giving rise to individual liability of its members.

FACT SUMMARY: Kunkel's Inc. (D) was indebted to Frontier Refining Company (Frontier) (P). Frontier (P) claimed that Kunkel's (D) was a partnership made up of Kunkel, who ran the business, and Beach (D) and Fairfield (D), who had agreed to loan money to Kunkel's (D) on the condition that it be incorporated. Kunkel's (D) was never incorporated, and Frontier (P) went after Beach (D) and Fairfield (D), alleging that they were indebted to it as members of the purported partnership.

🏛 RULE OF LAW
A business venture purporting to be a corporation is not a partnership giving rise to individual liability of its members, where the venture is not incorporated, where it is run by one individual in a doing-business-as capacity, and where the other participants in the venture have agreed to lend the venture money on condition that it be incorporated but do not know that it has not been incorporated.

FACTS: Kunkel wanted to take over a filling station owned by Frontier Refining Company (Frontier) (P), but he had no money, so he asked Beach (D) and Fairfield (D) to lend him money for that purpose. Beach (D) and Fairfield (D) agreed on condition that the business would be run as a corporation, but they left it to Kunkel to incorporate the business, which was called Kunkel's, Inc. (D). Kunkel failed to incorporate the business. Without Beach's (D) or Fairfield's (D) knowledge, Kunkel signed a sublease with Frontier (P) and commenced operating the station. The sublease agreement was with "CLIFFORD D. KUNKEL DBA KUNKEL'S, INC." Sales of gasoline by Frontier (P) were billed to "Clifford D. Kunkel dba Kunkel's, Inc." About a month after the initial sale, Frontier (P) discovered that through error, the products purchased by the station had not been paid for at the time of delivery, giving rise to a $5,000 debt. Around $11,000 was invested by Fairfield (D) and Beach (D) into the venture, but this was made after Kunkel opened the station. Frontier (P) claimed that Fairfield (D) had indicated that Fairfield (D) had represented to it that Kunkel's, Inc. (D) would be run as a corporation and that Fairfield (D) had given assurances that the delinquency would be paid, but Fairfield (D) denied these assertions. Also, Frontier (P) obtained from Kunkel a chattel mortgage in his individual capacity covering all the equipment used in the station. In another action, Frontier (P) prevailed on this

mortgage against Fairfield (D), who claimed that he owned the equipment. The trial court held that Kunkel's, Inc. (D) was not a partnership and dismissed the action. The state's highest court granted review.

ISSUE: Is a business venture purporting to be a corporation a partnership giving rise to individual liability of its members, where the venture is not incorporated, where it is run by one individual in a doing-business-as capacity, and where the other participants in the venture have agreed to lend the venture money on condition that it be incorporated but do not know that it has not been incorporated?

HOLDING AND DECISION: (Gray, J.) No. A business venture purporting to be a corporation is not a partnership giving rise to individual liability of its members, where the venture is not incorporated, where it is run by one individual in a doing-business-as capacity, and where the other participants in the venture have agreed to lend the venture money on condition that it be incorporated but do not know that it has not been incorporated. The facts, disputed as they are, show that the trial court was entitled to infer that Kunkel was the only source of any information given to Frontier (P) about a proposed corporation to be called Kunkel's, Inc. (D), and that neither Fairfield (D) nor Beach (D) authorized Kunkel to make such representations or to enter contracts with Frontier (P) in the name of Kunkel's, Inc. (D). This supports the conclusion that neither Beach (D) nor Fairfield (D) held themselves out as a corporation, thus negating an element of Frontier's (P) theory. The trial court could also infer that Frontier (P) knew that a corporation had not been formed, yet chose to do business with Kunkel as an individual. Thus, it could be inferred that the indebtedness was not incurred in the name of a pretended corporation. Under such circumstances, a creditor will be held to its bargain. Furthermore, Frontier's (P) position, as an equitable matter, is inconsistent. In its replevin action, where it prevailed against Fairfield (D), Frontier (P) accepted the fruit of a judgment that contained an inherent finding by the court that Kunkel, as an individual, was Frontier's (P) debtor and the owner of the property securing his debt. It would be unconscionable to allow Frontier (P) to disavow that judgment to the extent of imposing liability on Beach (D) and Fairfield (D). Affirmed.

▮ ANALYSIS

Beach (D) and Fairfield (D) avoided personal liability on the ground that they were creditors of the venture and not

Continued on next page.

partners in a partnership. However, by failing to ensure that Kunkel actually incorporated the venture, as agreed, they ran the risk that they would have been treated as partners rather than creditors. The case serves as a warning to investors to independently check to make sure that any required filings have been made to create the desired entity.

■■■■

Quicknotes

REPLEVIN An action to recover personal property wrongfully taken.

■■■■

CHAPTER 6

Disregard of the Corporate Entity

Quick Reference Rules of Law

Bartle v. Home Owners Cooperative, Inc.

Bankruptcy trustees (P) v. Parent corporation (D)

N.Y. Ct. App., 127 N.E.2d 832 (1955).

NATURE OF CASE: Action by trustee in bankruptcy to hold owner of subsidiary liable for latter's debts.

FACT SUMMARY: Home Owners Cooperative, Inc. (D) wholly owned Westerlea Builders, Inc. as a subsidiary and controlled its affairs but maintained separate outward indicia, did not mislead or defraud creditors of Westerlea, and caused no injury to Westerlea's creditors by depletion of assets.

> 🏛 **RULE OF LAW**
> Where there has been no fraud, misrepresentation, or illegality, the doctrine of "piercing the corporate veil" will not be invoked to hold a corporation liable for the debts of a wholly owned subsidiary.

FACTS: Home Owners Cooperative, Inc. (Home Owners) (D), a cooperative association of mostly veterans, unable to secure a contractor to build low-cost housing for its members, organized Westerlea Builders, Inc. (Westerlea) for that purpose. When Westerlea ran into financial difficulties, its creditors, pursuant to an extension agreement, took over the construction responsibilities. Four years later, even though Home Owners (D) contributed some $50,000 in original capital and additional sums, Westerlea went bankrupt. Westerlea's trustees in bankruptcy (P) sued Home Owners (D) for the contract debts of Westerlea. The trial court, in deciding for Home Owners (D), found that while Home Owners (D) controlled Westerlea's affairs, it maintained separate outward indicia at all times that credit was extended, did not mislead or defraud Westerlea's creditors, and performed no act injurious to them by depletion of assets or otherwise. The trial court also ruled that the trustees (P) were estopped by the extension agreement from denying the separate identities of the two corporations.

ISSUE: If there has been no fraud, misrepresentation, or illegality, should the doctrine of "piercing the corporate veil" be invoked to hold a corporation liable for the debts of the wholly owned subsidiary?

HOLDING AND DECISION: (Froessel, J.) No. Where there has been no fraud, misrepresentation, or illegality, the doctrine of "piercing the corporate veil" will not be invoked to hold a corporation liable for the debts of a wholly owned subsidiary. The trial court should not have "pierced the corporate veil" of Westerlea's corporate existence to see Home Owners (D) lurking in the background. Since the law permits the incorporation of a business for the very purpose of escaping personal liability, the doctrine of "piercing the corporate veil" is invoked only in instances of preventing fraud or to achieve equity. Home Owners' (D) purpose in placing its construction operation into a separate corporation was within the limits of public policy. Affirmed.

DISSENT: (Van Voorhis, J.) Westerlea is a wholly owned subsidiary of Home Owners (D), having the same directors and management. Business was done on such a basis that Westerlea could not make a profit (no allowance was made for profit by Westerlea). The benefit to the stockholders of Home Owners (D) from this arrangement is analogous to dividends. Westerlea, consequently, was no more than an agent of Home Owners (D).

▶ ANALYSIS

"Piercing the corporate veil" can take one of two routes: (1) The corporation is the "alter ego" of its shareholders—it is so dominated and used by them that, in reality, no separate entity is in existence. This is usually the case where the shareholders treat the corporation's assets as their own, drawing upon company funds for their personal use at will. (2) Recognizing the corporation as a legal entity would be to sanction a fraud or injustice. In these instances, where this approach is used, the purpose of incorporating was to prevent creditors from reaching personal debts, to run up debts in excess of assets, or, as charged in the present case, to minimize expected tort liabilities.

■=■

Quicknotes

CORPORATE VEIL Refers to the shielding from personal liability of a corporation's officers, directors or shareholders for unlawful conduct engaged in by the corporation.

SUBSIDIARY A company a majority of whose shares are owned by another corporation and which is subject to that corporation's control.

UNJUST ENRICHMENT The unlawful acquisition of money or property of another for which both law and equity require restitution made.

■=■

DeWitt Truck Brokers v. W. Ray Flemming Fruit Co.

Transportation provider (P) v. Produce agent (D)

540 F.2d 681 (4th Cir. 1976).

NATURE OF CASE: Appeal for award of damages on an unpaid debt.

FACT SUMMARY: DeWitt Truck Brokers (P) sought to pierce the corporate veil of W. Ray Flemming Fruit Co. (D) and impose individual liability on Flemming (D), the corporate president, for the indebtedness of the corporation.

🏛 RULE OF LAW
A court will pierce the corporate veil when recognition of the corporate form would extend the principle of incorporation beyond its legitimate purposes and would produce injustices or inequitable consequences.

FACTS: Flemming (D) was president of and ran a close, one-man corporation, W. Ray Flemming Fruit Co. (D), which acted as a commission-paid agent selling produce for growers. Corporate formalities were not observed, the corporation was undercapitalized, and no other stockholder or officer other than Flemming (D) ever received a salary or dividend. DeWitt Truck Brokers (P) brought an action to collect moneys due it for providing transportation. It sought to hold Flemming (D) personally liable on the debt, noting Flemming (D) had withdrawn funds from the corporation that could have been used to pay the debt. The lower court pierced the corporate veil and imposed personal liability on Flemming (D), who appealed.

ISSUE: Will the corporate veil be pierced where recognition of the corporate form would extend the principle of incorporation beyond its legitimate purposes and produce injustice or inequity?

HOLDING AND DECISION: (Russell, J.) Yes. The concept that a corporation is an entity, separate and distinct from its officers and stockholders, is merely a legal theory introduced to serve the ends of justice and for convenience. As such, the courts will refuse to recognize it and will pierce the corporate veil, where, as in this case, recognition of the corporate form would extend the principle of incorporation beyond its legitimate purposes and would produce injustices or inequitable consequences. One fact significant to such an inquiry (particularly so in the case of a one-man or closely held corporation) is whether the corporation was grossly undercapitalized for the purposes of the corporate undertaking. Here, undercapitalization of this one-man corporation and the presence of other factors, such as lack of corporate formalities, lead to the conclusion that the finding below that the corporate

entity should be disregarded was not clearly erroneous. Affirmed.

▶ ANALYSIS

Although courts are willing to pierce the corporate veil to hold an individual responsible for corporate debt, they are even more willing to pierce the corporate veil to hold a parent corporation responsible for the debt of a subsidiary whose stock it holds. Intermingling of the business affairs of parent and subsidiary, i.e., not delineating between their operations, has proven to be an almost certain way to ensure the veil will be pierced.

Quicknotes

ALTER EGO Other self; under the "alter ego" doctrine, the court disregards the corporate entity and holds the individual shareholders liable for acts done knowingly and intentionally in the corporation's name.

CAPITALIZATION The aggregate value of all securities issued by a company.

CORPORATE VEIL Refers to the shielding from personal liability of a corporation's officers, directors or shareholders for unlawful conduct engaged in by the corporation.

Baatz v. Arrow Bar

Injured motorist (P) v. Alcohol server (D)

S.D. Sup. Ct., 452 N.W.2d 138 (1990).

NATURE OF CASE: Appeal from summary judgment dismissing dram shop action.

FACT SUMMARY: The Baatzes (P) contended that Arrow Bar (D) was negligent in serving alcoholic beverages to McBride, who struck them with his car while intoxicated, and attempted to hold Arrow Bar's owners (D) personally liable.

🏛 RULE OF LAW
In determining whether the corporate veil should be pierced, the court must regard the corporation as a separate legal entity in the absence of sufficient evidence to the contrary.

FACTS: Kenny (P) and Peggy Baatz (P) were injured in a collision with McBride's car while riding on their motorcycle. The Baatzes (P) alleged that Arrow Bar (D) was negligent in serving alcoholic beverages to McBride while he was already intoxicated, thus contributing to their injuries. They also sued Edmond (D), LaVella (D), and Jacquette Neuroth (D) as individual defendants. Edmond (D) and LaVella Neuroth (D) formed Arrow Bar, Inc. (D) in 1980 and contributed $50,000 to the company. Edmond (D) served as president and Jacquette Neuroth (D) as manager. The trial court granted summary judgment for defendants. The Baatzes (P) appealed, and the case was remanded to trial court. The court granted Edmond (D), La Vella (D), and Jacquette's (D) motion for summary judgment, dismissing them as defendants. The Baatzes (P) appealed.

ISSUE: In determining whether the corporate veil should be pierced, must the court consider the corporation to be a separate legal entity in the absence of sufficient evidence to the contrary?

HOLDING AND DECISION: (Sabers, J.) Yes. In determining whether the corporate veil should be pierced, the court must regard the corporation as a separate legal entity in the absence of sufficient evidence to the contrary. The court may pierce the corporate veil and hold individual stockholders personally liable only where continuing to recognize the corporation would result in unfair consequences. In determining whether to disregard the corporate entity, the court must consider such factors as misrepresentation by the corporation, undercapitalization, failure to observe formalities, absence of records, payment of individual obligations, and the use of the corporate form to accomplish illegal ends. Shareholders are mandated to provide the corporation with a sufficient amount of capital required by the particular type of business. Where the corporation serves merely as a conduit for an individual to conduct his personal affairs, the court may pierce the corporate veil and hold the individual personally liable. Likewise, a failure to observe the formalities associated with a corporation may also justify such a result. However, failure must be continuous—one occasion is not sufficient. Here, the Baatzes (P) proffered no evidence of inequitable consequences justifying the court's piercing the corporate veil and imposing personal liability on the Neuroths (D). Affirmed.

DISSENT: (Henderson, J.) Arrow Bar (D) did not constitute a separate legal entity independent from its shareholders, officers, and employees.

▶ ANALYSIS

Courts draw a distinction between tort and contract claims when determining whether to pierce the corporate veil. The rationale for not piercing the veil in contract disputes is that contract claimants usually deal voluntarily with the corporation, and thus willingly assume the risk of loss. Moreover, if the contract creditor is concerned with the financial viability of the corporation, he has the alternative of securing a guarantee. In contrast, tort claimants are typically involuntary creditors, and thus should not be made to assume the risk of loss thrust upon them by an undercapitalized corporation.

■=■

Quicknotes

CAPITALIZATION The aggregate value of all securities issued by a company.

CORPORATE VEIL Refers to the shielding from personal liability of a corporation's officers, directors or shareholders for unlawful conduct engaged in by the corporation.

DRAM SHOP ACT Law, that imposes liability upon the seller of alcoholic beverages for injuries to a third party resulting from the intoxication of the buyer.

■=■

Radaszewski v. Telecom Corp.

Injured motorist (P) v. Truck owner (D)

981 F.2d 305 (8th Cir. 1992).

NATURE OF CASE: Appeal from dismissal of a suit to recover damages for personal injuries.

FACT SUMMARY: When a truck driven by an employee of a wholly owned subsidiary of Telecom Corp. (D) struck the motorcycle that Radaszewski (P) was riding, seriously injuring him, he filed this suit for damages for his injuries.

🏛 RULE OF LAW
To pierce the corporate veil, one must show control amounting to complete domination, use of that control for an improper motive which breaches a duty owed, and injury proximately caused by that breach.

FACTS: After Radaszewski (P) was seriously injured when the motorcycle he was riding was struck by a truck driven by an employee of Contrux, Inc., a wholly owned subsidiary of Telecom Corp. (D), Radaszewski (P) filed this suit to recover damages for his injuries. Radaszewski (P) sought to hold Telecom Corp. (D) liable for his injuries by piercing the corporate veil to reach its assets since Contrux was undercapitalized. Contrux initially had had basic and excess liability coverage, which would have covered Radaszewski's (P) damages. Unfortunately, two years after the accident, the excess liability insurance carrier became insolvent and went into receivership. The district court dismissed the complaint against Telecom (D), holding that the court lacked jurisdiction. Radaszewski (P) appealed.

ISSUE: To pierce the corporate veil, must one show control amounting to complete domination, use of that control for an improper motive which breaches a duty owed, and injury proximately caused by that breach?

HOLDING AND DECISION: (Arnold, C.J.) Yes. To pierce the corporate veil, one must show control amounting to complete domination, use of that control for an improper motive which breaches a duty owed, and injury proximately caused by that breach. Undercapitalizing a subsidiary is a sort of proxy for the second. Operating a corporation without sufficient funds to meet its obligations shows either an improper purpose or reckless disregard of the rights of others. Here, Contrux was undercapitalized in the accounting sense. However, it did carry $11 million worth of liability insurance. Insurance meets the policy behind the proper capitalization requirement just as well as a healthy balance sheet. There is no evidence that Telecom (D) or Contrux knew that the insurance company was going to become insolvent. The doctrine of limited liability would largely be destroyed if a parent corporation could be held liable simply on the basis of errors in business judgment. Affirmed but modified to dismiss with prejudice.

DISSENT: (Heaney, J.) Although Contrux's liability insurance is a relevant factor to be considered, a fact finder might nevertheless find that this factor alone does not require a verdict for Telecom (D).

▌ ANALYSIS

State courts have developed a variety of tests designed to guide courts in determining when the corporate veil should be pierced. All, however, tend to embody some sort of domination or abuse requirement and require proof of injustice should limited corporate liability be permitted. Studies have shown that, over the past forty years, courts have chosen to pierce the corporate veil in 40 percent of reported cases.

■═■

Quicknotes

CAPITALIZATION The aggregate value of all securities issued by a company.

CORPORATE VEIL Refers to the shielding from personal liability of a corporation's officers, directors or shareholders for unlawful conduct engaged in by the corporation.

LIMITED LIABILITY An advantage of doing business in the corporate form by safeguarding shareholders from liability for the debts or obligations of the corporation.

SUBSIDIARY A company a majority of whose shares are owned by another corporation and which is subject to that corporation's control.

■═■

Fletcher v. Atex, Inc.

Keyboard user (P) v. Keyboard maker (D)

68 F.3d 1451 (2d Cir. 1995).

NATURE OF CASE: Appeal from summary judgment dismissing defendant in design defect case.

FACT SUMMARY: Fletcher (P) brought suit against Atex, Inc. (D) and Eastman Kodak (D), its parent company, to recover for injuries incurred from the utilization of computer keyboards produced by Atex (D).

🏛 **RULE OF LAW**
Under applicable state law, the court may pierce the corporate veil of a company and hold its shareholders personally liable only in cases involving fraud, or where the company is a mere instrumentality or alter ego of its parent company.

FACTS: Atex, Inc. (D) was a wholly owned subsidiary of Eastman Kodak (Kodak) (D) until 1992, when Atex (D) sold substantially all of its assets to another party. Atex (D) then changed its name to 805 Middlesex Corp. (Middlesex). Kodak (D) continued as the sole shareholder of Middlesex. Fletcher (P) and other claimants (P) brought suit against Atex (D) and Kodak (D) to recover for stress injuries they incurred from utilizing keyboards produced by Atex (D). Fletcher (P) argued that Kodak (D) exercised undue control over Atex (D) by using a cash management system, exerting control over Atex's (D) major expenditures, and by dominating Atex's (D) board of directors. The lower court dismissed Kodak (D) as a defendant on summary judgment. Fletcher et al. (P) appealed.

ISSUE: May the court pierce the corporate veil of a company and hold its shareholders personally liable only in cases involving fraud, or where the company is a mere instrumentality or alter ego of its parent company?

HOLDING AND DECISION: (Cabranes, J.) Yes. Under applicable state law, the court may pierce the corporate veil of a company and hold its shareholders individually liable only in cases involving fraud, or where the company is a mere instrumentality or alter ego of its parent company. New York state law looks to the law of the state of incorporation to determine whether the court will disregard the corporate form and hold shareholders individually liable for the actions of the corporation. Since Atex (D) is a Delaware corporation, the law of that forum applies. Under Delaware law, an alter ego claim is demonstrated by a showing that the parent and its subsidiary acted as a single economic entity, and it would be unjust or inequitable to treat them as distinct from one another. Factors the court may consider in making its determination include the adequacy of capitalization, the corporation's

solvency, payment of dividends, observation of corporate formalities, and the intermingling of funds. Summary judgment may be granted for a defendant parent corporation where there has been an absence of sufficient evidence proffered to raise an issue of material fact as to the question of instrumentality. In this case, it would not be correct to disregard the corporate entity solely based on Kodak's (D) implementation of a cash management system. Such a system does not rise to the level of intermingling contemplated by the statute. Similarly, an overlap in the two companies' (D) boards of directors is not conclusive of Kodak's (D) domination over Atex (D). Fletcher (P) failed to demonstrate the degree of control necessary to pierce Atex's (D) corporate veil and hold Kodak (D) liable. Affirmed.

▶ **ANALYSIS**

It is not uncommon for publicly held corporations to own numerous subsidiaries. Subsidiaries are established in order to operate in areas that are either unrelated to the parent's main business, or that necessitate more centralized organization. Here, Atex (D) was in the business of manufacturing keyboards, an enterprise unrelated to Kodak's (D) primary business. Although Atex (D) looked to Kodak (D) for support on significant transactions, it is not unusual for a parent corporation or a majority shareholder to participate in such transactions involving the subsidiary.

■■■

Quicknotes

ALTER EGO Other self; under the "alter ego" doctrine, the court disregards the corporate entity and holds the individual shareholders liable for acts done knowingly and intentionally in the corporation's name.

CORPORATE VEIL Refers to the shielding from personal liability of a corporation's officers, directors or shareholders for unlawful conduct engaged in by the corporation.

■■■

United States v. Bestfoods

Federal government (P) v. Polluter (D)

524 U.S. 51 (1998).

NATURE OF CASE: Appeal from government suit to recover costs of cleaning up hazardous site under the Comprehensive Environmental Response, Compensation, and Liability Act of 1980 (CERCLA).

FACT SUMMARY: Bestfoods (D) alleged it could not be held liable for the actions of a corporate subsidiary.

🏛 RULE OF LAW

A corporate parent that actively participated in, and exercised control over, the operations of a polluting facility itself may, without more, be held directly liable in its own right as an operator of a facility.

FACTS: Bestfoods (D) incorporated a wholly owned subsidiary to purchase a chemical plant. The previous operator had dumped hazardous substances on the site, polluting the soil and ground water there. The new company continued production and pollution, as well. After the plant was sold to another company that filed for bankruptcy, the Michigan Department of Natural Resources found a buyer who agreed to clean up the site. The federal Environmental Protection Agency (EPA) had started cleaning up the site and filed suit to recover some of its costs. The various contribution-claims, cross-claims, and counter-claims were consolidated for trial. The first phase dealing with liability was completed. The district court said that operator liability could attach to a parent company both directly, when the parent itself operated the facility, and indirectly, when state law could be used to pierce the corporate veil. The court of appeals held that Bestfoods (D) was not liable since it did not utilize the subsidiary corporate form to perpetrate fraud or subvert justice. The United States Supreme Court granted certiorari to resolve a conflict among the Circuit courts over the extent to which parent corporations could be held liable under CERCLA for operating facilities ostensibly under the control of their subsidiaries.

ISSUE: May a corporate parent that actively participated in, and exercised control over, the operations of the polluting facility itself, without more, be held directly liable in its own right as an operator of a facility?

HOLDING AND DECISION: (Souter, J.) Yes. A corporate parent that actively participated in, and exercised control over, the operations of the polluting facility itself may, without more, be held directly liable in its own right as an operator of a facility. A parent company that actively participated in, and exercised control over, the operations of a subsidiary may not be held liable as an operator of a polluting facility owned or operated by the subsidiary, unless the corporate veil may be pierced. The appeals court erred in limiting direct liability under the statute to a parent's sole or joint venture operation, thereby eliminating any possible finding that Bestfoods (D) was liable as an operator here. Evidence an agent of Bestfoods (D) actively participated in, and exerted control over, environmental matters was sufficient to raise an issue of Bestfoods's (D) operation of the facility through its agent's actions. Prudence counsels that we remand, on the theory of direct operation, for reevaluation of this or any other agent's role in operation of the facility. Vacated and remanded.

▶ ANALYSIS

The Court did not resolve the question whether state or federal law applied to piercing in CERCLA cases. In some cases, persons with authority to control the subsidiary have been held liable even though that power had never been exercised. Similar issues arise in employment discrimination cases brought under title VII of the Civil Rights Act of 1964.

■==■

Quicknotes

CERCLA Enacted to fill gaps in environmental clean-up efforts left by Resource Conservation and Recovery Act of 1976.

CORPORATE VEIL Refers to the shielding from personal liability of a corporation's officers, directors or shareholders for unlawful conduct engaged in by the corporation.

SUBSIDIARY A company a majority of whose shares are owned by another corporation and which is subject to that corporation's control.

■==■

Stark v. Flemming

Farmer (P) v. HEW Secretary (D)

283 F.2d 410 (9th Cir. 1960).

NATURE OF CASE: Suit to obtain Social Security benefits.

FACT SUMMARY: Stark (P) started a corporation and paid herself wages so as to qualify for Social Security benefits.

🏛 RULE OF LAW
Where corporate formalities have been observed, the form cannot be disregarded unless authorized by statute.

FACTS: Stark (P) placed her assets in a newly formed corporation. She operated her farm and duplex for it and paid herself a $400 a month salary. This was done so as to qualify her for Social Security. Flemming (D), the Secretary of Health, Education and Welfare (HEW), denied Stark (P) her claimed benefits on the theory that the corporation was a mere sham. The district court found for Flemming (D) on this basis. It concluded that Stark's (P) only purpose in incorporating was to qualify for Social Security benefits.

ISSUE: Where not provided for by statute, may the government withhold benefits because a corporation was formed merely to qualify for them?

HOLDING AND DECISION: (Per curiam) No. If Congress has not specified that benefits are to be withheld in these cases, the Secretary of HEW (D) is not permitted to deny them. All corporate formalities were complied with by Stark (P), and regardless of her motive the corporation must be treated as a legitimate entity. Flemming (D) is permitted to make an independent appraisal of the salary paid to Stark (P) in order to determine if it is excessive. Flemming (D) may compare salaries paid to others in similar situations and commensurate with Stark's (P) responsibilities and the capital contribution to the business. The decision of the district court is vacated and remanded for further proceedings.

▌ ANALYSIS

Stark stands for the principle, that corporate form cannot be ignored. The motive of the incorporator is immaterial. Therefore, incorporation cannot be attacked because the incorporator's sole motive was to save taxes or to avoid personal liability. No legitimate business purpose is required. A person is free to adopt whatever form he desires, so long as he observes the formalities associated with his choice. There must be a compelling policy reason for piercing the form if statutory authority to do so is not granted.

■=■

Roccograndi v. Unemployment Comp. Bd. of Review

Benefits applicant (P) v. State agency (D)

Pa. Super. Ct., 178 A.2d 784 (1962).

NATURE OF CASE: Action to require payment of unemployment compensation benefits.

FACT SUMMARY: When business was slow, members of a family corporation were "laid off" and applied for unemployment compensation benefits.

🏛 RULE OF LAW
The corporate form may be ignored where applicants for unemployment compensation benefits exert sufficient control over the corporation to lay themselves off or rehire themselves at will and are considered self-employed.

FACTS: Roccograndi (P) and two other applicants filed for unemployment compensation benefits when they were "laid off." All were members and shareholders of a family business that during slow periods laid off various family members so as to qualify for these benefits. The Unemployment Compensation Board denied the claim based on the fact that the applicants were really self-employed. A referee reversed. The Board of Review (D) reversed the referee.

ISSUE: May corporate form, be disregarded for the purpose of unemployment benefits where the applicants exert sufficient control over the corporation to lay themselves off and/or rehire themselves at will?

HOLDING AND DECISION: (Montgomery, J.) Yes. Where the applicants can exert sufficient control over a corporate entity to lay themselves off when business is bad, they are really self-employed. The Unemployment Compensation Act provides that no benefits shall be given the self-employed. Case law on the Act has held that in cases of close family corporations, such as Roccograndi's (P), the corporate form may be disregarded. The decision of the Unemployment Compensation Board of Review (D) is sustained.

▶ *ANALYSIS*

To qualify for benefits from the State, an applicant must be able to bring himself within the class sought to be benefited. The self-employed are excluded. The courts have defined self-employed as members of a close corporation in which they retain a substantial amount of control after being laid off. This is a public policy decision that said parties are not within the class sought to be benefited by the legislation.

■▬▬■

Cargill, Inc. v. Hedge

Creditor (P) v. Debtor (D)

Minn. Sup. Ct., 375 N.W.2d 477 (1985).

NATURE OF CASE: Appeal from affirmance of judgment for defendant debtors in action on execution by judgment creditor.

FACT SUMMARY: The Hedges (D), whose land was held by them through a family farm corporation, contended that the corporation's corporate veil could be reverse pierced so they would not lose their homestead exemption to judgment creditor Cargill, Inc. (P).

🏛 RULE OF LAW
The corporate veil of a family farm corporation may be reverse pierced so that the owner-occupants of the farm, by placing their land in the corporation, do not lose their homestead exemption from judgment creditors.

FACTS: Sam (D) and Annette Hedge (the Hedges) purchased a 160-acre farm and then assigned their vendee rights to Hedge Farm, Inc., a family farm corporation. Annette was the sole shareholder. For several years, Sam (D) purchased farm supplies and services on account from Cargill, Inc. (P). After Cargill (P) commenced suit on the account, it discovered the Hedges' corporation. Eventually, judgment was entered against Sam (D) and the corporation, and an execution sale was held, with Cargill (P) as the successful bidder. Annette intervened, and the trial court held that the Hedges had a right to be exempt from the execution of 80 acres, which constituted their homestead under the state's constitution. The state's intermediate appellate court affirmed, finding that Annette, as sole shareholder, had an equitable interest in the corporate property, that when coupled with occupancy, satisfied the homestead exemption requirements. The state's highest court granted review.

ISSUE: May the corporate veil of a family farm corporation be reverse pierced so that the owner-occupants of the farm, by placing their land in the corporation, do not lose their homestead exemption from judgment creditors?

HOLDING AND DECISION: (Simonnet, J.) Yes. The corporate veil of a family farm corporation may be reverse pierced so that the owner-occupants of the farm, by placing their land in the corporation, do not lose their homestead exemption from judgment creditors. Although the result reached by the trial and appellate courts is correct, the approach taken by the appellate court is not well suited to resolving the issues presented by this case, which involves not only a creditor's rights, but also the relationship of a shareholder to a corporation. That is because if Annette is the sole "owner" of the corporation, there is no need to assert a homestead exemption since she is not the debtor. However, a reverse pierce of the corporate veil may be used. Through a reverse pierce, the corporate entity is disregarded to promote strong policy interests. To do so, however, there must be a close identity between the shareholders and the corporation, so that it may be said the corporation is the shareholders' alter ego. Another important consideration as to whether to permit reverse piercing is whether a third party will be injured thereby. Here, there was a very close identity between the Hedges and the corporation. They operated the farm as their own, had no lease with the corporation, paid no rent, and used the farmhouse as their home. All family members were officers and directors of the corporation, but none received a salary. Here, too, there is a very strong policy reason to reverse pierce, i.e., to promote the purpose of the homestead exemption. Accordingly, the corporation is disregarded and the farm is treated as if it were owned by Sam (D) and Annette. As a co-owner, Sam (D) is entitled to claim the homestead exemption, and Cargill's (P) execution sale of the exempted 80 acres is void. Affirmed.

▶ ANALYSIS

A reverse piercing claim may be brought by either the corporate insider, as was the case here, or by one with a claim against the corporate insider. In either case, the corporation is disregarded so that the corporate insider and the corporation are treated as one. As the court and critics have noted, however, there is the danger that a debtor will be able to use the corporation to escape personal liability while also using the reverse piercing doctrine to prevent creditors from reaching the corporation's assets. The court's answer to this danger is that "a reverse pierce should be permitted in only the most carefully limited circumstances."

■—■

Quicknotes

CORPORATE VEIL Refers to the shielding from personal liability of a corporation's officers, directors or shareholders for unlawful conduct engaged in by the corporation.

JUDGMENT CREDITOR A creditor who has obtained an enforceable judgment against a debtor and who may collect on that debt once the debtor has been given notice of the action.

■—■

Pepper v. Litton

Bankruptcy trustee (D) v. Corporation owner (P)

308 U.S. 295 (1939).

NATURE OF CASE: Action to recover salary claims against a bankrupt corporation.

FACT SUMMARY: Litton (P) was the sole shareholder and head of a bankrupt corporation. He filed a wage claim in bankruptcy.

🏛 RULE OF LAW
Where a claimant in bankruptcy has dominated and controlled a corporation, his claim may be subordinated or even disallowed upon a showing that enforcement of the claim would be unfair to other creditors.

FACTS: Litton (P) was the sole owner of a small corporation. When the corporation became insolvent, Litton (P) brought suit and recovered a judgment against it for "wage" claims. When bankruptcy was declared, Litton (P) filed a priority claim for wages with Pepper (D), the trustee. Pepper (D) disallowed the claim. Litton (P) brought suit in district court. The court found that Litton (P) had engaged in a scheme to defraud creditors and dismissed Litton's (P) claim under its broad equity powers. It found that Litton (P) totally controlled the corporation and had dealt unfairly with it. Finally, allowing Litton (P) to enforce his claim would be unfair to other creditors.

ISSUE: May the bankruptcy court disallow a claim by a party who dominated and controlled the bankrupt corporation?

HOLDING AND DECISION: (Douglas, J.) Yes. The bankruptcy court may disallow a claim by a party who dominated and controlled the bankrupt corporation. The parties to be protected in a bankruptcy proceeding are the corporation's innocent creditors. Therefore, a party owning and controlling the corporation who files a claim must be carefully scrutinized. Where he has dealt with the corporation unfairly and has attempted to defraud creditors, or where the corporate form may be disregarded, his claim should be subordinated or even disallowed. To hold otherwise would work an injustice upon those who innocently bestowed credit to the bankrupt corporation. In one-man or family corporations, claims will normally be subordinated. Here, the court found that Litton (P) had initiated a plan to defraud creditors. The fact that his claim has been reduced to judgment is immaterial. The bankruptcy court has broad equity powers to disallow claims that would be unfair to innocent creditors. The decision of the district court is affirmed and the judgment of the circuit court of appeals reversed.

▶ ANALYSIS

By way of explanation, wage claims take precedence over creditor claims in bankruptcy. By filing a wage claim, Litton (P) tried to put himself ahead of the corporation's creditors. This is known as the "Deep Rock" doctrine. This doctrine also applies to a dominant or controlling stockholder or group of stockholders. *Southern Pacific Company v. Bogert*, 250 U.S. 483 (1919).

Quicknotes

FIDUCIARY DUTY A legal obligation to act for the benefit of another, including subordinating one's personal interests to that of the other person.

Nissen Corp. v. Miller

Successor corporation (D) v. Injured consumer (P)

Md. Ct. App., 594 A.2d 564 (1991).

NATURE OF CASE: Appeal from reversal of summary judgment in product liability action.

FACT SUMMARY: Brandt (P) purchased and was injured by a treadmill manufactured by American Tredex Corp. Nissen Corp. (D) was the successor corporation to American Tredex, and Brandt (P) sued Nissen (D) and others for product liability.

RULE OF LAW
Corporate successor liability does not include an exception for "continuity of enterprise."

FACTS: Brandt (P) purchased a treadmill from Atlantic Fitness Products (Atlantic). The machine had been designed, manufactured, and marketed by American Tredex Corp. That same year, Nissen Corp. (D) bought the assets of American Tredex, but expressly excluded assumption of liability for injuries arising from any American Tredex product. Five years later, Brandt (P) was injured by the treadmill, and a year after that, American Tredex (known as AT Corp. pursuant to the asset sale) was administratively dissolved. Yet a year after that, Brandt (P) and his wife sued American Tredex, AT Corp., Nissen, and Atlantic for negligence, strict liability, breach of express and implied warranties, and loss of consortium. Atlantic cross-claimed against Nissen (D) for indemnity and contribution; and Nissen (D) was granted summary judgment by the trial court. On appeal, the intermediate court reversed, and the state's highest court granted review.

ISSUE: Does corporate successor liability include an exception for "continuity of enterprise"?

HOLDING AND DECISION: (Chasanow, J.) No. Corporate successor liability does not include an exception for "continuity of enterprise." The issue is whether the general, traditional rule of corporate successor liability, which has four exceptions, should be expanded to include a fifth exception for "continuity of enterprise." This exception focuses on the continuation of the business operation or enterprise where there is no continuation in ownership. Under a mere continuation of entity exception, which would not apply here, there is no successor liability unless there is a continuation of directors and management. Here, there is no contention that Nissen (D) was a "mere continuation" of American Tredex or that the sale of assets falls within any of the traditional exceptions. Therefore, to proceed, Brandt (P) must convince the court to use the continuity of enterprise exception. His policy argument is that this exception is necessary for injured consumers to have recourse against "some entity" where the manufactur-er no longer exists. Nissen (D) counters that the traditional exceptions are sufficient and strike a balance between the rights of creditors and successor corporations by preserving principles of corporate law and promoting the free alienability of business assets while still protecting consumers from fraudulent corporate transactions. However, the principles underlying strict products liability is that it is the seller who places defective and unreasonably dangerous products on the market who is held accountable; a corporate successor is not a seller and bears no blame in bringing the product and the user together. By adopting the continuity of enterprise exception, the court would potentially spread liability unfairly, not only to major corporations, but also to small businesses that may not be in the position to spread the risk or insure against it. Moreover, here, Nissen (D) did more than was required of it, because it maintained a network to service American Tredex customers and furnished replacement parts to them. Having done so, Nissen (D) should not be penalized for such beneficial actions, or for retaining some of American Tredex's employees or for assuming some of American Tredex's commitments—Nissen (D) was not one of those responsible for Brandt's injuries. Finally, the Restatement (Second) of Torts, on which the state's strict liability in tort is based, does not contemplate successor corporation liability. Therefore, the continuity of enterprise theory of successor corporate liability is rejected. Reversed.

DISSENT: (Eldridge, J.) The "continuity of enterprise" exception should be added to the general rule of nonliability of successor corporations with regard to defective products.

ANALYSIS

As the court intimates, the policy considerations involved in the imposition of successor liability must be carefully balanced. On the one hand, imposition of successor liability makes the alienability of assets more difficult. On the other hand, there is the omnipresent risk that corporate assets will be sold for less than fair consideration or that the proceeds of the sale will be siphoned off by the shareholders. Thus the interests of creditors, including tort victims, must be adequately balanced against the interests of the shareholders.

■■■■

Continued on next page.

Quicknotes

BREACH OF EXPRESS WARRANTY The breach of an express promise made by one party to a contract that the other party may rely on a fact, relieving that party from the obligation of determining whether the fact is true and indemnifying the other party from liability if that fact is shown to be false.

LOSS OF CONSORTIUM An action brought based on willful interference with the marital relationship.

NEGLIGENCE Conduct falling below the standard of care that a reasonable person would demonstrate under similar conditions.

STRICT LIABILITY Liability for all injuries proximately caused by a party's conducting of certain inherently dangerous activities without regard to negligence or fault.

SUMMARY JUDGMENT Judgment rendered by a court in response to a motion by one of the parties, claiming that the lack of a question of material fact in respect to an issue warrants disposition of the issue without consideration by the jury.

CHAPTER 7

Financial Matters and the Corporation

Quick Reference Rules of Law

Hanewald v. Bryan's Inc.

Store owner (P) v. Purchaser (D)

N.D. Sup. Ct., 429 N.W.2d 414 (1988).

NATURE OF CASE: Appeal from judgment in an action for breach of a lease agreement and promissory note.

FACT SUMMARY: After Bryan's, Inc. (D) went out of business without paying off a promissory note or the lease on his store, Hanewald (P) filed suit against the corporation and the Bryan (D) family members, to whom the corporate stock had been issued, seeking to hold them personally liable.

🏛 RULE OF LAW
A shareholder is liable to corporate creditors to the extent his stock has not been paid for.

FACTS: After the Bryans (D) incorporated Bryan's, Inc. (D) to operate a general retail clothing store, they issued stock to themselves, lent the corporation some cash, and personally guaranteed a bank loan. However, they failed to pay the corporation for the stock that was issued. Bryan's, Inc. (D) then purchased Hanewald's (P) inventory and assets in a dry goods store for cash and for a corporate promissory note. It also signed a lease on Hanewald's (P) store. When Bryan's, Inc. (D) closed after a few months, it paid off all its creditors except Hanewald (P), sending him a notice of rescission in an attempt to avoid the lease. Hanewald (P) sued Bryan's, Inc. (D) and the Bryans (D) for breach of the lease agreement and the promissory note, seeking to hold the Bryans (D) personally liable. The trial court ruled against Bryan's, Inc. (D) but refused to hold the Bryans (D) personally liable. Hanewald (P) appealed.

ISSUE: Is a shareholder liable to corporate creditors to the extent his stock has not been paid for?

HOLDING AND DECISION: (Meschke, J.) Yes. A shareholder is liable to corporate creditors to the extent his stock has not been paid for. A corporation that issues its stock as a gratuity commits a fraud upon creditors who deal with it on the faith of its capital stock. Where, as here, a loan was repaid by the corporation to the shareholders before its operations were abandoned, the loan cannot be considered a capital contribution. The Bryans (D) had a statutory duty to pay for shares that were issued to them by Bryan's, Inc. (D). However, Bryan's, Inc. (D) did not receive any payment, either in labor, services, money, or property, for the stock issued to Keith and Joan Bryan (D). The Bryans (D) have not challenged this finding of fact on appeal. Thus, the trial court erred as a matter of law in refusing to hold the Bryans (D) personally liable for the corporation's debt to Hanewald (P). Affirmed in part, reversed in part, and remanded.

▶ ANALYSIS

The Bryans' (D) failure to pay for their shares in the corporation made them personally liable under the court's application of § 25 of the Model Business Corporation Act (MBCA). The court also applied Article XII, § 9, of the state's constitution, stating that no corporation shall issue stock or bonds except for money, labor done, or money or property actually received. The purpose of the constitutional and statutory provisions is to protect the public and those dealing with the corporation.

■━■

Quicknotes

CONSIDERATION Value given by one party in exchange for performance, or a promise to perform, by another party.

LIMITED LIABILITY The maximum amount a person participating in a corporation can lose resulting from a lawsuit against the corporation or other losses suffered by the corporation.

PAR VALUE The stated value of a security.

RESCISSION The canceling of an agreement and the return of the parties to their positions prior to the formation of the contract.

■━■

Securities and Exchange Commn. v. Ralston Purina Co.

Government agency (P) v. Stock issuer (D)

346 U.S. 119 (1953).

NATURE OF CASE: Action to enjoin the unregistered offerings of stock under the Securities Act of 1933.

FACT SUMMARY: Ralston Purina Co. (D) offered treasury stock to their key employees, which the Securities and Exchange Commission (SEC) (P) attempted to enjoin.

🏛 RULE OF LAW
The exemption in § 4(1) of the Securities Act of 1933, which exempts transactions not involving any public offering from the registration requirement, applies only when all the offerees have access to the same kind of information that would be available if registration were required.

FACTS: Since 1911, Ralston Purina Co. (D) has had a policy of encouraging stock ownership among its employees and, since 1942, has made unissued common shares available to some of them. Ralston Purina (D) had sold nearly $2,000,000 of stock to employees between the years of 1947 and 1951. They had attempted to avoid the registration requirements of the Securities Act of 1933, under the exemption contained in § 4(1) of the Act, which exempted transactions by an issuer not involving any public offering. Each year between 1947 and 1951, Ralston Purina (D) authorized the sale of common stock to employees who, without any solicitation by the Company (D) or its officers or employees, inquired as to how to purchase common stock of Ralston Purina (D). The branch and store managers were advised that only the employees who took the initiative and were interested in buying stock at the present market prices would be able to purchase the stock. Among those taking advantage of the offer were employees with the duties of artist, bakeshop foreman, chow-loading foreman, clerical assistant, copywriter, electrician, stock clerk, mill office clerk, order credit trainee, production trainee, stenographer, and veterinarian. The buyers resided in 50 widely separated communities scattered throughout the United States. The record shows that in 1947, 243 employees bought stock, 20 in 1948, 414 in 1949, and 411 in 1950; and, in 1951, 165 made applications to purchase the stock. No actual records were kept showing how many employees were offered the stock, but it is estimated that, in 1951, at least 500 employees were offered the stock. Ralston Purina (D) had approximately 7,000 employees during the years in question. Ralston Purina (D) bases its exemption claim on the classification that all the offerees were key employees in its organization. Its position at trial was that a key employee included an individual who is eligible for promotion; an individual

who especially influences others or who advises others; a person whom the employees look to in some special way; one who carries some special responsibility and who is sympathetic to management; and one who is ambitious and who the management feels is likely to be promoted to a greater responsibility. They admit, however, that an offering to all of its employees would be a public offering. The district court held that the exemption applied and dismissed the suit, and the court of appeals affirmed the decision.

ISSUE: Does an offer of stock by a company to a limited number of its employees automatically qualify for the exemption for transactions not involving any public offering?

HOLDING AND DECISION: (Clark, J.) No. The Securities Act does not define what a private offering is and what a public offering is. It is clear that an offer need not be open to the whole world to qualify as a public offering. If Ralston Purina (D) had made the stock offer to all of its employees, it would have been a public offering. The court looked at the intent of the Securities Act, which is to protect investors by promoting full disclosure of information thought to be necessary for informed investment decisions. When the Act grants an exemption, the class of people involved was not considered as needing the disclosure that the Act normally requires. Therefore, when an offering is made to people who can fend for themselves, the transaction is considered to be one not involving a public offering. Most of the employees purchasing the stock from Ralston Purina (D) were not in a position to know or have access to the kind of information which registration under the Act would disclose and, therefore, were in need of the protection of the Act. Stock offers made to employees may qualify for the exemption if the employees are executive personnel who, because of their position, have access to the same kind of information that the Act would make available in the form of a registration statement. Absent such a showing of special circumstances, employees are just as much members of the investing public as any of their neighbors in the community. The burden of proof is on the issuer of the stock, who is claiming an exemption to show that he qualifies for the exemption. Also, since the right to an exemption depends on the knowledge of the offerees, the issuer's motives are irrelevant. It didn't matter that Ralston Purina's (D) motives may have been good because it did not show that its employees had the requisite information. Therefore, judgment reversed.

Continued on next page.

▶ *ANALYSIS*

The exemption discussed above is now found in § 4(2) instead of § 4(1). This case is considered to be the leading case in this area. The test established in this case is still used in determining whether an offering qualifies for the nonpublic offering exemption of § 4(2). Some of the factors used in determining whether the offerees have sufficient access to information concerning the stock are the number of offerees, the size of the offering, the relationship of the offerees, the manner of the solicitation of the offerees, and the amount of investment experience of the offerees.

■━■

Quicknotes

SECURITIES ACT, § 4 Exempts nonpublic offerings from registration requirements.

■━■

Smith v. Gross

Stock buyer (P) v. Stock seller (D)

604 F.2d 639 (9th Cir. 1979).

NATURE OF CASE: Appeal from dismissal of an action charging violation of federal securities laws.

FACT SUMMARY: The Smiths' (P) suit charging Gross (D) with violation of federal securities laws was dismissed on the ground that there was no security involved in the transactions between the parties.

🏛 **RULE OF LAW**
The test as to whether something constitutes an investment contract type of security is whether the scheme (1) involves an investment of money (2) in a common enterprise (3) with profits to come solely from the efforts of others.

FACTS: The Smiths (P) responded to a newsletter in which Gross (D) solicited buyer-investors to raise earthworms, promising they would double every 60 days and he would buy back all the worms produced at $2.25 per pound. He (D) told the Smiths (P) little work was required, success was guaranteed by the repurchase agreement, etc. A suit the Smiths (P) filed charging Gross (D) with violation of the federal securities laws was dismissed on the ground that no "security" was involved. On appeal, the Smiths (P) argued that there had been an investment contract type security involved. They claimed the worms did not multiply at the promised rate and that a profit could be made only if the promised multiplication rate were reached and if Gross (D) bought back the entire production at the higher-than-market price of $2.25 he had promised. As it turned out, he could pay that price only by selling worms to new worm farmers at inflated prices.

ISSUE: Does an investment contract exist when a scheme (1) involves an investment of money (2) in a common enterprise (3) with profits to come solely from the efforts of others?

HOLDING AND DECISION: (Per curiam) Yes. An investment contract type of security exists when a scheme (1) involves an investment of money (2) in a common enterprise (meaning one in which the fortunes of the investor are interwoven with and dependent upon the effort and success of those seeking the investment or of third parties) (3) with profits to come solely from the efforts of others. In this case, these three criteria are met. Thus, a security was involved. Reversed.

▶ *ANALYSIS*

The definition of "security" that has been adopted in this line of cases is quite broad. The result has been to permit investors suckered into a number of ingenious investment schemes to utilize the protection of the securities laws. However, in *International Brotherhood of Teamsters v. Daniel*, 439 U.S. 551 (1979), the United States Supreme Court refused to characterize a noncontributory pension plan as a "security."

■■■

Quicknotes

FRANCHISE AGREEMENT A contract pursuant to which a supplier of goods or services agrees to permit a reseller to sell the good or service or to otherwise conduct business on behalf of the franchise.

SECURITIES ACT, § 4 Exempts non-public offerings from registration requirements.

■■■

Stokes v. Continental Trust Co. of City of New York

Shareholder (P) v. Corporation (D)

N.Y. Ct. App., 78 N.E. 1090 (1906).

NATURE OF CASE: Action by shareholder to compel the corporation to sell him his proportionate share of a new issue of stock.

FACT SUMMARY: Stokes (P), a shareholder of Continental Trust Co. of City of New York (D), demanded that it sell him an equivalent number of newly issued shares of stock to the proportion he now holds.

🏛 RULE OF LAW
A corporation must allow a shareholder to purchase newly issued stock at the fixed price to allow him to keep his proportionate share of the stock.

FACTS: Continental Trust Co. of City of New York (Continental) (D) had 500,000 shares of outstanding stock of which Stokes (P) owned 221 shares. The par value of the stock was $100, but the market value was $550. Blair and Company offered to buy 500,000 newly issued shares of Continental (D) at $450, if those shares were issued. Continental (D) held a shareholders' meeting, and the new issue was voted. Stokes (P) demanded that he be sold enough of the new shares to keep his percentage of stock ownership the same before and after the new issue. He also demanded that he be sold these shares at par value; however, these demands were turned down.

ISSUE: Is a stockholder entitled to purchase enough shares of newly issued stock to insure that his proportionate share of ownership will remain constant?

HOLDING AND DECISION: (Vann, J.) Yes. A corporation must allow a shareholder to purchase newly issued stock (at the fixed sales price) to allow him to maintain his proportionate share of the stock of the corporation. Stockholders may elect to do so as a matter of right. Unless this opportunity is extended to each shareholder and either executed or effectively waived, the corporation may not issue new shares without at least incurring liability for the damage done to the shareholder's interest. If the stockholder elects to buy, however, he must do so at the fixed sales price, not the par value. (It would be unfair to allow him to buy at par, since this would inflate his proportionate interest.) Here, Stokes (P) had a right to purchase a proportionate interest of new stock. Since he offered to do so (though at an incorrect price), he cannot be said to have waived his right, so damages are appropriate. Since again, however, his offer was at par, which was incorrect, his damages must be measured as the difference between that price and the market value. Reversed and the judgment of the trial court modified.

▶ ANALYSIS

This case represents the common-law view on preemptive rights, or the right of first refusal of new issues of stock. The prevailing view is that these rights apply only to common stock.

■═■

Quicknotes

PAR VALUE The stated value of a security.

PREEMPTIVE RIGHTS The right of existing shareholders to the first purchase of new issuances of stock in proportion to their share in ownership.

■═■

Katzowitz v. Sidler

Shareholder (P) v. Shareholder (D)

N.Y. Ct. App., 249 N.E.2d 359 (1969).

NATURE OF CASE: Declaratory judgment action to establish rights in corporate assets.

FACT SUMMARY: Two of three directors of a closed corporation voted an additional issuance of stock, which they opted to purchase and which the third director refused. When the corporate assets were sold, the proceeds were distributed in proportion to the stock owned, and the third director sought to have this distribution set aside.

🏛 RULE OF LAW
Where new shares are offered in a closed corporation, existing shareholders who do not want to or are unable to purchase their share of the issuance are not estopped from bringing an action based on a fraudulent dilution of their interest where the price for the shares is inadequate.

FACTS: Katzowitz (P), Sidler (D), and Lasker (D) were the sole shareholders and directors in the Sulburn Corporation. Sidler (D) and Lasker (D) had joined forces in an attempt to oust Katzowitz (P) from his position in the corporation, and by stipulation Katzowitz (P) agreed to withdraw from active participation. At the time of Katzowitz's (P) withdrawal, the corporation owed each of the directors $2,500, and Sidler (D) and Lasker (D) proposed a new issuance of stock to ameliorate the debt. Over Katzowitz's (P) objections, they passed a resolution whereby each of the three could purchase 25 shares at $100 per share when the stock was actually worth $1,800 per share. Katzowitz (P) did not opt to purchase, and when the company was dissolved he received $3,147.59 to Sidler's (D) and Lasker's (D) $18,885.52. Katzowitz (P) brought this action to set aside the distribution to allow Sidler (D) and Lasker (D) the return of their purchase price of the 25 shares, and to compel an equal distribution of the remaining assets.

ISSUE: Can a shareholder who did not purchase from a new issuance of shares set aside that issuance as fraudulent where the new shares are offered in a closed corporation at a totally inadequate price causing dilution of the shareholders' interest in the corporation?

HOLDING AND DECISION: (Keating, J.) Yes. Where new shares are offered in a closed corporation, existing shareholders who do not want to or are unable to purchase their share of the issuance are not estopped from bringing an action based on a fraudulent dilution of their interest where the price for shares was inadequate. The concept of preemptive rights was fashioned by the courts to protect against dilution of shareholders' interest and is particularly applicable to the situation of a closed corporation. Although the courts and the legislature are reluctant to regulate the price at which shares can be offered, if issuing stock for less than fair value results in a fraudulent dilution of the shareholders' interests, it will be set aside. Here, Sidler (D) and Lasker (D) issued stock at $100 per share when the true value of the stock was over $1,800 per share, knowing that Katzowitz (P) would not elect to purchase his proportionate share and thereby diluting his interest. Thus, the issuance was fraudulent, and after allowing Sidler (D) and Lasker (D) the amount they paid for the additional shares of stock, the remaining assets of the corporation will be divided among the shareholders in proportion to their interests held before the issuance. Reversed.

▌ ANALYSIS

Although the courts are reluctant to fix prices at which corporate stock can be issued, they can find little justification for issuing stock far below its fair value. Generally, the only time stock can be issued far below its book value is when book value is not reflective of the actual worth of the corporation or where a publicly held corporation experiences difficulties floating a new issue. The Model Corporations Act, § 26, provides that preemptive rights exist only to the extent that such rights are provided, if at all, in the articles of incorporation.

■=■

Quicknotes

CLOSE CORPORATION A corporation whose shares (or at least voting shares) are held by a closely knit group of shareholders or a single person.

PAR VALUE The stated value of a security.

PREEMPTIVE RIGHTS The right of existing shareholders to the first purchase of new issuances of stock in proportion to their share in ownership.

■=■

Lacos Land Company v. Arden Group, Inc.

Shareholders (P) v. Corporation (D)

Del. Ch. Ct., 517 A.2d 271 (1986).

NATURE OF CASE: Action to void issuance of class of corporate stock.

FACT SUMMARY: Briskin, an officer, director, and the main shareholder of Arden Group, Inc. (D), threatened actions adverse to the corporation if a new class of stock was not issued.

🏛 RULE OF LAW
Adoption of a new class of stock is voidable if the adoption was influenced by threats from a fiduciary.

FACTS: Briskin was an officer, director, and the main shareholder of Arden Group, Inc. (D). A proposal was made to issue a new class of voting stock. The stock was of a nature that only Briskin would be interested in purchasing. The new class would concentrate control with Briskin. Briskin made it known that he might interfere with ventures profitable to Arden Group (D) if the recapitalization was not approved. Following approval, Lacos Land Co. (P) and other shareholders filed an action seeking to enjoin the recapitalization.

ISSUE: Is adoption of a new class of stock voidable if the adoption was influenced by threats from a fiduciary?

HOLDING AND DECISION: (Allen, Chan.) Yes. Adoption of a new class of stock is voidable if the adoption was influenced by threats from a fiduciary. A fiduciary is under an obligation, at all times, to act with the interests of the corporation uppermost in mind. While a shareholder is not usually a fiduciary, directors and officers are. For an officer or director to use coercion upon the shareholders of a corporation to induce them to approve a measure is improper. Here, Briskin, who was not only a shareholder but a director and officer as well, made it clear he would block beneficial transactions if he did not get his way. This was quite unseemly and clearly a breach of fiduciary duty. This makes the transaction approved by the coercion voidable. Injunction issued.

▌ ANALYSIS

Coercion alone does not make a corporate transaction invalid. Individual shareholders can and often do use coercive tactics in corporate power struggles. Rather, it is improper coercion, here by a fiduciary, which brings a transaction into question.

Quicknotes

FIDUCIARY Person holding a legal obligation to act for the benefit of another.

FIDUCIARY DUTY A legal obligation to act for the benefit of another, including subordinating one's personal interests to that of the other person.

RECAPITALIZATION The restructuring of the capital of a corporation.

Dodge v. Ford Motor Co.

Shareholder (P) v. Corporation (D)

Mich. Sup. Ct., 170 N.W. 668 (1919).

NATURE OF CASE: Shareholder action to compel dividend.

FACT SUMMARY: Ostensibly to lower the price of its autos and increase jobs, the Ford Motor Co. (D) decided to discontinue the payment of dividends.

🏛 RULE OF LAW
Ordinarily, the directors of a corporation alone have the power to declare a dividend, but the courts will intervene to require that a dividend be paid if it is discovered that the refusal of the directors to do so is based in fraud or an intention to conduct the affairs of the corporation not for the shareholders.

FACTS: In the 1916 sales year, Ford Motor Co. (D) looked forward to a $60 million profit, $132 million in assets, $54 million in cash and municipal bonds, and a $112 million surplus—all set against a mere $20 million in liabilities. Despite this, President and Board Chairman Henry Ford announced that he was forthwith discontinuing the payment of dividends to stockholders. Two general reasons were given. First, he anticipated an $11.3 million construction program to go into effect in order to erect a smelter for the company. Second, and more importantly, he had determined to dedicate the company to the welfare of the general public by increasing jobs and lowering the price of cars annually. The Dodge Brothers (P), shareholders in Ford Motor Co. (D), objected to the latter reason for not declaring dividends so they filed this action to compel their payment. From decree for Dodge (P), this appeal followed.

ISSUE: May the courts intervene to require payment of a corporate dividend where the avowed motive of the directors for not paying it is to benefit the interests of third parties not participating in the ownership of the corporation?

HOLDING AND DECISION: (Ostrander, C.J.) Yes. Ordinarily, the directors of a corporation alone have the power to declare a dividend, but the courts will intervene to require that a dividend be paid if it is discovered that the refusal of the directors to do so is based in fraud or an intention to conduct the affairs of the corporation not for the shareholders. It is manifestly improper for the directors of a corporation to refuse to exercise their powers for the benefit of the shareholders. In following Chairman Ford's reasoning, here, however, the directors have done just that. As such, the Ford Motor Co. (D) is directed to pay a dividend to its stockholders this year in an amount consistent only with the legitimate expansion and business interests of the corporation. The decree of the court below is affirmed.

CONCURRENCE: (Moore, J.) The very fact here of the extraordinary accumulation of surplus should, by itself, be enough to establish a sufficient abuse of discretion to justify the intervention of equity.

▶ ANALYSIS

Though many public interest groups have urged changes in it, the general rule still is that a corporation may not legally put the public interest above the interests of its shareholders. As a general rule, however, there is no right to a dividend for any shareholder (except in those cases in which dividends are made mandatory for preferred shareholders, by the Articles of Incorporation, in cases in which proper sources are available). Note finally that *Dodge* is one of very few cases in which equity has ever considered a refusal to pay a dividend so improper and/or in such bad faith as to justify interference with the normal corporate decision process. Of course, since Henry Ford dominated that process in the Ford Motor Co. (D), it was ineffective to protect the (soon-to-depart) minority interests of the Dodges (P).

Quicknotes

DIVIDEND The payment of earnings to a corporation's shareholders in proportion to the amount of shares held.

MINORITY SHAREHOLDER A stockholder in a corporation controlling such a small portion of those shares outstanding that its votes have no influence in the management of the corporation.

CHAPTER 8

Management and Control of the Corporation

Quick Reference Rules of Law

McQuade v. Stoneham

Director (P) v. Majority stockholder (D)

N.Y. Ct. App., 189 N.E. 234 (1934).

NATURE OF CASE: Appeal from an action to compel specific performance.

FACT SUMMARY: After McQuade (P) was removed as an officer and director of the New York Giants Baseball Club, he alleged that his removal violated an agreement between the parties to use best efforts to keep the parties as officers and directors of the club.

🏛 RULE OF LAW
A contract is illegal and void so far as it precludes the board of directors, at the risk of incurring legal liability, from changing officers, salaries, or policies or retaining individuals in office, except by consent of the contracting parties.

FACTS: Stoneham (D) was the majority stockholder in the National Exhibition Company (New York Giants Baseball Club) and held 1,306 shares. McQuade (P) and McGraw (D) were the only other stockholders. Each held 70 shares for which each paid Stoneham (D) $50,338.10. The three entered into an agreement by which they promised to use their "best endeavors" for the purpose of continuing themselves as directors and officers of the club, with Stoneham (D) as president at $45,000 per year, McGraw (D) as vice president at $7,500 per year, and McQuade (P) as treasurer at $7,500 per year. The agreement could not be changed without unanimous consent of the parties. The board of directors had four other members controlled by Stoneham (D). McQuade (P), who also happened to be a city magistrate, served as treasurer for seven years when Bondy was elected to succeed him. At the meeting, Stoneham (D) and McGraw (D) abstained from voting. McQuade (P) voted for himself, and the other four directors voted for Bondy. Stoneham (D) and McGraw (D) acquiesced in this election and in the failure to reelect McQuade (P) as a director at the following shareholders' meeting. The trial court would not reinstate McQuade (P) in his action to compel specific performance but gave him damages for wrongful discharge. Stoneham (D) and McGraw (D) appealed.

ISSUE: Is a contract illegal and void so far as it precludes the board of directors, at the risk of incurring legal liability, from changing officers, salaries, or policies or retaining individuals in office, except by consent of the contracting parties?

HOLDING AND DECISION: (Pound, C.J.) Yes. A contract is illegal and void so far as it precludes the board of directors, at the risk of incurring legal liability, from changing officers, salaries, or policies or retaining individuals in office, except by consent of the contracting parties. While McQuade (P) argued that the agreement should be enforceable so long as the officer is loyal to the interests of the corporation, holding such agreements unenforceable is preferable to one where the courts would have to pass on the motives of directors in the lawful exercise of their trust. The decision should also be reversed because, by statute, no city magistrate shall engage in any business other than the duties of his office. McQuade's (P) employment with the club was more than an occasional business transaction or voluntary assistance. He was receiving a substantial salary. Reversed and complaint dismissed.

► ANALYSIS

Generally, an agreement made by a person who is a director, or expects to become one, that requires that the director to vote in a certain way, or puts the director under pressure to do so, is illegal and void, except in some cases where all the shareholders are parties. Also, an agreement placing restrictions on a shareholder that wholly deprive the director of any functions as a shareholder or as a director, if he or she were to become one, is illegal. Such an agreement would, under Delaware law, insofar as it concerns a close corporation and stockholders holding a majority of the outstanding voting shares, be valid.

◼═◼

Quicknotes

MINORITY STOCKHOLDER A stockholder in a corporation controlling such a small portion of those shares outstanding that its votes have no influence in the management of the corporation.

SPECIFIC PERFORMANCE An equitable remedy whereby the court requires the parties to perform their obligations pursuant to a contract.

◼═◼

Galler v. Galler

Shareholder (P) v. Shareholder (D)

Ill. Sup. Ct., 203 N.E.2d 577 (1964).

NATURE OF CASE: Action for specific performance on a contract between shareholders in a close corporation.

FACT SUMMARY: Suit by Emma Galler (P) to compel specific performance of a shareholder agreement made between her deceased husband, Benjamin Galler, and Isadore Galler (D), his brother and business partner. The agreement bound the shareholders to vote for specific individuals and directors and called for mandatory dividends.

🏛 RULE OF LAW
Close corporations will not be held to the same standards of corporate conduct as publicly held corporations in the absence of a showing of fraud or prejudice toward minority shareholders or creditors.

FACTS: Two brothers, Isadore (D) and Benjamin, incorporated their partnership in 1924 and operated as such for over 30 years. In 1955, the two brothers drew up a shareholders' agreement to provide for the financial security of their respective families in the event of either brother's death. The agreement provided for salary continuation payments to the surviving widow. It further allowed the surviving widow to remain on the board of directors and to name a successor to her husband. Specific dollar amounts of dividends were mandated by the agreement. However, these payments were qualified so as not to impair the capital of the corporation. After Benjamin's death, his wife Emma (P) sought enforcement of the agreement. Isadore (D) repudiated the agreement, claiming it violated the Corporations Code of Illinois and the public policy of that state.

ISSUE: Can shareholder agreements pertaining to dividend policy and selection of directors be enforced in the case of a close corporation when such agreements would not be permissible in a publicly held corporation?

HOLDING AND DECISION: (Underwood, J.) Yes. Shareholder agreements pertaining to dividend policy and selection of directors can be enforced in the case of a close corporation when such agreements would not be permissible in a publicly held corporation. The unique nature of close corporations—close relationship of shareholders, lack of marketability of shares, and overlapping of shareholders and officers—creates a situation that should allow "slight deviations from corporate norms." These deviations should be permitted so long as they do not operate to defraud or prejudice the interests of minority shareholders or creditors. Since the principals in a close corporation usually have a close relationship, their agreements should be enforced where no clear statutory prohibitions are violated. Since the agreement did not imperil creditors and there were no minority shareholders' interests involved in this instance, the agreement was valid and enforceable. Affirmed in part, reversed in part, and remanded.

▶ ANALYSIS

This case is representative of the growing acceptance by most jurisdictions of the basic differences between publicly held and closely held (close) corporations. There is recognition that the parties in a close corporation regard themselves, in fact, as partners. This view allows for latitude in enforcing shareholders' agreements that would be unacceptable in publicly held corporations. Many statutes regulating corporations are intended to protect the interests of the shareholders and creditors. Where the shareholders are few in number and operating, in essence, as partners, the need for such rigid protection is absent. As long as the rights of minority shareholders and creditors are not infringed, the close corporation can be given a relatively free reign as regards internal structure and operation.

■══■

Quicknotes

CLOSE CORPORATION A corporation whose shares (or at least voting shares) are held by a closely knit group of shareholders or a single person.

SPECIFIC PERFORMANCE An equitable remedy whereby the court requires the parties to perform their obligations pursuant to a contract.

ULTRA VIRES An act undertaken by a corporation that is beyond the scope of its authority pursuant to law or its articles of incorporation.

■══■

Zion v. Kurtz

Minority shareholder (P) v. Principal shareholder (D)

N.Y. Ct. App., 405 N.E.2d 681 (1980).

NATURE OF CASE: Appeal from entry of summary judgment granting enforcement of shareholder's agreement.

FACT SUMMARY: Zion (P) sought enforcement of a shareholder's agreement that prohibited the corporation from entering into any business transaction without his consent.

🏛 RULE OF LAW
A shareholder's agreement requiring minority shareholder approval of corporate activities is enforceable between the original parties to it.

FACTS: Kurtz (D) was the principal shareholder of a corporation in which Zion (P) was a minority shareholder. They executed an agreement that precluded the corporation from entering into any business transaction without Zion's (P) consent. The corporation subsequently breached the agreement, and Zion (P) sued to enforce it. The trial court granted summary judgment for Zion (P), and Kurtz (D) appealed, contending the agreement violated state law by delegating the control over corporate actions from the board of directors to a minority shareholder. The appellate court reversed, and the court of appeals granted certiorari.

ISSUE: Is a shareholder's agreement requiring minority shareholder approval of corporate activities enforceable between the original parties to it?

HOLDING AND DECISION: (Meyer, J.) Yes. A shareholder's agreement requiring minority shareholder approval of corporate activities is enforceable between the original parties to it. Reasonable restrictions on director discretion are not against public policy and are not precluded by statute. Since all stockholders assented to the agreement and it is not prohibited by statute or public policy, it is enforceable. Reversed.

DISSENT IN PART: (Gabrielli, J.) A shareholder agreement of this type illegally transfers control of the corporation from the board of directors to a minority shareholder.

▌ ANALYSIS

Agreements of the type discussed in this case are usually found in closely held corporations. Although the corporation in this case was not formed as a close corporation, the court found this inconsequential. It reasoned that because the articles of incorporation granted the board power to take all steps necessary to enforce the terms of the articles, the corporation could easily gain close status in order to render the shareholder agreement valid.

◼◼◼

Quicknotes

8 DEL. C. § 141 The authority to manage corporate affairs rests solely with the Board of Directors.

CERTIORARI A discretionary writ issued by a superior court to an inferior court in order to review the lower court's decisions; the Supreme Court's writ ordering such review.

MINORITY STOCKHOLDER A stockholder in a corporation controlling such a small portion of those shares outstanding that its votes have no influence in the management of the corporation.

◼◼◼

Matter of Auer v. Dressel

[Parties not identified.]

N.Y. Ct. App., 118 N.E.2d 590 (1954).

NATURE OF CASE: Appeal from a mandamus ordering that a special stockholders' meeting be called.

FACT SUMMARY: Stockholders (P) sought a special stockholders' meeting to vote on amendments to the bylaws, but the president (D) refused to call one.

🏛 RULE OF LAW
Corporate management must call a special stockholders' meeting when the necessary number of voting shares back such a request and no purpose for the meeting is improper.

FACTS: Stockholders of Hoe & Co. Inc. (P) sought to compel Hoe's president (D) to call a special stockholders' meeting after stockholders of more than the required 50 percent of the voting class A stock requested such meeting which the president (D) refused to call. The president (D) claimed that he did not have information sufficient to confirm the adequacy of the number of shares backing the request. He also claimed that none of the four stated purposes for the meeting was proper. Those purposes were as follows: (1) to recommend reinstatement of the former president (Auer) who had been ousted by the directors; (2) to amend the bylaws so that any vacancy on the board be filled by a vote of only those stockholders whom the director represents; (3) to vote upon charges against four particular directors; and (4) to amend the bylaws regarding the number of directors necessary for a quorum. The court summarily ordered the president (D) to call the requested meeting, and he appealed.

ISSUE: Must corporate management call a special meeting when the necessary number of voting shares backs such a request and when no purpose for the meeting is improper?

HOLDING AND DECISION: (Desmond, J.) Yes. Corporate management must call a special stockholders' meeting when the necessary number of voting shares back such a request and no purpose for the meeting is improper. Here, there was no reason why the stockholders could not show their approval of their former president. As for purpose "B," stockholders who are empowered to elect directors have the inherent power to remove them for cause. Furthermore, stockholders of one class can exclude those of another from filling vacancies when the director only represents a particular class. The important right of stockholders to have such meetings called will be of little practical value if corporate management can ignore the requests, force the stockholders to commence legal proceedings, and then, by purely formal denials, put the stockholders to lengthy and extensive litigation to establish facts as to stockholdings which are peculiarly within the knowledge of the corporate officers. Affirmed.

DISSENT: (Van Voorhis, J.) The president (D) was justified in not calling a meeting no matter how many shares supported the request if none of the proposals could be acted upon by the stockholders. It would have been an idle gesture for the shareholders to show their support for the former president because the management of the corporation is vested in its board of directors. As for only allowing class A stockholders to fill class A directorships, class A stockholders could not exclude other shareholders from voting on a proposal which would prevent them from voting on certain directorships in the future. Further, while stockholders can recall directors for cause, they cannot recall directors before their terms have expired simply to change corporate policy.

▶ ANALYSIS

One aspect of the case barely discussed by the majority was the alleged impracticability and unfairness of constituting the numerous stockholders as a tribunal to hear charges made by themselves and the incongruity of letting the stockholders hear and pass on those charges by proxy. The dissent feared that "the consequence is that these directors are to be adjudged guilty of fraud or breach of faith in absentia by shareholders who have neither heard nor ever will hear the evidence against them or in their behalf." The majority simply stated that this question was not before the court on the appeal and that any director who believed he was illegally removed could seek his remedy in the courts.

■■■■

Quicknotes

MANDAMUS A court order issued commanding a public or private entity, or an official thereof, to perform a duty required by law.

■■■■

Salgo v. Matthews

Corporate president (D) v. Shareholder (P)

Tex. Civ. App., 497 S.W.2d 620 (1973).

NATURE OF CASE: Suit seeking a mandatory injunction.

FACT SUMMARY: A corporate election inspector (D) appointed by Salgo (D) refused to accept several proxies which, if accepted, would have enabled Matthews (P) to win his proxy fight against Salgo (D).

🏛 **RULE OF LAW**
Shares of stock may be voted only by an authorized representative of the party designated in the corporate records as legal owner of the shares.

FACTS: Matthews (P) headed a group of stockholders who desired to wrest control of General Electrodynamics Corporation from Salgo (D), the president of the corporation. Matthews's (P) faction intended to accomplish its objective by waging a successful proxy fight. A special stockholders' meeting was convened, and Salgo (D) appointed Meer (D) to serve as election inspector. Numerous proxies were submitted to Meer (D) by Matthews (P), but Meer (D) refused to accept certain of these, including some that had been executed in Matthews's (P) favor by Pioneer Casualty Company (Pioneer), registered owner of nearly 30,000 shares of General Electrodynamics stock. Pioneer was in receivership, and beneficial title to its shares had been transferred to Shepherd, who was bankrupt. A court order had authorized Pioneer's receiver to give Shepherd a proxy to vote Pioneer's shares, but Meer (D) refused to accept any proxy executed by Shepherd. Meer (D) took the position that only Shepherd's bankruptcy trustee, as beneficial owner of the General Electrodynamics stock, had a right to vote the shares. Matthews (P) filed suit against Salgo (D) and Meer (D), and the trial court issued an order requiring Salgo (D) to reconvene the shareholders' meeting for the purpose of declaring Matthews (P) and his slate as winners of the company election. Salgo (D) did so but then appealed from the court's order.

ISSUE: May a corporation require that shares of its stock be voted by their beneficial owner?

HOLDING AND DECISION: (Guittard, J.) No. Shares of stock may be voted only by an authorized representative of the party designated in the corporate records as legal owner of the shares. General Electrodynamics' corporate records show that nearly 30,000 shares of its stock are owned by Pioneer, and Meer (D) had no right to insist that those shares be voted only by their beneficial owner. Pioneer was entitled to vote the shares, and, because of Pioneer's insolvency, its receiver was the only representative authorized to act on the company's behalf. The receiver did, in fact, act, and the fact that he chose to do

so through Shepherd does not change the fact that the receiver was acting on behalf of the duly registered owner of the stock. As election inspector, Meer (D) was entitled to use his discretion in assessing the validity of disputed proxies, but he had no right to go beyond the corporate records to determine the identities of those shareholders entitled to vote. However, although Meer (D) exceeded his authority, the proper remedy for his abuse of discretion was a proceeding quo warranto. Since Matthews (P) should have availed himself of that statutory remedy, the court had no right to grant the mandatory relief which it decreed. Reversed and rendered.

▶ **ANALYSIS**

The individuals listed in a corporation's stock book are designated its "shareholders of record." Only those persons who were shareholders of record on a specified date may vote in corporate elections. Ordinarily, a list of all shareholders is maintained and kept current, and interested parties are entitled to inspect the list if certain statutory requisites are met. Shareholders of record enjoy various other privileges as well, including the right to bring derivative suits against the corporation and the right to receive such dividends as may from time to time be declared.

■━■

Quicknotes

BENEFICIAL OWNER A party holding equitable but not legal title to property that is held by a third party for his benefit.

BYLAWS Rules promulgated by a corporation regulating its governance.

MANDATORY INJUNCTION A court order that (1) requires the defendant to do particular thing; (2) prohibits defendant from refusing to do some thing or act to which the plaintiff is legally entitled; or (3) prevents the defendant from continuing the previous wrongful act, thus compelling him to undo it.

PROXY CONTEST A solicitation of proxies in order to oppose another proxy solicitation regarding the election or removal of a corporation's directors.

QUO WARRANTO By what right; a writ brought for the purpose of determining whether a person or entity has the legal authority to hold an office or franchise.

RECORD OWNER A party who holds title to property as reflected by an official record.

■━■

Humphrys v. Winous Co.

Shareholder (P) v. Corporation (D)

Ohio Sup. Ct., 133 N.E.2d 780 (1956).

NATURE OF CASE: Suit to invalidate a director classification scheme.

FACT SUMMARY: Winous Co. (D) established separate classifications for each of its three directors. Humphrys (P) contended that this had been done in order to nullify the effectiveness of cumulative voting.

🏛 RULE OF LAW
A statute prohibiting restrictions upon the exercise of cumulative voting rights should not be construed as guaranteeing minority representation on a company's board of directors.

FACTS: The board of directors of Winous Co. (D) consisted of three members. The company (D) created separate classifications for each of the three directors so that no two would be required to stand for reelection at the same time. Humphrys (P) filed suit against the company (D), contending that its classification scheme nullified the effectiveness of cumulative voting. A state statute expressly conferred the right to vote cumulatively and prohibited the restriction or qualification of that right. Classification of directors was also authorized by statute. The trial court rejected Humphrys's (P) argument, but the appellate court reversed. Winous Co. (D) then appealed.

ISSUE: Does a statute prohibiting interference with the exercise of cumulative voting rights ensure that minority stockholders will be represented on a company's board of directors?

HOLDING AND DECISION: (Bell, J.) No. A statute prohibiting restrictions upon the exercise of cumulative voting rights should not be construed as guaranteeing minority representation on a company's board of directors. The value of cumulative voting as a restraint upon a potentially oppressive majority was first recognized by the bar association of this state. And cases in other jurisdictions have held that cumulative voting may not be negated by charter amendments, by removing minority directors without cause, or by reducing the membership of a board of directors. But the Ohio cumulative voting statute, while it precludes interference with the right to vote cumulatively, cannot be interpreted as ensuring minority representation. Any scheme for classifying directors necessarily diminishes the potential effectiveness of cumulative voting. But since the legislature has chosen to permit the classification of directors, it seems illogical to contend that classification should not be permitted merely because it may tend to nullify the potential success of cumulative voting. Therefore, the appellate court erred in deciding that the Winous Co. (D) classification scheme violated the cumulative voting statute, although the scheme would be void today because of a code revision prohibiting the creation of classes consisting of fewer than three directors. Reversed.

DISSENT: (Weygandt, C.J.) In authorizing classification of directors, the legislature could not have intended the practice to be used to defeat cumulative voting. This is evidenced by the fact that the same act as permitted classification of directors also included the provision prohibiting restriction or qualification of the right to vote cumulatively.

▶ ANALYSIS

Cumulative voting is designed to enable minority shareholders to secure some representation on a corporation's board of directors. It permits a shareholder to cast his total number of votes (the number of shares he owns × the number of slots to be filled) for one director, instead of casting one vote per share for each vacancy. A simple formula may be used to determine the number of shares needed to elect a given number of directors. Where S equals the total number of shares voting, D equals the number of slots to be filled, and N equals the number of directors the minority hopes to be able to elect, the following equation will reveal the number of shares needed to elect the desired number of directors: $D + 1 + 1 =$ number of shares minority shareholders needed in order to elect a director.

◼▬◼

Quicknotes

CUMULATIVE VOTING RIGHTS Method of shareholder voting whereby the shareholder is entitled to as many votes as he or she has shares of stock multiplied by the number of directors to be elected.

MINORITY STOCKHOLDER A stockholder in a corporation controlling such a small portion of those shares outstanding that its votes have no influence in the management of the corporation.

◼▬◼

Ringling Bros.-Barnum & Bailey Combined Shows v. Ringling

Corporation (D) v. Shareholder (P)

Del. Sup. Ct., 53 A.2d 441 (1947).

NATURE OF CASE: Appeal from finding of validity of a stock policy agreement.

FACT SUMMARY: Ringling (P) and Haley (D) entered into a stock pooling agreement by which they agreed to always vote their shares together, but when Haley (D) refused to agree on a vote for directors or vote as directed by the arbitrator, who was provided for in the agreement, Ringling (P) sought to enforce the arbitrator's decision.

> ## RULE OF LAW
> A group of shareholders may lawfully contract with each other to vote in such a way as they determine.

FACTS: Two of the stockholders of Ringling Bros. (D), Ringling (P) and Haley (D), entered into an agreement by which they always would vote their shares together, but if they could not agree, they would vote in accordance with the decision of an arbitrator, one Loos. They made this agreement because together they would have enough votes to elect five of the seven directors, while North, the third stockholder, could only elect two. In 1946, Ringling (P) and Haley (D) agreed to elect themselves, Ringling's (P) son, and Haley's (D) husband, but they could not agree on a fifth director. Ringling (P) demanded arbitration, and Loos decided that Ringling's (P) proposed director, Dunn, should receive the votes of Haley (D). Haley (D) refused to vote for Dunn and voted for just herself and her husband. If the vote was figured according to Loos's direction, Dunn was elected, but if not, one of North's candidates, Griffin, was chosen. Ringling (P) brought suit to enforce the arbitrator's decision, while Haley (D) argued that their voting agreement was illegal. The agreement was upheld and a new election directed in accordance with the agreement. Haley (D) appealed.

ISSUE: May a group of shareholders lawfully contract with each other to vote in the future in such a way as they, or a majority of their group, from time to time determine?

HOLDING AND DECISION: (Pearson, J.) Yes. A group of shareholders may lawfully contract with each other to vote in the future in such a way as they determine. First, the agreement in question did not give Loos the power to enforce his decision. His decision could only be enforced if one of the parties attempted to enforce it. Second, the agreement was not illegal. The law does not purport to deal with agreements whereby shareholders attempt to bind each other as to how they shall vote their shares. Various forms of pooling agreements have been held valid and have been distinguished from voting trusts. The provision for submission to an arbitrator was clearly for the purpose of breaking deadlocks. The agreement did not allow the parties to take unlawful advantage of each other or any other person. As for a remedy, only the votes of Ringling (P) and North should have been counted. While that would leave one board vacancy, because the next board meeting follows closely, the board can fill the vacancy itself. As modified, affirmed.

► ANALYSIS

Generally, a stockholder may exercise wide liberality of judgment in the matter of voting of his shares. It is not objectionable that his motives may be for personal profit, or determined by whims or caprice, so long as he violates no duty owed to his fellow shareholders. The remedy in the above case was made possible by Delaware law which permits the Chancery Court, when reviewing an election, to reject the votes of a registered stockholder where his voting of them is found to be in violation of the rights of another person.

Quicknotes

CORPORATION LAW, REV. CODE § 18 One or more stockholders may have a written agreement to deposit capital stock with a trustee for the purpose of voting as agreed for a period of time.

VOTING TRUST An agreement establishing a trust, whereby shareholders transfer their title to shares to a trustee who is authorized to exercise their voting powers.

Brown v. McLanahan

[Parties not identified.]

148 F.2d 703 (4th Cir. 1945).

NATURE OF CASE: Appeal from dismissal of an action to set aside a corporate amendment.

FACT SUMMARY: The trustees (D) of voting common and preferred stock of a corporation approved an amendment that diluted the power of the preferred stock and enhanced their privately owned debentures.

🏛 RULE OF LAW
Under a corporate voting trust agreement, "a trustee may not exercise powers granted in a way that is detrimental to the cestuis que trustent (i.e., actual owner of the voting shares); nor may one who is trustee for different classes favor one class at the expense of another."

FACTS: In 1935, debentures and preferred stock of the corporation were issued to the holders of first lien bonds in a bankruptcy reorganization of the company. Under this reorganization, only the preferred stock (and common stock) enjoyed voting power. After the issuance of the stock, all preferred and common shares were placed in a 10-year voting trust, with the voting trustees (D) given the right to vote with respect to amendment of the articles of incorporation, "as well as every other right of an absolute owner of said shares." Although the debenture holders and preferred stockholders were the same people at the time of the reorganization, subsequent transfers of the preferred stock created two separate classes of security holders (i.e., preferred and debenture holders). The trustees (D) of the voting trust were holders of substantial amounts of debentures and were also a majority of the corporation's directors (having elected themselves by using their voting power as trustees of preferred shares). Since these trustees were afraid of losing power after the termination of the trust, shortly before its termination, they voted for an amendment of the corporation's charter. This amendment diluted the control of the preferred shares by bestowing voting rights on the debentures. In response, a holder (P) of voting trust certificates representing 500 preferred shares brought a class action to set aside the amendment. The district court, though, granted the trustees' (D) motion to dismiss, and this appeal followed.

ISSUE: Can a trustee, under a corporate voting trust agreement, exercise his voting rights in such a way that is detrimental to the actual owner of the shares held in trust?

HOLDING AND DECISION: (Dobie, J.) No. Under a corporate voting trust agreement, "a trustee may not exercise powers granted in a way that is detrimental to the cestuis que trustent (i.e., actual owner of the voting shares held in trust); nor may one who is a trustee for different classes favor one class at the expense of another." This is based upon the rationale that "the voting strength attaching to shares of stock is as much a property right as any element of dominion possessed by an owner of realty," and, as such, a trustee of voting shares should not be allowed to dilute such strength. Here, the voting trustees (D) diminished the voting strength of the preferred shares (which they held in trust) in order to enhance the value of their own debentures (i.e., in order to maintain control of the corporation). Such action was beyond their authority, and, as such, the amendment must be declared void. Reversed and remanded.

▶ ANALYSIS

This case illustrates the general rule regarding voting trusts. Although at common law such trusts were not recognized, most states now recognize their validity. Most states, though, require the trust to be written and filed with the corporation, and most states limit the duration of such trusts to 21 years. Note that under such a trust the shareholder turns over his right to vote to a trustee, but he maintains his right to dividends, to inspect corporate records (for proper purposes), and to bring derivative suits. Furthermore, as this case illustrates, the shareholder can bring an action against the trustee if he uses the shares to the shareholder's detriment.

◼◼

Quicknotes

CESTUI QUE TRUST Beneficiary; the party for whose benefit a trust is established.

CREDITOR'S LIEN A claim against the property of another in order to secure the payment of a debt.

DEBENTURES Long-term unsecured debt securities issued by a corporation.

VOTING TRUST An agreement establishing a trust, whereby shareholders transfer their title to shares to a trustee who is authorized to exercise their voting powers.

◼◼

Lehrman v. Cohen

Shareholder (P) v. Shareholder (D)

Del. Sup. Ct., 222 A.2d 800 (1966).

NATURE OF CASE: Action for breach of contract and fiduciary duty.

FACT SUMMARY: Dispute between rival factions, Lehrman (P) and Cohen (D), over issuance of Class AD stock and its voting power.

🏛 RULE OF LAW
The creation of a new class of voting stock does not divest and separate the voting rights, which remain vested in the stockholders who created it, from the other attributes of the ownership of that stock.

FACTS: The Lehrman and Cohen families, stockholders in Giant Food Inc., held equal voting stock of Class AC common (owned by the Cohen family) and Class AL common (the Lehrman family). Each class elected two members of a four-member board of directors. When founder Sam Lehrman died, a dispute among his children over an inter vivos gift to Jacob Lehrman (P) was resolved by allowing Jacob Lehrman (P) to acquire all of the outstanding Class AL stock. The Cohen family demanded that a fifth directorship be created to deal with possible deadlocks arising between AL and AC stock. An agreement was reached whereby the certificate of incorporation was amended creating a third class of stock, designated AD. The AD stock was issued to Joseph Danzansky, corporate counsel, giving him the power to elect a fifth director and all other common stock privileges except to receive dividends. He was issued one share with par value of $10, and the corporation reserved redemption rights. Danzansky elected himself as the fifth director. The present dispute arose when the stockholders adopted a resolution giving Danzansky a 15-year executive employment contract of $67,600 annual salary, plus stock options. AC and AD stock voted in favor of the resolution, but AL stock voted against. The same day, Danzansky was elected president of the company by a 3-2 vote, the two AL directors voting against him. Danzansky resigned as director and elected as fifth director one Millard West, a former AL director. The board ratified these actions. Jacob Lehrman (P) brought action against N. M. Cohen (D), former president of the company, on grounds that (1) issuance and voting of the single AD share resulted in an illegal voting trust under Delaware law and (2) Danzansky's election as president and his employment contract violated the deadlock agreement and was a breach of contract and fiduciary duty. The Court of Chancery granted N. M. Cohen's (D) motion for summary judgment, and Jacob Lehrman (P) appealed.

ISSUE: Does the creation of a new class of voting stock separate the voting rights from the other attributes of ownership in the old voting stock held by the stockholders who created the new class?

HOLDING AND DECISION: (Herrmann, J.) No. The AD arrangement did not separate the voting rights of the AC or AL from the other attributes of ownership of that stock. Each AC and AL stockholder retained complete control over his stock. It is true that creation of the AD stock may have diluted the voting power of the AC-AL stock. But even though the voting power of the AC and AL stock was reduced, this doesn't mean, as Lehrman (P) asserts, that the percentage of reduction (10 percent each of AL and AC) became the res of a voting trust. The first element in a test of whether a voting agreement constitutes a voting trust is that the voting rights of the stock in question are separated from the other attributes of that stock's ownership. Since this element is not met here, no voting trust was created. Thus, this disposes of Lehrman's (P) other contention that the voting trust was illegal under the laws of Delaware on grounds that it was not limited to a 10-year period as required. However, Lehrman (P) contends that even if the Class AD stock arrangement is not a voting trust, it is still illegal because the creation of a class of stock having only voting rights and no participating ownership interest in the corporation is contra to Delaware law. There is no requirement that all stock of a Delaware corporation must have both voting rights and proprietary interests (see Del. C. § 218). Nonvoting stock is specifically authorized by § 151 (a). The main purpose of a voting trust statute is to avoid secret uncontrolled combinations of stockholders from acquiring voting control to the detriment of other shareholders. But there is nothing inherently wrong about a device, such as the AD agreement, designed by shareholders to break a deadlock among directors. Affirmed.

▶ ANALYSIS

To be upheld, a voting trust or a pooling agreement must be created for a legitimate purpose. Some legitimate purposes are to aid in reorganization, to fulfill some bona fide corporate policy, or to prevent rival concerns from gaining control of the corporation. However, a voting trust or pooling agreement will not be upheld where it is established to gain control by minority shareholders, to guarantee employment or salaries for management, or to freeze domination in an incumbent group or protect a minority interest in the corporation.

Continued on next page.

Quicknotes

INTER VIVOS   Between living persons.

RES   Thing; subject matter of a dispute to establish rights therein.

VOTING TRUST   An agreement establishing a trust, whereby shareholders transfer their title to shares to a trustee who is authorized to exercise their voting powers.

■■■

Ling and Co. v. Trinity Savings and Loan Assn.

Borrower (D) v. Lender (P)

Tex. Sup. Ct., 482 S.W.2d 841 (1972).

NATURE OF CASE: Action to recover a debt and to foreclose on a security interest.

FACT SUMMARY: To secure a loan from Trinity Savings and Loan Association (P), Bowman (D) pledged 1,500 shares of Ling and Co., Inc. (D) stock. Ling (D) contended that the transfer of its stock was subject to certain limitations.

🏛 **RULE OF LAW**
A corporation may impose restrictions upon the transfer of its stock as long as those restrictions do not constitute unreasonable restraints.

FACTS: Bowman (D) borrowed money from Trinity Savings and Loan Association. (Trinity) (P), executing a promissory note and pledging a certificate for 1,500 shares of Class A Common Stock in Ling and Co., Inc. (Ling) (D). When Bowman (D) failed to repay the entire loan, Trinity (P) sued to recover the balance and to foreclose on the stock certificate. Trinity (P) made Ling (D) a party to the action when Ling (D) objected to the foreclosure and public sale of its stock on the ground that the shares were subject to certain transfer restrictions. Specifically, Ling's (D) articles of incorporation required a stockholder to obtain the prior written approval of the New York Stock Exchange before selling or encumbering his or her shares and required that the company (D) and all shareholders of the same class be given a right of first refusal in the event that a stockholder decided to sell his or her shares. The trial court entered a summary judgment for Trinity (P), and the appellate court, after ruling that the Ling (D) stock restrictions were invalid, affirmed the trial court's order. Trinity (P) then appealed to the state supreme court.

ISSUE: May a corporation place restrictions upon the transfer of its stock?

HOLDING AND DECISION: (Reavley, J.) Yes. A corporation may impose restrictions upon the transfer of its stock as long as those restrictions do not constitute unreasonable restraints. As the court of civil appeals noted, a restriction upon transfer must be expressly set forth in the corporation's articles of incorporation and must be conspicuously stated or referred to in the stock certificate itself. No sufficiently conspicuous legend appears on the Ling (D) stock to place a reasonable person on notice of the restrictions, but this deficiency did not entitle Trinity (P) to a summary judgment absent conclusive proof of the fact that Trinity (P) lacked actual notice of the restrictions on transfer. The lower court also found that Ling's (D) restrictions were unreasonable, but this conclu-sion is not sound. The provision requiring stock exchange approval was apparently inserted in response to a rule that once required all member firms to impose such a condition upon sale. And the provision requiring that the corporation (D) and other shareholders be given a right of first refusal cannot be considered unreasonable because there has been no showing that the other stockholders are so numerous as to render the requirement truly burdensome. The court of civil appeals ruled that the second transfer restriction violated a statute that permits the imposition of restrictions upon buy-and-sell agreements only if the class of shareholders affected consists of 20 or fewer persons. But it was error even to consider whether Ling's (D) restriction violated that statute. The Ling (D) restriction pertained to options, not buy-and-sell agreements. Thus, the statute cited by the court of civil appeals has no applicability to the Ling (D) restriction. Since there is no basis for any of the grounds relied upon by the lower courts in declaring the Ling (D) stock transfer restrictions invalid, the order granting a summary judgment in favor of Trinity (P) is reversed and the case remanded.

▶ *ANALYSIS*

Although the Model Business Corporation Act contains no specific provisions pertaining to share transfer restriction, many states have enacted statutes that expressly permit restrictions of certain types. Such statutes are often similar to those involved in the *Ling and Co.* case. The laws generally include a requirement that any restrictions be conspicuously stated or specifically referred to on the face of all stock certificates to which the restrictions are applicable. The effect of transfer restrictions is to impose upon each shareholder a contractual obligation that may be enforced by the corporation.

◼︎◼︎◼︎

Quicknotes

TEXAS BCA 2-22 Provides that a corporation may impose restrictions on stock transfers if they are set forth in Articles of Incorporation and copied on back of stock certificates.

TEXAS U.C.C. § 8-204 Transfer restrictions must be noted conspicuously on security.

◼︎◼︎◼︎

In the Matter of Drive-In Development Corp.

[Parties not identified.]

371 F.2d 215 (7th Cir. 1966).

NATURE OF CASE: Appeal from an order disallowing a claim in a bankruptcy proceeding.

FACT SUMMARY: National Boulevard Bank (P) loaned money to Drive-In Development Corp.'s (Drive-In) (D) parent company after proof was furnished that Drive-In's (D) directors had authorized Maranz to guarantee payment of the loan.

RULE OF LAW

Statements of a corporate officer, if made while acting within the scope of his authority, are binding upon the corporation.

FACTS: Tastee Freez Industries, Inc., parent company of Drive-In Development Corp. (Drive-In) (D), wanted to borrow money from the National Boulevard Bank of Chicago (the "Bank") (P). The Bank (P) agreed to advance the money if Drive-In (D) would guarantee the loan. Maranz, as "Chairman" of Drive-In (D), was willing to execute a guaranty, but the Bank (P) also requested a copy of a resolution authorizing Maranz to sign the document on behalf of Drive-In (D). Pursuant to the Bank's (P) demand, Dick, secretary of Drive-In (D), provided a certified copy of what purported to be the resolution adopted by the board of directors. No such resolution ever appeared in Drive-In's (D) Corporate Minutes Book, however, and some doubt eventually arose as to whether or not it had ever been adopted by the board. Drive-In (D) ultimately petitioned for an arrangement under Chapter XI of the Bankruptcy Act, and the Bank (P) filed a claim in the amount of its unpaid loan. The referee disallowed the claim, concluding that Maranz had lacked the authority to bind Drive-In (D) to the loan guaranty agreement. From a judgment confirming the decision of the referee, the Bank (P) appealed.

ISSUE: Is a party who enters into a transaction with a corporation entitled to rely upon statements made by the corporation's officers?

HOLDING AND DECISION: (Swygert, J.) Yes. Statements of a corporate officer, if made while acting within the scope of his authority, are binding upon the corporation. It is the duty of a corporation's secretary to maintain the company's records, and it was well within Dick's authority to certify that the resolution in question was actually adopted. The Bank (P) had no duty to make further inquiry once Dick had provided assurance that Maranz had authority to act. Thus, Drive-In (D) is estopped from denying that it was bound by Maranz's agreement to guarantee the Tastee Freez loan. Drive-In (D) argues that, inasmuch as one of the Bank's (P) officers was also a director of Tastee Freez, the Bank (P) is chargeable with knowledge that no authorizing resolution had been adopted. The simple answer to this contention is that individual's contacts with Tastee Freez did not put the Bank (P) on notice of the nonexistence of the resolution. Therefore, the bankruptcy referee erred in dismissing the Bank's (P) claim. Reversed in part and affirmed in part.

ANALYSIS

A corporation may be bound by the statements, agreements, etc., of one of its officers or directors who appears to outsiders to be acting pursuant to authority duly conferred upon him by the board of directors. Such ostensible authority may result from either the actions or representations of the officer himself or from the corporation's failure to disclaim his authority to act. The corporation will not be bound by the unauthorized acts of one of its officers unless the outsider's belief that the officer possessed the requisite authority was a reasonable one. And, of course, an outsider who had actual knowledge of the officer's lack of authority may not bind the corporation.

■■■

Quicknotes

OSTENSIBLE AGENCY The apparent authority granted to an agent to act on behalf of the principal in order to effectuate the principal's objective.

■■■

Lee v. Jenkins Bros.

Employee (P) v. Employer (D)

268 F.2d 357 (2d Cir. 1959).

NATURE OF CASE: Appeal from a judgment denying a pension.

FACT SUMMARY: Lee (P) sought to enforce a promise made by the president of Jenkins Brothers (Jenkins) (D) in 1920, when Lee (P) was hired, that Jenkins (D) would pay Lee (P) a $1,500 pension at age 60, "regardless of what happens."

🏛 RULE OF LAW
A president has authority only to bind his company by acts arising in the usual and regular course of business but not for contracts of an extraordinary nature.

FACTS: Jenkins Brothers (Jenkins) (D), after purchasing a factory from Crane, sought to hire Crane's business manager, Lee (P). The president of Jenkins (D), Yardley, and one of the vice-presidents met with Lee (P) in 1920 to make Lee (P) an offer. Yardley promised Lee (P) that Jenkins (D) would pay Lee (P) his Crane pension, and if anything came up, he would pay Lee (P) himself. The pension was $1,500 a year to be paid at age 60; "regardless of what happens, you will get that pension if you join our company." This promise was made orally. At age 55, after serving as a vice-president and director of Jenkins (D), Lee (P) was discharged. He sought to recover his pension at age 60. Jenkins (D) argued that Yardley had no authority to bind Jenkins (D) to such an extraordinary contract, and the trial court agreed as a matter of law. Lee (P) appealed.

ISSUE: Does a president have authority only to bind his company by acts arising in the usual and regular course of business and not for contracts of an extraordinary nature?

HOLDING AND DECISION: (Medina, J.) Yes. A president has authority only to bind his company by acts arising in the usual and regular course of business but not for contracts of an extraordinary nature. Many courts have noted the injustice caused by permitting corporations to act commonly through their executives and then allowing them to disclaim an agreement as beyond the authority of the contracting officer, when the contract no longer suited its convenience. Generally, a president can hire and discharge employees and fix their compensation. But employment contracts for life or on a "permanent" basis are generally regarded as extraordinary and unauthorized. Jenkins (D) argued that the indefinite nature of the pension promise should be treated similarly. Such lifetime contracts have been enforced in situations where the employee gave additional consideration such as quitting another job, giving up a competing business, or where the services were "peculiarly necessary" to the corporation. The only similarity that a pension promise bears to an unenforceable lifetime contract is that it is of an indefinite period. Such an agreement is not unreasonable: it is necessary and beneficial to the corporation and is a common corporate fringe benefit. Apparent authority is a question of fact and depends upon the nature of the promise, the officer negotiating, and the corporation's usual mode of business. Accordingly, reasonable men could differ on the question of whether Yardley had apparent authority to make the contract, and the trial court erred in determining the issue as a matter of law. Reversed.

▶ ANALYSIS

The general reasons for finding a contract extraordinary include the following: an undue restriction on shareholder power and that of future boards on questions of managerial policy; an undue subjection of the corporation to an inordinately substantial amount of liability; and a long and indefinite running period. Unlike the case with life employment contracts, courts have often gone out of their way to find pension promises binding and definite even when labeled gratuitous by the employer. With such promises, the consideration given to the employee involved is not at all dependent on profits or sales, nor does it involve some other variable suggesting direction discretion.

■■■

Quicknotes

APPARENT AUTHORITY The authority granted to an agent to act on behalf of the principal in order to effectuate the principal's objective, which is not expressly granted but which is inferred from the principal's conduct.

PROMISSORY ESTOPPEL A promise that is enforceable if the promisor should reasonably expect that it will induce action or forbearance on the part of the promisee, and does in fact cause such action or forbearance, and it is the only means of avoiding injustice.

RATIFICATION Affirmation of a prior action taken by either the individual himself or by an agent on behalf of the principal, which is then treated as if it had been initially authorized by the principal.

■■■

Management and Control of the Publicly Held Corporation

Quick Reference Rules of Law

In the Matter of Caterpillar, Inc.

[Parties not identified.]

SEC Rel. No. 34-30532 (Adm. Proceeding File No. 3-7692, 1992).

NATURE OF CASE: Securities and Exchange Commission (SEC) hearing on compliance with reporting requirements of the Securities and Exchange Act.

FACT SUMMARY: Caterpillar, Inc. (D) failed, in its annual and quarterly reports, to adequately comply with the disclosure requirements of § 13(a) of the Securities Exchange Act of 1934.

🏛 RULE OF LAW
Disclosure is required where a known trend, demand, commitment, event, or uncertainty is likely to occur, and, where such a determination cannot be made, an objective evaluation must be made of the consequences of such an occurrence on the assumption that it will occur.

FACTS: Caterpillar, Inc. (D) had a wholly owned subsidiary, Caterpillar Brasil, S.A. (CBSA), which accounted for about a quarter of Caterpillar's (D) net profits. Before Caterpillar (D) filed the reports required by § 13(a) of the Securities Exchange Act of 1934, management recognized that CBSA's future performance would be exceptionally difficult to predict. Brazil was volatile, and the impact was significant enough to reduce Caterpillar's (D) 1990 projected results. However, nothing in the Management Discussion and Analysis (MD & A) in its reports suggested the disproportionate impact of CBSA's profits on Caterpillar's (D) overall profitability or adequately mentioned management's uncertainty about CBSA's 1990 performance.

ISSUE: Is disclosure required where a known trend, demand, commitment, event, or uncertainty is likely to occur, and, where such a determination cannot be made, must an objective evaluation be made of the consequences of such an occurrence on the assumption that it will occur?

HOLDING AND DECISION: [Judge not stated in casebook excerpt.] Yes. Disclosure is required where a known trend, demand, commitment, event, or uncertainty is likely to occur, and, where such a determination cannot be made, an objective evaluation must be made of the consequences of such an occurrence on the assumption that it will occur. Caterpillar's (D) disclosure should have discussed the impact of the expected changes in CBSA on Caterpillar's (D) overall results of operations. Further, its annual and quarterly reports should have discussed future uncertainties of CBSA's operations and the possible risk of Caterpillar's (D) having materially lower earnings as a result and, to the extent reasonably practicable, quantified the impact of such risk. Caterpillar (D) failed to do so.

▶ ANALYSIS

A Management Decision and Analysis (MD & A) is intended to give the investor an opportunity to look at the company through the eyes of management by providing both a short- and long-term analysis of the business of the company. Caterpillar's (D) failure to include required information about CBSA in its MD & A left investors with an incomplete picture of Caterpillar's (D) financial condition and results of operations. Investors were thus denied the opportunity to see the company through the eyes of management.

■═■

Quicknotes

REGULATION S-K, ITEM 303 If a discussion of segment information of the registrant's business would be appropriate the discussion should focus on each reportable subdivision of the business.

■═■

TSC Indus., Inc. v. Northway, Inc.

Corporation (D) v. Shareholder (P)

426 U.S. 438 (1976).

NATURE OF CASE: Action charging violation of federal securities laws.

FACT SUMMARY: Northway, Inc. (P), a TSC Indus., Inc. (TSC) (D) shareholder, claimed that the proxy statement issued in connection with a liquidation and sale of TSC's (D) assets to National omitted material facts.

🏛 RULE OF LAW
A fact omitted from a proxy solicitation is "material" if there is a substantial likelihood that a reasonable shareholder would consider it important in deciding how to vote.

FACTS: After National acquired 34 percent of TSC Indus., Inc.'s (TSC) (D) stock, the Board of Directors of TSC (D) approved a proposal to liquidate and sell all of TSC's (D) assets to National via an exchange of stock. The National nominees to the Board did not vote. Northway, Inc, (P), a TSC (D) stockholder, brought suit claiming the resulting proxy solicitation violated § 14a-9 of the Securities Exchange Act of 1934, which bars the use of proxy statements that are false or misleading with respect to the presentation or omission of material facts. The alleged material omission involved the failure to reveal the degree of National's control over TSC (D). The district court denied Northway's (P) motion for summary judgment, but the court of appeals reversed and granted partial summary judgment on the ground that the omitted facts were material as a matter of law. In so doing, it reasoned that any fact a reasonable shareholder might consider important was material. TSC (D) appealed.

ISSUE: Is the test of the "materiality" of a fact omitted from a proxy statement whether there is a substantial likelihood a reasonable shareholder would consider it important in deciding how to vote?

HOLDING AND DECISION: (Marshall, J.) Yes. The proper standard for determining the materiality of a proxy statement is whether there is a substantial likelihood that a reasonable shareholder would consider it important in deciding how to vote. The "might-consider-important" test used by the court below simply sets too low a threshold for the imposition of liability under Rule 14a-9. The issue of materiality may be characterized as a mixed question of law and fact, involving the application of a legal standard to a particular set of facts. Only if the established omissions are "so obviously important to an investor that reasonable minds cannot differ on the question of materiality" is the ultimate issue of materiality appropriately resolved "as a matter of law" by summary judgment. That was not the case here. So, a summary judgment was improper. Reversed and remanded.

▶ ANALYSIS

The "materiality" standard the Court adopted in this case was supported by the Securities and Exchange Commission (SEC). There had been a split among the courts, some adopting the "facts a reasonable shareholder might consider important" standard at issue in this case and others, notably the Second and Fifth Circuits, opting for the conventional tort test of materiality, i.e., whether a reasonable man would attach importance to the fact. The Court adopted a test midway between these extremes.

Quicknotes

MATERIALITY Importance; the degree of relevance or necessity to the particular matter.

PROXY STATEMENT A statement, containing specified information by the Securities and Exchange Commission, in order to provide shareholders with adequate information upon which to make an informed decision regarding the solicitation of their proxies.

RULE 14a-9 No proxy solicitation shall contain false and misleading statements or omissions regarding material facts.

SECURITIES EXCHANGE ACT, § 14(a) Prevents management from obtaining illegal proxies.

Virginia Bankshares, Inc. v. Sandberg

Corporation (D) v. Minority shareholder (P)

501 U.S. 1083 (1991).

NATURE OF CASE: Appeal from a jury award of damages in a minority shareholder action.

FACT SUMMARY: After a freeze-out merger, in which the minority shareholders of First American Bank of Virginia (Bank) lost their interest, Sandberg (P) and other minority shareholders sued for damages, alleging violation of § 14(a) and Rule 14a-9 and a breach of the fiduciary duties.

🏛 RULE OF LAW
(1) An individual is permitted to prove a specific statement of reason knowingly false or materially misleading, even when the statement is couched in conclusory terms.
(2) Causation of damages compensable through a federal implied private right of action cannot be demonstrated by minority shareholders whose votes are not required to authorize the transaction giving rise to the claim.

FACTS: In a freeze-out merger, the First American Bank of Virginia (Bank) merged into Virginia Bankshares, Inc. (VBI) (D). First American Bankshares, Inc., (D) (FABI), the parent company of VBI (D), hired an investment banking firm to give its opinion on the appropriate price for shares of the minority holders who would lose their interest as a result of the merger. The investment banking firm concluded that $42 a share would be a fair price based on market quotations and unverified information from FABI (D). The merger proposal was approved at that price, according to the directors' proxy solicitation, because it was an opportunity for the minority shareholders to achieve a high value and a fair price for their minority stock. Sandberg (P), who had not voted for the merger, then filed suit against VBI (D) and FABI (D), alleging violation of § 14(a) and Rule 14a-9 and breach of fiduciary duties owed the minority shareholders under state law. The jury held for Sandberg (P), finding that she would have received $60 per share had her stock been properly valued. The court of appeals affirmed, and VBI (D) appealed.

ISSUE:
(1) Is an individual permitted to prove a specific statement of reason knowingly false or materially misleading, even when the statement is couched in conclusory terms?
(2) Can causation of damages compensable through a federal implied private right of action be demonstrated by minority shareholders whose votes are not required to authorize the transaction giving rise to the claim?

HOLDING AND DECISION: (Souter, J.)
(1) Yes. An individual is permitted to prove a specific statement of reason knowingly false or materially misleading, even when the statement is couched in conclusory terms. Here, there was evidence of a "going concern" value for the Bank in excess of $60 per share of common stock, a fact never disclosed. Thus the directors' statement was materially misleading on its face. The evidence invoked by VBI (D) fell short of compelling the jury to find that the facial materiality of the misleading statement was neutralized or that the risk of real deception was nullified by any true statements in the proxy solicitation.
(2) No. Causation of damages compensable through a federal implied private right of action cannot be demonstrated by minority shareholders whose votes are not required to authorize the transaction giving rise to the claim. Application of the "essential link" causation test to the facts of this case would extend the private right of action beyond the scope congressionally intended by the Securities Exchange Act of 1934. Causation would then turn on inferences about what the corporate directors would have thought and done without the minority shareholder approval unneeded to authorize action. Assuming that the material facts about the merger were not accurately disclosed, the minority votes were inadequate to ratify the merger under state law, and there was no loss of a state appraisal remedy to connect the proxy solicitation with harm to minority shareholders. The judgment of the court of appeal is reversed.

CONCURRENCE: (Scalia, J.) Sometimes a sentence with the word "opinion" in it actually represents facts as facts rather than opinions—and in that event no more need be done than apply the normal rules for § 14(a) liability. That is the situation here.

CONCURRENCE AND DISSENT: (Stevens, J.) Shareholders may bring an action for damages under § 14 (a) whenever materially false or misleading statements are made in proxy statements. That the solicitation of proxies is not required by law or by the bylaws of a corporation does not authorize corporate officers, once they have decided for whatever reason to solicit proxies, to avoid the constraints of the statute. Thus, the judgment of the court of appeals should be affirmed.

CONCURRENCE AND DISSENT: (Kennedy, J.) The severe limits the majority place upon possible proof

Continued on next page.

of nonvoting causation in a § 14(a) private action are justified neither by the Court's precedents nor by any case in the court of appeals. Causation is established where the proxy statement is an essential link in completing the transaction, even if the minority lacks sufficient votes to defeat a proposal of management.

▶ *ANALYSIS*

While a materially misleading statement may lose its deceptive edge, simply by joinder with others that are true, not every mixture with the true will neutralize deception. Sandberg (P) invoked language from the Court's opinion in *Mills v. Electric Auto-Lite Co.*, 396 U.S. 375 (1970), permitting the jury could find for the plaintiff without a showing of her own reliance on the alleged misstatements, so long as the misstatements were material and the proxy solicitation was an "essential link" in the merger process. Justice Souter, however, distinguished *Mills*, where a majority stockholder controlled just over half of the corporation's shares and a two-thirds vote was needed to approve the merger proposal, from the instant case.

■══■

Quicknotes

MATERIALITY Importance; the degree of relevance or necessity to the particular matter.

RULE 14a-9 No proxy solicitation shall contain false and misleading statements or omissions regarding material facts.

SECURITIES EXCHANGE ACT, § 14(a) Prevents management from obtaining illegal proxies.

■══■

Rauchman v. Mobil Corp.

Shareholder (P) v. Corporation (D)

739 F.2d 205 (6th Cir. 1984).

NATURE OF CASE: Appeal from entry of summary judgment denying relief for refusal to include proposed amendment in proxy statement.

FACT SUMMARY: Rauchman (P) sued, contending Mobil Corp. (D) had to include his proposed amendment to the corporation's bylaws in its proxy statement.

🏛 RULE OF LAW
A corporation may refuse to include in its proxy statement a proposal to amend its bylaws to prevent a foreign citizen from becoming a board member.

FACTS: Rauchman (P), owner of voting shares of Mobil Corp. (D) stock, submitted a proposed bylaw amendment to be included in the proxy statement sent out for shareholder information. The amendment sought to preclude a citizen of an OPEC [Organization of the Petroleum Exporting Countries] country from sitting on the board of directors. Mobil (D) obtained a Securities and Exchange Commission (SEC) statement indicating no action would be taken if the proposal were excluded as it related to an election to office of a director. The trial court granted Mobil's (D) motion for summary judgment, and Rauchman (P) appealed.

ISSUE: May a corporation refuse to include in its proxy statement a proposal to amend its bylaws to prevent a foreign citizen from becoming a board member?

HOLDING AND DECISION: (Engel, J.) Yes. A corporation may refuse to include in its proxy statement a proposal to amend its bylaws to prevent a foreign citizen from becoming a board member. Because Mobil (D) had a director who was up for reelection and who was a citizen of Saudi Arabia, the proposal related to the election of a director and was properly excludable at Mobil's (D) discretion. Therefore, there was no triable factual issue, and summary judgment was properly entered. Affirmed.

▌ANALYSIS

The holding in this case follows the language in SEC Rule 14a-8(c)(8). This rule allows the corporation to exclude proposals of this type. Corporations are not compelled to engage in "electioneering" in the preparation of proxy statements. It can, however, include recommendations from the board regarding who should be elected.

Quicknotes

OPEC Organization of the Petroleum Exporting Countries; an international organization whose mission is to coordinate and unify the petroleum policies of its member countries and ensure the stabilization of oil markets.

RULE 14a-8 Requires companies to include shareholder proposals in the company's proxy statement. Subsections of the rule permit companies to omit proposals that deal with certain matters.

CHAPTER 10

Duty of Care and the Business Judgment Rule

Quick Reference Rules of Law

Shlensky v. Wrigley

Minority shareholder (P) v. Controlling shareholder (D)

Ill. App. Ct., 237 N.E.2d 776 (1968).

NATURE OF CASE: Appeal from dismissal.

FACT SUMMARY: Wrigley (D), the majority shareholder in the Chicago Cubs, refused to install lights at Wrigley Field in order to hold night games, and Shlensky (P), a minority shareholder, filed a derivative suit to compel the installation.

🏛 RULE OF LAW
A shareholder's derivative suit can only be based on conduct by the directors that borders on fraud, illegality, or conflict of interest.

FACTS: Wrigley (D) was the majority shareholder and a director of the Chicago Cubs baseball team. Shlensky (P), a minority shareholder, sought to bring a shareholders' derivative action to compel the directors to equip Wrigley Field (the Cub's home field) with lights so that night games could be played and revenues could be increased. The trial court sustained Wrigley's (D) motion to dismiss over Shlensky's (P) contention that the refusal to install lights was a personal decision of Wrigley's (D) and not in the best interest of the shareholders.

ISSUE: Can a shareholder's derivative suit only be based on conduct by the directors that borders on fraud, illegality, or conflict of interest?

HOLDING AND DECISION: (Sullivan, J.) Yes. A shareholder's derivative suit can only be based on conduct by the directors that borders on fraud, illegality, or conflict of interest. Shlensky (P) is attempting to use the derivative suit to force a business judgment on the board of directors of the Chicago Cubs, but there is no showing of fraud, illegality, or conflict of interest. There are valid reasons for refusal to install lights in the stadium. Though Shlensky (P) alleges that night games haven't been considered due to Wrigley's (D) personal feelings about the sport, Wrigley (D) has suggested that night games in the Wrigley Field area would have a detrimental effect on the neighborhood. Additionally, there is no showing that night games would significantly increase revenues or even that additional expenses wouldn't be required. Affirmed.

▶ ANALYSIS

Though the "business judgment rule" is typically stated as relating to the functions of directors, the rule is equally applicable to officers of the corporation while acting in their official capacities, and it may apply to controlling shareholders as well if these persons assert their more extraordinary management functions, e.g., mergers or sale of their complete interest.

■=■

Quicknotes

BUSINESS JUDGMENT RULE Doctrine relieving corporate directors and/or officers from liability for decisions honestly and rationally made in the corporation's best interests.

STOCKHOLDER DERIVATIVE SUIT Action asserted by a shareholder in order to enforce a cause of action on behalf of the corporation.

■=■

Smith v. Van Gorkom

Shareholder (P) v. Director (D)

Del. Sup. Ct., 488 A.2d 858 (1985).

NATURE OF CASE: Appeal from denial of damages for breach of director's duties.

FACT SUMMARY: The trial court held that because Van Gorkom (D) and the other Trans Union directors had three opportunities to reject the merger proposal, they acted with due deliberation and their conduct fell within the business judgment rule.

🏛 RULE OF LAW
Directors are bound to exercise good faith informed judgment in making decisions on behalf of the corporation.

FACTS: In order to fully realize a favorable tax situation, Trans Union's chief executive, Van Gorkom (D), solicited a merger offer from an outside investor. Van Gorkom (D) acted on his own and arbitrarily arrived at a $55 per share price. Without any form of investigation, the full Trans Union board accepted the offer. The offer was proposed two subsequent times before its formal acceptance by the board. Smith (P) and other shareholders brought this derivative suit on the basis that the board had not given due consideration to the offer. The trial court held that because it considered the offer three times before formally accepting it, the board's action fell within the business judgment rule. The appellate court affirmed, and this appeal was taken.

ISSUE: Are directors bound to exercise good faith informed judgment in making corporate decisions?

HOLDING AND DECISION: (Horsey, J.) Yes. Directors are bound to exercise good faith informed judgment in making corporate decisions. In this case, the directors tentatively approved the merger the first time it was presented to them. They had no, and requested no, substantiating data regarding the feasibility of the $55 per share price. No consideration was given to allowing time to study the proposal or to gain more information. As a result, their decision to accept the offer can be classified as nothing short of gross negligence. As a result, their actions cannot be foisted on the shareholders under protection of the business judgment rule. Reversed and remanded for a determination of the value of the shares and an appropriate damage award.

DISSENT: (McNeilly, J.) The Board consisted of extremely well-educated, experienced, and successful business people. They were well aware of their duties and of the merits of the offer. Although their actions seem subjectively imprudent, this does not preclude application of the business judgment rule.

▶ ANALYSIS

The decisions of a corporation are left up to the board of directors. Some major decisions, such as mergers and acquisitions, require shareholder approval or ratification. Within certain parameters, decisions of the board are upheld on review based on the business judgment rule. This rule grants immunity from liability for decisions a board makes based on its business experience. In the absence of gross negligence, such decisions are generally upheld as falling within the board's discretion.

▣▬◼

Quicknotes

8 DEL. C. § 141(e) Allows directors to rely on reports from officers and other experts.

BUSINESS JUDGMENT RULE Doctrine relieving corporate directors and/or officers from liability for decisions honestly and rationally made in the corporation's best interests.

CASH-OUT MERGER Occurs when a merging company prematurely redeems the securities of a holder as part of the merger.

▣▬◼

In re Caremark Intern. Inc. Derivative Litigation

Health maintenance organization (D) v. Shareholders (P)

Del. Ch. Ct., 698 A.2d 959 (1996).

NATURE OF CASE: Motion to approve a settlement of a consolidated derivative action.

FACT SUMMARY: Caremark International, Inc., a managed health-care provider, entered into contractual arrangements with physicians and hospitals, often for "consultation" or "research," without first clarifying the unsettled law surrounding prohibitions against referral fee payments.

🏛 RULE OF LAW
A board of directors has an affirmative duty to attempt in good faith to assure that a corporate information-and-reporting system exists and is adequate.

FACTS: Caremark International Inc. (Caremark) was involved in providing patient health care and managed health-care services. Much of Caremark's revenue came from third-party payments, insurers, and Medicare and Medicaid reimbursement programs. The Anti-Referral Payments Law (ARPL) applied to Caremark, prohibiting payments to induce the referral of Medicare or Medicaid patients. Caremark had a practice of entering into service contracts, including consultation and research, with physicians who at times prescribed Caremark products or services to Medicare recipients. Such contracts were not prohibited by the ARPL, but they raised the issue of unlawful kickbacks. Caremark's board of directors (D) attempted to monitor these contracts internally, seeking legal advice and devising guidelines for employees. However, the government began investigating Caremark. Caremark began making structural changes in response to the investigation, centralizing management. In spite of this, Caremark and two officers were indicted. Several shareholder derivative actions were subsequently filed, charging the board of directors (D) with failure to adequately monitor as part of its duty of care. Settlement negotiations began. Caremark agreed in the settlement to cease all payments to third parties that referred patients to Caremark and to establish an ethics committee, which it had, in effect, already done. Caremark also agreed to make reimbursement payments to private and public parties totaling $250 million. All other claims were waived in the proposed settlement. The proposed settlement was submitted to the court for approval.

ISSUE: Does a board of directors have an affirmative duty to attempt in good faith to assure that a corporate information-and-reporting system exists and is adequate?

HOLDING AND DECISION: (Allen, Chan.) Yes. A board of directors has an affirmative duty to attempt in good faith to assure that a corporate information-and-reporting system exists and is adequate. Directors generally do not monitor day-to-day operations in a company. The Supreme Court has said, where there is no basis for suspicion, directors cannot be liable. However, it would be extending this holding too far to say that directors have no obligation whatsoever to determine whether they are receiving accurate information. The duty of care implies that a board will make a good faith effort to ensure that a corporation's information and reporting system is adequate. In this case, acts that resulted in indictments do not, by themselves, prove that the Caremark board (D) was not adequately monitoring corporate behavior. On the contrary, the board (D) appears to have been making structural changes all along to gain greater centralized control of the company. And an ethics monitoring group was in place well before the settlement was reached. Given that the evidence on the record suggests that success in the derivative suit was unlikely, but that Caremark is giving up little in the way of concessions not already in place, the settlement is fair.

▶ ANALYSIS

A duty to monitor does not require a board to be aware of all the details of corporate activity. In fact, such oversight would be physically impossible in a large company. The duty does, however, require the board to be aware of major activities and related issues that could pose a threat to the company. The choice of what structure to use in informational gathering is still subject to the safe harbor of the business judgment rule; therefore, a claim that the duty to monitor has been breached is tremendously difficult to prove successfully.

■=■

Quicknotes

SHAREHOLDERS' DERIVATIVE ACTION Action asserted by a shareholder in order to enforce a cause of action on behalf of the corporation.

■=■

Stone v. Ritter

Shareholder (P) v. Corporate directors (D)

Del. Sup. Ct., 911 A.2d 362, *en banc* (2006).

NATURE OF CASE: Appeal from judgment dismissing derivative action.

FACT SUMMARY: Shareholders (P) bringing a derivative action against AmSouth Bancorporation (AmSouth) directors (D) contended that demand was excused because the directors (D) breached their oversight duty, which breach allegedly resulted in around $50 million in penalties the corporation had to pay as a consequence of its employees' failure to file certain reports required by federal banking regulations.

🏛 RULE OF LAW
A derivative action will be dismissed for failure to make demand where alleged particularized facts do not create a reasonable doubt that the corporation's directors acted in good faith in exercising their oversight responsibilities.

FACTS: AmSouth Bancorporation (AmSouth) and a subsidiary paid $40 million in fines and $10 million in civil penalties arising from the failure of bank employees to file certain reports required by the federal Bank Secrecy Act (BSA) and various federal anti-money-laundering (AML) regulations. There was evidence that the corporation dedicated considerable resources to its BSA/AML compliance program, put in place numerous procedures and systems to attempt to ensure compliance, and that these procedures and systems enabled the directors (D) to periodically monitor the corporation's compliance with BSA/AML regulations and requirements. The board (D) regularly received reports and training in these BSA/AML compliance systems and enacted written policies and procedures to ensure BSA/AML compliance. AmSouth shareholders (P) brought a derivative action against the corporation's directors (D) based on these events, alleging breach of their oversight duties, without first making demand on the board. They contended that demand was excused because the directors (D) faced a likelihood of personal liability that would render them incapable of exercising independent and disinterested judgment in response to a demand request. AmSouth's certificate of incorporation contained a provision that would exculpate its directors for breaches of their duty of care, provided they acted in good faith. The Chancery Court held that the shareholders (P) had failed to adequately plead that demand would have been futile, finding that the directors (D) had not been alerted by any "red flags" that violations of law were occurring. The state's highest court granted review.

ISSUE: Will a derivative action be dismissed for failure to make demand where alleged particularized facts do not

create a reasonable doubt that the corporation's directors acted in good faith in exercising their oversight responsibilities?

HOLDING AND DECISION: (Holland, J.) Yes. A derivative action will be dismissed for failure to make demand where alleged particularized facts do not create a reasonable doubt that the corporation's directors acted in good faith in exercising their oversight responsibilities. The standard to determine demand futility in this situation, where a business decision was not involved, is whether the particularized factual allegations create a reasonable doubt that, as of the time the complaint was filed, the directors could have exercised their independent and disinterested business judgment in response to a demand. The shareholders (P) attempt to satisfy this standard by asserting that the directors (D) face a substantial likelihood of personal liability, thus rendering them interested in the outcome. However, this argument must take into account the certificate of incorporation's exculpatory clause, which can exculpate the directors (D) from a breach of the duty of care, but not a breach of their duty of loyalty or a breach that is not in good faith. The failure to act in good faith is a condition to finding a breach of the fiduciary duty of loyalty and imposing fiduciary liability. "[A] failure to act in good faith is not conduct that results, ipso facto, in the direct imposition of fiduciary liability." The failure to act in good faith may result in liability because the requirement to act in good faith is a condition of the duty of loyalty. Therefore, since a showing of bad faith conduct is essential to establish director oversight liability, the fiduciary duty violated by that conduct is the duty of loyalty. Second, and as a corollary, the duty to act in good faith does not establish an independent fiduciary duty that stands on the same footing as the duty of care and loyalty. A failure to act in good faith gives rise to liability only indirectly. Also, as a corollary, the fiduciary duty of loyalty is not limited to financial or similar conflicts of interest, but encompasses cases where a director has failed to act in good faith. Oversight liability itself is determined by the standards articulated in the *Caremark* case (*In re Caremark Int'l. Deriv. Litig.*, 698 A.2d 959 (Del. Ch. 1996)). The predicates to oversight liability occurs where (1) the directors utterly fail to implement any reporting or information system or controls, or (2) having implemented such a system or controls, consciously fail to monitor or oversee its operations, thus disabling themselves from being informed of risks or problems requiring their attention. In either case, liability requires a showing that the directors knew that

Continued on next page.

they were not discharging their fiduciary obligations. When these standards are applied to the facts pleaded by the shareholders (P), it becomes clear that the directors (D) did not fail to act in good faith. The facts showed that the directors (D) had established a reasonable information and reporting system and had set up numerous departments and committees to oversee AmSouth's compliance with federal banking regulations. This system also permitted the board to periodically monitor such compliance. While it is clear with hindsight that the organization's internal controls were inadequate there were also no "red flags" to put the board on notice of any wrongdoing. The directors (D) took the steps they needed to ensure that reasonable information and reporting system existed. Therefore, although there ultimately may have been failures by employees to report deficiencies to the board, there is no basis for an oversight claim seeking to hold the directors personally liable for such failures by employees. Affirmed.

▶ ANALYSIS

This case makes it clear that in Delaware directors do not have a fiduciary duty of good faith that is separate from other fiduciary duties. Instead, as the court makes a point of explaining, the duty of good faith is a component of the duty of loyalty. The case also teaches that in the context of breach of oversight claims, a bad (and very costly) outcome does not per se equate to bad faith.

■■■

Quicknotes

BREACH OF FIDUCIARY DUTY The failure of a fiduciary to observe the standard of care exercised by professionals of similar education and experience.

DEMAND REQUIREMENT Requirement that a shareholder make a demand for corrective action by the board of directors before commencing a derivative suit.

DUTY OF CARE Duty that an officer or director owes to the corporation, by virtue of his fiduciary relationship, to act for the benefit of the corporation.

DUTY OF LOYALTY A director's duty to refrain from self-dealing or to take a position that is adverse to the corporation's best interests.

SHAREHOLDERS' DERIVATIVE ACTION Action asserted by a shareholder in order to enforce a cause of action on behalf of the corporation.

■■■

Malone v. Brincat

Shareholders (P) v. Corporation (D)

Del. Sup. Ct., 722 A.2d 5, *en banc*, (1998).

NATURE OF CASE: Appeal from dismissal with prejudice of a class action suit alleging breach of fiduciary duty.

FACT SUMMARY: Malone (P) and other stockholders alleged that Brincat (D) and the other directors of Mercury Finance Company, a Delaware corporation, had breached their fiduciary duty of disclosure by overstating the company's earnings.

🏛 RULE OF LAW
When the directors disseminate information to stockholders when no stockholder action is sought, the fiduciary duties of care, loyalty and good faith apply.

FACTS: Malone (P) and other shareholders alleged that Brincat (D) and the other directors had intentionally inflated the company's earnings and had thereby breached their fiduciary duties. The Court of Chancery held that directors have no fiduciary duty of disclosure under Delaware law in the absence of a request for shareholder action, reasoning that the shareholders must seek a remedy under federal securities law. The Court of Chancery dismissed the complaint with prejudice pursuant to rule 12(b)(6) for failure to state a claim upon which relief may be granted. Malone (P) appealed.

ISSUE: When the directors disseminate information to stockholders when no stockholder action is sought, do the fiduciary duties of care, loyalty and good faith apply?

HOLDING AND DECISION: (Holland, J.) Yes. When the directors disseminate information to stockholders when no stockholder action is sought, the fiduciary duties of care, loyalty and good faith apply. Dissemination of false information could violate one or more of those duties. Directors who knowingly disseminate false information that results in corporate injury or damage to an individual stockholder violate their fiduciary duty, and may be held accountable in a manner appropriate to the circumstances. If Malone (P) intends to assert a derivative claim, he should be permitted to replead to assert such a claim. The Court of Chancery properly dismissed the complaint before it against the individual director defendants, in the absence of well-pleaded allegations stating a derivative, class or individual cause of action and remedy. We disagree, however, with the Court of Chancery's holding that such a claim cannot be articulated on these facts. The case should have been dismissed without prejudice. Reversed in part and remanded.

▶ ANALYSIS

The court in this case decided that the plaintiffs should be allowed to amend their complaint. Delaware law may provide a basis for equitable relief. This court found that federal securities law may not be involved since the purchase or sale of securities was not at issue. The court stated that the 1998 Securities Litigation Uniform Standards Act would not apply retroactively to the case at bar.

■▬■

Quicknotes

1998 SECURITIES LITIGATION UNIFORM STANDARDS ACT Requires securities class actions such as these to be brought exclusively in federal court.

■▬■

CHAPTER 11

Duty of Loyalty and Conflict of Interest

Quick Reference Rules of Law

Marciano v. Nakash

Shareholder (P) v. Shareholder (D)

Del. Sup. Ct., 535 A.2d 400 (1987).

NATURE OF CASE: Appeal of order validating a claim in liquidation.

FACT SUMMARY: A loan to Gasoline, Ltd. by certain board members was validated as a fair transaction.

🏛 RULE OF LAW
A transaction by a corporation with its insiders will be valid if intrinsically fair.

FACTS: Gasoline, Ltd. was a Delaware corporation, with 50 percent of its shares owned by the Marciano (P) faction and 50 percent by the Nakash (D) faction. The board was comprised of six members, each faction having three seats. During Gasoline's lifetime, a loan was extended to Gasoline by the Nakashes (D). Gasoline eventually became insolvent. A claim was made against the insolvent estate by the Nakashes (D). The Marcianos (P) challenged the claim, contending it was voidable per se as an interested transaction not approved by a majority of shareholders. The Chancery Court validated the loan as inherently fair. The Marcianos (P) appealed.

ISSUE: Will a transaction by a corporation with its insiders be valid if intrinsically fair?

HOLDING AND DECISION: (Walsh, J.) Yes. A transaction by a corporation with its insiders will be valid if intrinsically fair. Certain older precedents suggest that a transaction by a corporation with insiders that is not approved by a majority of shareholders will be per se voidable. However, the weight of modern authority, which this court is inclined to follow, is that such a transaction will be valid if intrinsically fair. Delaware has enacted General Statutes § 144, which establishes certain conditions which, when met, will make an interested transaction valid. All parties concede that these conditions were not met here. However, this court believes that § 144 was not enacted to preempt the intrinsic fairness rule, but rather to create a "... safe haven." Here, the Chancery Court applied the intrinsic fairness rule, and this was proper. Affirmed.

▌ ANALYSIS

At early common law, interested transactions were looked upon with great disfavor. They were generally held to be void ab initio or voidable per se. The more common rule today, either by statute or judicial decision, comports with the rule stated here.

Quicknotes

8 DEL. C. § 144 Governs rules for interested director transactions.

FIDUCIARY DUTY A legal obligation to act for the benefit of another, including subordinating one's personal interests to that of the other person.

PER SE RULE OF VOIDABILITY Transactions by interested directors can be voided.

In re El Paso Corp. Shareholder Litigation

[Parties not identified.]

Del. Ch. Ct., 41 A.3d 432 (2012).

NATURE OF CASE: Motion for preliminary injunction in action challenging a merger on the grounds, inter alia, that it was tainted by disloyalty and self-dealing.

FACT SUMMARY: Shareholders of El Paso Corporation sought to preliminarily enjoin a merger of El Paso with Kinder Morgan, Inc. on the grounds that the merger was tainted by the disloyalty and self-dealing of El Paso's chief executive officer, as well as its financial advisor, Goldman, Sachs & Co., which had a significant interest in Kinder Morgan.

🏛 RULE OF LAW

Notwithstanding that a merger negotiation process has been tainted by disloyalty and self-dealing, and in violation of a board's duties to maximize the price for shareholders, a shareholder vote on the merger will not be enjoined where there is no other bid on the table and the shareholders may decide for themselves whether to accept the merger consideration as adequate in light of prevailing economic conditions.

FACTS: Foshee, the chief executive officer (CEO) of El Paso Corporation, undertook sole responsibility for negotiating the sale of El Paso to Kinder Morgan, Inc., in a merger. Kinder Morgan intended to keep El Paso's pipeline business and sell off El Paso's exploration and production, or "E&P," business to finance the purchase. Foshee did not disclose to the El Paso board of directors his interest in working with other El Paso managers in making a bid to buy the E&P business from Kinder Morgan in a manager buyout (MBO). He kept that motive secret, negotiated the merger, and then approached Kinder Morgan's CEO on two occasions to try to interest him in the idea. In other words, when Foshee was supposed to be getting the maximum price from Kinder Morgan, he actually had an interest in not doing that. Additionally, the board and management of El Paso relied in part on advice given by a financial advisor, Goldman, Sachs & Co. (Goldman), which owned 19 percent of Kinder Morgan (a $4 billion investment) and controlled two Kinder Morgan board seats. Although Goldman's conflict was known, inadequate efforts to cabin its role were made, and Goldman was able to intervene in the merger process and promote its interests. Further, the senior Goldman banker working on the spinoff owned an interest in approximately $340,000 of Kinder Morgan stock. El Paso ended up taking a package that was valued at $26.87 as of signing, comprised of $25.91 in cash and stock, and a warrant with a strike price of

$40—some $13 above Kinder Morgan's then-current stock price of $26.89 per share—and no protection against ordinary dividends. At no time did El Paso or its bankers reach out to other parties to conduct a market test to see if this price was appropriate. Still, the deal was at a substantial premium to market, and the board was advised by Morgan Stanley (and also by the analyses of Goldman, which had, and continued to, advise El Paso on the spin-off of the E&P business) that the offer was more attractive in the immediate term than doing the spin-off and had less execution risk, because Kinder Morgan had agreed to a great deal of closing certainty. However, as a result of Goldman's influence, Morgan Stanley would only be paid if it approved the merger, but not if it counseled the board to go with the spinoff or some other option. The deal also included a termination fee that represented 3.1 percent of the equity value and 1.69 percent of the enterprise value of El Paso, and that would make it very expensive for a bidder to buy the pipeline business. The board approved the merger. El Paso shareholders brought suit seeking to preliminarily enjoin the merger, contending that despite the premium over market offered by the merger, the merger was tainted by the selfish motivations of both Foshee and Goldman, and there were numerous decisions made by the El Paso board during the process that were questionable and tainted by self-dealing, including the board's failure to shop El Paso as a whole, or its key divisions separately. The Delaware Court of Chancery considered the motion for a preliminary injunction.

ISSUE: Notwithstanding that a merger negotiation process has been tainted by disloyalty self-dealing, and in violation of a board's duties to maximize the price for shareholders, will a shareholder vote on the merger be enjoined where there is no other bid on the table and the shareholders may decide for themselves whether to accept the merger consideration as adequate in light of prevailing economic conditions?

HOLDING AND DECISION: (Strine, Chan.) No. Notwithstanding that a merger negotiation process has been tainted by disloyalty self-dealing, and in violation of a board's duties to maximize the price for shareholders, a shareholder vote on the merger will not be enjoined where there is no other bid on the table and the shareholders may decide for themselves whether to accept the merger consideration as adequate in light of prevailing economic conditions. Here, the plaintiffs have a reasonable likelihood of success in proving that the merger was tainted by disloyalty and breaches of fiduciary duties. Although a

Continued on next page.

reasonable mind might debate the tactical choices made by the El Paso board, these choices would provide little basis for enjoining a third-party merger approved by a board overwhelmingly comprised of independent directors, many of whom had substantial industry experience. Nevertheless, the record indicated there was a reason to conclude that debatable tactical decisions were motivated not by a principled evaluation of the risks and benefits to the company's stockholders, but by Foshee's consideration of his own financial or other personal self-interests. Thus, the plaintiff shareholders have made out a creditable case that more faithful, unconflicted parties could have secured a better price from Kinder Morgan, and that there were numerous debatable tactical choices that in retrospect seemed to have been made in large measure based on Foshee's advice and with important influence from Goldman. Goldman's assertions that it was not influenced by its own economic incentives to maximize its $4 billion investment in Kinder Morgan by steering El Paso towards a deal with Kinder Morgan at a suboptimal price, are unconvincing, because it is difficult to believe that Goldman would not seek to maximize the value of its multi-billion dollar investment in Kinder Morgan at the expense of El Paso, but instead would be keen on obtaining an investment banking fee in the tens of millions. Moreover, Goldman continued to play an advisory role on the spinoff, which is significant, since the board was assessing the attractiveness of the merger relative to the attractiveness of the spinoff. Further, Goldman was able to effectively compromise Morgan Stanley's independence by ensuring that Morgan Stanley was paid only if it approved the merger. In sum, Goldman exerted significant influence over the merger. Given Foshee's failure to disclose his pursuit of the MBO, and Goldman's self-interested dealings, the plaintiffs have a probability of showing that more faithful, unconflicted parties could have secured a better price from Kinder Morgan. Notwithstanding the plaintiffs' probability of success on the merits of their case, and even assuming the likelihood of irreparable damage absent an injunction, the requested injunction is denied out of fear such an injunction might do more harm than good. El Paso stockholders arguably have much to gain by seeing the merger proceed, since the price being offered by Kinder Morgan is one that reasonable El Paso stockholders might find very attractive and since there are no other bidders. Given that the El Paso stockholders are well positioned to turn down the Kinder Morgan price if they do not like it, they should not be deprived of the chance to make that decision for themselves. Although an after-the-fact monetary damages claim against the defendants is not a perfect tool, it has some value as a remedial instrument, and the likely prospect of a damages trial is no doubt unpleasant to Foshee, other El Paso managers who might be added as defendants, and to Goldman—especially since discovery might uncover even more troubling information than had already surfaced. Motion for a preliminary injunction is denied.

▶ *ANALYSIS*

Although Chancellor Strine expressed his skepticism of the possibility of meaningful monetary damages, noting that Foshee was possibly liable for hundreds of millions of dollars but could not personally pay that amount, and that the other El Paso directors were most likely not liable because they acted in good faith, while Kinder Morgan was merely doing what was expected of it, and Goldman's conflicts were disclosed, this case left open the possibility of significant money damages. Apparently based in part on Chancellor Strine's harsh assessment of Foshee's and Goldman's self-dealing and disloyal conduct, the parties ultimately settled for $110 million. Moreover, Goldman—for the first time in its history—also agreed to forego its $20 million fee as part of the settlement.

■━■

Quicknotes

BREACH OF FIDUCIARY DUTY The failure of a fiduciary to observe the standard of care exercised by professionals of similar education and experience.

SELF-DEALING Transaction in which a fiduciary uses property of another, held by virtue of the confidential relationship, for personal gain.

■━■

Heller v. Boylan

[Parties not identified.]

N.Y. Sup. Ct., 29 N.Y.S.2d 653 (1941).

NATURE OF CASE: Stockholders' derivative action.

FACT SUMMARY: Heller (P) and six other stockholders in American Tobacco Company claimed that the bonuses paid top executive officers bore no relation to the services for which they were given.

🏛 RULE OF LAW
If a bonus payment has no relation to the value of services for which it is given, it is in reality a gift in part, and the majority stockholders have no power to give away corporate property against the protest of the minority.

FACTS: Heller (P) and six other stockholders out of the 62,000 holding shares in the American Tobacco Company brought a derivative action challenging the high bonuses paid to top officers under a concededly legally passed 1912 bylaw. Salary and bonus payments to the company president alone topped $1,000,000 yearly in 1930 and 1931 and averaged $400,000 per year from 1929 to 1939. Heller (P) contended that the payments bore no relation to the value of the services for which they were given and that, consequently, they were, in reality, a gift in part and that the majority stockholders committed waste and spoliation in giving away corporate property against the protest of the minority. In a prior suit, *Rogers v. Hill*, 289 U.S. 582, 88 A.L.R. 744 (1933), in which the same bylaw was challenged, a compromise judgment was entered into by which the bonus payments were reduced. However, Heller (P) argued that that judgment should be set aside because Rogers, the successful plaintiff, received a $525,000 fee for his efforts, the fee in effect being a bribe.

ISSUE: If a bonus payment has no relation to the value of services for which it is given, is it in reality a gift in part?

HOLDING AND DECISION: (Collins, J.) Yes. If a bonus payment has no relation to the value of services for which it is given, it is in reality a gift in part, and the majority stockholders have no power to give away corporate property against the protest of the minority. Here, Heller (P) proffered no testimony whatever in support of his charge of waste. He argued that the figures spoke for themselves. Without such evidence, the court is left without any guide for reducing the payments. "To act out of whimsy or caprice or arbitrariness would be more than inexact—it would be the precise antithesis of justice; it would be a farce." It was not clear by which standard the payments should be measured. Society does not always compensate merit fully while it often rewards commercial mediocrity. While the court does not necessarily approve the large payments, it has no valid ground for disapproving what this great majority of stockholders have approved.

▶ ANALYSIS

In a general comment on the nature of the object of the type of suit brought by Heller (P), the court noted: "Courts are ill-equipped to solve or even grapple with these entangled economic problems. Indeed, their solution is not within judicial province. Courts are concerned that corporations be honestly and fairly operated by its [sic] directors, with the observance of the formal requirements of the law; but what is reasonable compensation for its officers is primarily for its stockholders to decide. This does not mean that fiduciaries are to commit waste, or misuse or abuse trust property, with impunity. A just case will find the courts at guard and implemented to grant redress. But the stockholder must project a less amorphous plaint than is here presented."

Quicknotes

SHAREHOLDER DERIVATIVE ACTION Action asserted by a shareholder in order to enforce a cause of action on behalf of the corporation.

Wilderman v. Wilderman

Director (P) v. President (D)

Del. Ch. Ct., 315 A.2d 610 (1974).

NATURE OF CASE: Suit to compel the return of unauthorized corporate disbursements.

FACT SUMMARY: Joseph Wilderman (D), as president of a family-owned business, paid himself large sums without the approval of his wife, Eleanor (P), who was the company's only other director, officer, and shareholder.

🏛 RULE OF LAW
In the absence of a specific authorization by the company's board of directors, a corporate executive may receive only compensation that is reasonably commensurate with his functions and duties.

FACTS: Eleanor Wilderman (P) and her husband Joseph (D) founded, and later incorporated, the Marble Craft Company (D). The business was engaged in the installation of ceramic tile and marble facings. Both Eleanor (P) and Joseph (D) had some knowledge of the craft, but from the inception of the company (D), Joseph (D) performed most of the duties of the business, while Eleanor (P) served as bookkeeper. After incorporation, Joseph (D) and Eleanor (P), as the company's (D) only stockholders, elected themselves as directors and chose Joseph (D) as president, while Eleanor (P) was designated vice president, secretary, and treasurer. Both Joseph (D) and Eleanor (P) received salaries that had been fixed by agreement, although they elected not to pay themselves dividends because that practice would have subjected them to double taxation. Although the company (D) became extremely successful, the Wildermans' marital relationship ultimately proved unsatisfactory. They separated and later divorced, and Joseph (D) increased the amount of compensation he paid to himself. Although Joseph (D) had been authorized to receive an annual salary of only $20,800, he paid himself more than $90,000 in salary and bonuses in 1971, received $35,000 in 1972, and accepted a total compensation of nearly $87,000 in 1973. Eleanor's (P) salary from 1971 to 1973 was $7,800 per year. During this period, the court appointed a custodian to assist in the management of the company (D), and he succeeded in having a $20,000 dividend declared, Eleanor (P) and Joseph (D) dividing the amount equally. But when the custodian's intervention failed to eliminate or reduce the disparity in salaries, Eleanor (P) filed suit against both Joseph (D) and the company (D). Suing both as an individual and in her capacity as a shareholder, Eleanor (P) sought the return of excessive amounts paid to Joseph (D), an injunction against additional unauthorized disbursements, and an order directing that the company's (D) management continue to be sub-jected to the supervision of the custodian. Eleanor (P) also sought an order compelling the company (D) to pay dividends and asked that the corporate pension plan be adjusted to reflect the fact that the excessive compensation paid to Joseph (D) had been declared improper.

ISSUE: May the president of a corporation arbitrarily pay himself more compensation than the company's board of directors has authorized?

HOLDING AND DECISION: (Marvel, V. Chan.) No. In the absence of a specific authorization by the company's board of directors, a corporate executive may receive only compensation that is reasonably commensurate with his functions and duties. Joseph Wilderman (D) was authorized to receive a salary of only $20,800 per year. Any agreement pursuant to which he may have been entitled to more compensation had been rescinded prior to 1971. Thus, the excessive amounts which he received in 1971, 1972, and 1973 may be justified, if at all, only by application of the quantum meruit theory. And, on the basis of the evidence presented, it does not appear that the compensation to which Joseph (D) unilaterally and arbitrarily declared himself entitled was reasonable in light of the services he performed for the company (D). An expert witness testified that $35,000 per year was the highest salary which should reasonably have been paid to Joseph (D). Moreover, the Internal Revenue Service permitted Marble Craft (D) to deduct only $52,000 of the more than $92,000 that Joseph (D) received in 1971. Since Joseph (D) has produced no evidence that would justify his receipt of compensation as generous as that which he paid himself, it is appropriate to require the return of any excess over $45,000 received in any of the years in question. Appropriate adjustments in the corporate pension fund must also be made, and dividends may be declared at the insistence of the company's (D) board of directors or, in the event of a deadlock, the custodian.

▶ ANALYSIS

The salaries of corporate executives are ordinarily fixed by the company's board of directors and are incorporated into each executive's employment contract, whether it is oral or written. Any person who renders services for another has some chance of recovering compensation if he brings an action based on quantum meruit. However, only rarely would such a suit prove beneficial to a corporate executive since, in order to recover, he would have to prove that his services were performed on behalf of the company but

Continued on next page.

were in addition to the duties that were required of him in the usual conduct of his employment.

■═■

Quicknotes

8 DEL. C. § 122(5) Board of directors has the authority to compensate officers.

QUANTUM MERUIT Equitable doctrine allowing recovery for labor and materials provided by one party, even though no contract was entered into, in order to avoid unjust enrichment by the benefited party.

■═■

Brehm v. Eisner

Stockholders (P) v. Board of directors (D)

Del. Sup. Ct., 746 A.2d 244 (2000).

NATURE OF CASE: Appeal of stockholder derivative complaint.

FACT SUMMARY: Brehm (P) sued Eisner (D) for approving an employment agreement and subsequent non-fault termination of Disney's president, Ovitz.

🏛 **RULE OF LAW**
A complaint that is mostly conclusory does not meet the rules required for a stockholder to pursue a derivative remedy.

FACTS: Disney hired Ovitz as its president. He was a friend of Disney's Chairman, Eisner (D). Ovitz lacked experience managing a diversified public company. Ovitz's Employment Agreement with Disney was unilaterally negotiated by Eisner (D) and approved by the Disney's Board of Directors (D). The Agreement had an initial term of five years and required Ovitz to devote his full time and best efforts exclusively to the Company. In return he received a base salary of $1 million, a discretionary bonus, and options to purchase 5 million shares of Disney's common stock. Certain options would vest immediately upon termination. Per the Agreement, Ovitz's employment could end by his contract not being renewed in five years; Disney's terminating him for good cause prior to the five years expiring; or Ovitz's resigning voluntarily. Non-fault termination would entitle Ovitz to the present value of his remaining salary payments through September 2000, a $20 million severance payment, an additional $7.5 million for each fiscal year remaining under the agreement, and the immediate vesting of the first $3 million stock options. Problems arose soon after Ovitz began to work, and Brehm (P) alleges that these problems were sufficient to let Ovitz go for cause. Eisner (D) and Ovitz, however, agreed to arrange for Ovitz to leave Disney on the non-fault basis provided in the Agreement, and a New Disney Board (D) approved his decision. Brehm (P) alleges that the Old Disney Board of Directors (D) breached its fiduciary duty in approving the wasteful Agreement; that the New Disney Board (D) breached its fiduciary duty by agreeing to a non-fault termination of the Agreement, and that the Directors (D) were not disinterested and independent. Brehm (P) alleged that the Old Disney Board (D) failed to properly inform itself about the total costs and incentives of the Agreement, especially the severance package. The Board (D) had relied on a corporate compensation expert in connection with its decision to approve the Agreement. The expert, however, had not quantified for the Board (D) the maximum payout to Ovitz under the non-fault termination scenario. The expert

later stated that he should have done so at the time. Brehm (P) also charges the Board (D) with waste in that the severance package was over $140 million when Disney really owed Ovitz nothing because he either resigned or could have been fired for cause.

ISSUE: Do the particularized facts alleged in the Complaint provide a reason to believe that the conduct of the New and Old Disney Boards (D) constituted a violation of their fiduciary duties?

HOLDING AND DECISION: (Veasey, C.J.) No. The particularized facts as alleged in the Complaint do not provide a reason to believe that the conduct of the New and Old Disney Boards (D) constituted a violation of their fiduciary duties. Although the Boards' (D) actions probably did not demonstrate good business judgment of directors in that the compensation and termination payout to Ovitz were lucrative compared to his value to Disney, and the Boards' (D) handling of the termination of the Agreement was sloppy, the 88-page Complaint is conclusory, inartfully drafted, and was properly dismissed because it didn't meet the pleading standards for derivative suits. The pleading standards required are particularized factual statements that are essential to the claim, and they must be simple, concise, and direct. The plaintiff must allege with particularity facts raising a reasonable doubt that the corporate action being questioned was properly the product of business judgment. Conclusory allegations are not considered as expressly pleaded facts or factual inferences. In this case, the Complaint does not comply with these fundamental pleading mandates as it is full of conclusory language. First, Brehm's (P) theory that the New Disney Board (D) was not disinterested because it was beholden to Eisner (D), and a lavish contract to Ovitz would result in Eisner's (D) own compensation increasing, is not supported by well-pleaded facts, only illogical and counterintuitive conclusory allegations. No reasonable doubt can exist as to Eisner's (D) disinterest in the approval of the Agreement, and Brehm (P) thus has not demonstrated a reasonable doubt that Eisner (D) was disinterested in granting Ovitz a non-fault termination. A majority of the New Disney Board (D) was therefore disinterested and independent. Second, the Complaint does not set forth particularized facts creating a reasonable doubt that the decisions of the Boards (D) were not protected by the business judgment rule. Brehm (P) contends that the Directors (D) did not avail themselves of all material information reasonably available in approving the Agreement and therefore, that they violated their fiduciary duty of care. The particularized facts in the

Continued on next page.

complaint must create a reasonable doubt that the informational component of the Directors' (D) decision making, measured by concepts of gross negligence, included consideration of all material information reasonably available. The economic exposure of Disney to the payout scenarios of the Agreement was material for purposes of the Directors' (D) decision making and the dollar exposure numbers were reasonably available. The Complaint charges that the expert admitted that neither he nor the Directors (D) made the calculation, although all the necessary information was at hand to do so. The trial court's reading of the Complaint, that only the expert and not the Board (D) itself failed to bring to bear all the necessary information, was too restrictive, but such error was harmless. The Directors (D) relied in good faith on a qualified expert and therefore have presumption that they exercised proper business judgment. Brehm (P) must rebut the presumption that the Directors (D) properly exercised their business judgment, including their good faith reliance on his expertise. The trial court's error is harmless because it is not a sufficient rebuttal to say what the expert now believes in hindsight as to what he and the Board (D) should have done in 1995. The Complaint was therefore subject to dismissal. Brehm (P), however, should be provided the opportunity to properly replead this issue. Third, the Complaint failed to set forth particularized facts creating a reasonable doubt that the Directors' (D) decision to enter into the Agreement was a product of the proper exercise of business judgment. The agreement was not a wasteful transaction for Disney. It was not an exchange that is so one sided that no business person of ordinary, sound judgment could conclude that the corporation has received adequate consideration. The Boards' (D) decision on executive compensation is entitled to great deference. There are outer limits, but those are confined to unconscionable cases when directors irrationally squander or give away corporate assets. Fourth, the Complaint as currently pled does not set forth particularized facts that Ovitz resigned or unarguably breached his Agreement. There are no facts that show he actually resigned before the Board (D) acted on his non-fault termination. Also, the Complaint is inconsistent because it states that Ovitz would not actually resign before he could achieve a lucrative payout under the generous terms of his Agreement. Fifth, the Complaint also alleges that it was waste to pay Ovitz under non-fault termination when the Boards could have fired him for cause. The facts in the Complaint show Ovitz's performance as president was disappointing at best and arguable grounds existed to fire him for cause. However, what is alleged is only an argument that his conduct constituted negligence or malfeasance. Disney would have had to persuade a trier of fact in litigation which would have been expensive, distracted executives, company resources, caused lost opportunity costs, bad publicity, and an uncertain outcome. The Complaint does not show that no reasonable business person would have made the decision that the New Disney Board (D) made under these circumstances. Brehm (P) therefore will have another opportunity on remand to replead. The lower court's ruling is reversed, only as to its ruling of dismissal with prejudice as to claims for breach of fiduciary duty and waste which shall now be dismissed without prejudice. Remanded.

▶ *ANALYSIS*

Absent properly pled seriously egregious conduct on a board's behalf, it is evident from this case that it is unlikely that a court will hold a board liable for approving an employment agreement, and subsequent termination agreement, which costs the company a tremendous amount of money.

■══■

Quicknotes

SHAREHOLDER DERIVATIVE CLAIM Action asserted by a shareholder in order to enforce a cause of action on behalf of the corporation.

■══■

In re Walt Disney Co. Derivative Litigation (Brehm v. Eisner)

Shareholders (P) v. Directors (D)

Del. Sup. Ct., 906 A.2d 27 (2006).

NATURE OF CASE: Appeal from judgment for defendants in an action for the breach of the fiduciary duty of care.

FACT SUMMARY: Disney shareholders (P) contended that the corporation's compensation committee (D) breached its duty of care in approving an employment agreement to Ovitz that had the potential for granting him a severance package worth around $130 million in its first year; that the committee (D) and remaining directors (D) breached their duty of care in hiring Ovitz as Disney's president because they acted in bad faith; and that, in any event, the payment of the severance package to Ovitz constituted waste.

🏛 RULE OF LAW

(1) Corporate directors who are members of a compensation committee do not breach their fiduciary duty of care in approving a compensation package where they have based their approval on knowledge of the financial purpose and potential consequences of the package.

(2) The appropriate standard for bad faith is an intentional dereliction of duty and a conscious disregard for one's responsibilities.

(3) A severance package does not constitute waste where it may be attributed to a rational business purpose.

FACTS: Disney's compensation committee (D) approved an employment agreement for Ovitz to serve as Disney's president. This Ovitz Employment Agreement (OEA) contained No Fault Termination (NFT) terms that provided, inter alia, that in the event of a non-fault termination, Ovitz would receive: (1) the present value of his salary ($ 1 million per year) for the balance of the contract term, (2) the present value of his annual bonus payments (computed at $ 7.5 million) for the balance of the contract term, (3) a $ 10 million termination fee, and (4) the acceleration of his options for 3 million shares, which would become immediately exercisable at market price. In approving the OEA with the NTF terms, the committee (D) met twice. At the first meeting, the directors (D) on the committee considered a "term sheet" that summarized all the OEA's material terms. The committee members (D) were informed that the value of the option component of the severance package could reach the $ 92 million order of magnitude if they terminated Ovitz without cause after one year. Their sources of information were the value of benchmark options previously granted to Disney employees, valuations of the proposed Ovitz options that were

explained to them, and the amount of downside protection Ovitz was demanding to leave a job that would have paid him between $150 million and $200 million in commissions over five years. This meant that if Ovitz was terminated without cause, the earlier in the contract term the termination occurred the larger the severance amount would be to replace the lost commissions. Ovitz was terminated without cause after about a year, and he was paid the severance package provided by the OEA. Disney shareholders (P) brought suit claiming that the compensation committee members (D) had breached their duty of care by failing to properly inform themselves of material facts and hence were grossly negligent in approving the NFT provisions; that the compensation committee (D) and the remaining Disney directors (D) had breached their duty of care by approving the hiring of Ovitz; and that even if the approval of the OEA was protected by the business judgment rule, the payment of the severance constituted corporate waste. The Chancery Court rendered judgment for the directors (D) on all claims, finding that even though the committee's (D) decision-making process fell far short of corporate governance "best practices," the committee members (D) breached no duty of care in considering and approving the NFT terms of the OEA; that the business judgment rule presumptions protected the decisions of the compensation committee (D) and the remaining directors (D), not only because they had acted with due care but also because they had not acted in bad faith; and that the record did not support the contention that the NFT provisions of the OEA were wasteful because they incentivized Ovitz to perform poorly in order to obtain payment of the NFT provisions. The state's highest court granted review.

ISSUE:

(1) Do corporate directors who are members of a compensation committee breach their fiduciary duty of care in approving a compensation package where they have based their approval on knowledge of the financial purpose and potential consequences of the package?

(2) Is the appropriate standard for bad faith an intentional dereliction of duty and a conscious disregard for one's responsibilities?

(3) Does a severance package constitute waste where it may be attributed to a rational business purpose?

HOLDING AND DECISION: (Jacobs, J.)

(1) No. Corporate directors who are members of a compensation committee do not breach their fiduciary duty of care in approving a compensation package where they have based their approval on knowledge of the

Continued on next page.

financial purpose and potential consequences of the package. Although the committee's (D) decision-making process here was not ideal, it did not rise to the level of a breach of the fiduciary duty of care. The record shows that the committee members (D) were informed of the possible value and cost to Disney of the NFT terms, and that the OEA was specifically structured to compensate Ovitz for walking away from $150 million to $200 million of anticipated commissions. Even if some of the directors (D) did not review valuation spreadsheets provided to them, as alleged by the shareholders (P), such failure was harmless since they were adequately informed of the spreadsheets' contents by others. Affirmed as to this issue.

(2) Yes. The appropriate standard for bad faith is an intentional dereliction of duty and a conscious disregard for one's responsibilities. The Chancery Court defined bad faith as intentional dereliction of duty and a conscious disregard for one's responsibilities, saying that deliberate indifference and inaction in the face of a duty to act is the epitome of faithless conduct. That court also noted that this is an appropriate, though not the only, standard for determining whether a fiduciary has acted in good faith. The shareholders (P) assert that this is not the correct legal standard for bad faith. There are three categories where there might be bad faith. First, bad faith might occur where the fiduciary has deliberately intended to do harm—but that is not being asserted here. Second, it is asserted that bad faith can occur where there has been gross negligence. However, gross negligence, without more, cannot constitute bad faith. Such a conclusion is supported by the distinction made by legislative history and common law between the duties to exercise due care and to act in good faith, and the highly significant consequences that flow from that distinction. The legislature has permitted corporations to exculpate their directors from liability for breaches of the duty of care, but not for conduct that is not in good faith. A definition of bad faith that would cause a violation of the duty of care to automatically become a bad faith act or omission would eviscerate such exculpatory protections. Similarly, directors or officers can be indemnified for liability for breaches of their duty of care, but not for a violation of the duty to act in good faith. The third category of possible bad faith is a category of conduct between subjective bad faith and gross negligence. This is the category addressed by the Chancery Court—where there has been an intentional dereliction of duty, a conscious disregard for one's responsibilities. The question is whether this category of misconduct is properly treated as a non-exculpable, non-indemnifiable violation of the fiduciary duty to act in good faith. The answer is that it is. This type of conduct does not involve self-interest and disloyalty to the corporation, but is more culpable than mere inattention or failure to be informed. To protect the shareholders and the corpora-

tion, such conduct must be proscribed. The state's corporation statute expressly denies exculpation from liability for "acts or omissions not in good faith or which involve intentional misconduct or a knowing violation of law." Thus, the statute distinguishes between subjective bad faith on the one hand, and acts that are not in good faith on the other, but nonetheless denies exculpation for both. Because the statute exculpates directors only for conduct amounting to gross negligence, the statutory denial of exculpation for "acts . . . not in good faith" must encompass the intermediate category of misconduct addressed by the Chancery Court's definition of bad faith. Thus, this definition is upheld. Affirmed as to this issue.

(3) No. A severance package does not constitute waste where it may be attributed to a rational business purpose. To recover on a claim of corporate waste, the shareholders (P) must shoulder the burden of proving that the exchange was "so one sided that no business person of ordinary, sound judgment could conclude that the corporation has received adequate consideration." The issue here is thus not whether the actual payment to Ovitz constituted waste, but whether the amounts required to be paid in the event of an NFT were a wasteful obligation. As the Chancery Court found, and contrary to the shareholders' (P) assertions, the NFT provisions did not provide an irrational incentive to Ovitz to perform just poorly enough to be terminated for no cause. Instead, the OEA had a rational purpose—to induce Ovitz to join Disney as President, and leave a very lucrative position to do so. The record showed that Ovitz had no control over whether or not he would be fired, either with or without cause; there was no proof to even suggest that at the time he entered into the OEA Ovitz would engineer an early departure at the cost of his extraordinary reputation in the entertainment industry and his historical friendship with Disney's chairman. Such a claim is entirely speculative. Accordingly, the shareholders (P) have failed to show that the approval of the NFT terms of the OEA was not a rational business decision. Affirmed as to this issue.

▶ ANALYSIS

The court lays out a veritable road map for compensation committees to follow in carrying out best practices regarding compensation packages. The court said: "In a 'best case' scenario, all committee members would have received, before or at the committee's first meeting . . . a spreadsheet or similar document prepared by (or with the assistance of) a compensation expert. . . . Making different, alternative assumptions, the spreadsheet would disclose the amounts that Ovitz could receive under the OEA in each circumstance that might foreseeably arise. One variable in that matrix of possibilities would be the

Continued on next page.

cost to Disney of a non-fault termination for each of the five years of the initial term of the OEA. The contents of the spreadsheet would be explained to the committee members, either by the expert who prepared it or by a fellow committee member similarly knowledgeable about the subject. That spreadsheet, which ultimately would become an exhibit to the minutes of the compensation committee meeting, would form the basis of the committee's deliberations and decision. . . . Had that scenario been followed, there would be no dispute (and no basis for litigation) over what information was furnished to the committee members or when it was furnished." Any compensation committee that wants to avoid being accused of breaching its duty of care regarding compensation packages should follow this "map."

■━■

Quicknotes

DUTY OF CARE Duty that an officer or director owes to the corporation, by virtue of his fiduciary relationship, to act for the benefit of the corporation.

■━■

Sinclair Oil Corp. v. Levien

Corporation (D) v. Minority stockholder (P)

Del. Sup. Ct., 280 A.2d 717 (1971).

NATURE OF CASE: Derivative suit for an accounting by parent company.

FACT SUMMARY: A minority stockholder in Sinven, Levien (P) accused Sinclair (D), the parent company, of using Sinven assets to finance its operations.

🏛 RULE OF LAW

Where a parent company controls all transactions of a subsidiary, receiving a benefit at the expense of the subsidiary's minority stockholders, the intrinsic fairness test will be applied, placing the burden on the parent company to prove the transactions were based on reasonable business objectives.

FACTS: Sinclair Oil Corp. (Sinclair) (D) is a holding company that markets, produces, and explores for oil. Sinclair (D) owned 97 percent of the stock of Sinclair Venezuelan Oil Company (Sinven), a company engaged in petroleum operations in South America. Levien (P) owns about 3,000 of Sinven's 120,000 publicly held shares. Sinclair (D) controls the directors of Sinven. From 1960 to 1966, Sinclair (D) caused Sinven to pay out excessive dividends of $108,000,000, $38,000,000 above its earnings. In 1961, Sinclair (D) created Sinclair International (International) to coordinate Sinclair's (D) foreign operations, and then caused Sinven to contract to sell crude oil to International at specified rates and minimum quantities. When International failed to live up to the contract, Levien (P) and other minority shareholders of Sinven brought this derivative action requiring Sinclair (D) to account for damages sustained by Sinven as a result of the excessive dividends and causing Sinven not to enforce the contract with International. The Court of Chancery found for Levien (P), and Sinclair (D) appealed.

ISSUE: Does the business judgment rule protecting fiduciaries from judicial scrutiny also protect a parent company where it exerts such complete control over its subsidiary that the parent receives a benefit at the subsidiary's expense?

HOLDING AND DECISION: (Wolcott, C.J.) No. Under the business judgment rule a court will not interfere with a board of director's judgment unless there is a showing of gross and palpable overreaching. But this rule does not apply to a situation where a parent company appears to have benefited from its control over a subsidiary to the detriment of the subsidiary's minority stockholders. In such a situation, any transactions will be tested by their intrinsic fairness if there is evidence of breach of the parent company's fiduciary duty coupled with self-dealing. For instance, in the present case, the allegation that Sinclair (D) caused excessive dividends to be paid out of Sinven is not enough to create a cause of action against the parent company for intrinsic unfairness. Levien (P) must meet the burden of proving the dividend was not based on a reasonable business objective. However, the court found that the dividends were not self-dealing since Sinclair (D) had received nothing to the exclusion of Sinven and its minority shareholders. Thus, as to the dividends, the business judgment rule applied. As to the allegations that the dividends had prevented Sinven from expanding, the court held that Levien (P) had proved no loss of business opportunities due to the drain of cash from Sinven, so again the business judgment rule protected Sinclair (D). However, the court held that there was self-dealing by Sinclair (D) in contracting with its dominated subsidiary, International. Sinclair (D) caused International to breach its contract with Sinven to the detriment of Sinven's minority shareholders. But Sinclair (D) received products from Sinven through International and thus benefited from the transaction. However, Sinclair (D) failed to cause Sinven to enforce the contract. Therefore, Sinclair's (D) inherent duty to its subsidiary, Sinven, coupled with its self-dealing shifted the burden to it to show its breach of the International-Sinven contract was intrinsically fair. The court found that Sinclair (D) failed to meet the burden. Reversed in part, affirmed in part, and remanded.

▶ ANALYSIS

The business judgment rule is an expression of the court's reluctance to interfere with corporate decision making. It is a rule of evidence rather than a rule of law, and the standard of intrinsic fairness is an extension of the business judgment rule in this respect. For instance, in the present case, the court applied the business judgment rule and refused to interfere with Sinclair's (D) decisions on the dividends. In short, the burden to prove overreaching in order to knock down the business judgment rule was on Levien (P), and it was not met. But as to the breach of the International-Sinven contract, the burden shifted to Sinclair (D) to prove it was intrinsically fair, a burden it failed to meet. In such cases, the shift of burden of proof from the controlling stockholder-management to the accusing minority pivots on evidence of overreaching and self-dealing by the majority.

Continued on next page.

Quicknotes

INTRINSIC FAIRNESS STANDARD A defense to a claim that a director engaged in an interested director transaction by showing the transaction's fairness to the corporation.

■■■

Weinberger v. UOP, Inc.

Former shareholder (P) v. Corporation (D)

Del. Sup. Ct., 457 A.2d 701, *en banc* (1983).

NATURE OF CASE: Class action to rescind a merger.

FACT SUMMARY: Claiming that a cash-out merger between UOP (D) and Signal (D) was unfair, Weinberger (P), a former minority shareholder of UOP (D), brought a class action to have the merger rescinded.

🏛 RULE OF LAW
When seeking to secure minority shareholder approval for a proposed cash-out merger, the corporations involved must comply with the fairness test, which has two basic interrelated aspects: (1) fair dealings—which imposes a duty on the corporations to completely disclose to the shareholders all information germane to the merger and (2) fair price—which requires that the price being offered for the outstanding stock be equivalent to a price determined by an appraisal where "all relevant nonspeculative factors" were considered.

FACTS: Signal, Inc. (D) owned 50.5 percent of UOP (D) stock. Seven of UOP's (D) 13 directors, including the president, were also directors or employees of Signal (D). Arledge and Chitiea, who were directors of UOP (D) and Signal (D), prepared a feasibility study for Signal (D). The study reported that it would be a good investment for Signal (D) to acquire the remaining 49.5 percent of UOP (D) shares through a cash-out merger at any price up to $24 per share. The study was given to all the Signal (D) directors, including those who also served as a director on UOP's (D) board. However, the evidence dictates that the study was never disclosed to UOP's (D) six non-Signal, i.e., outside, directors. Nor was it disclosed to the minority shareholders who owned the remaining 49.5 percent of UOP (D) stock. On February 28, Signal (D) offered UOP (D) a cash-out merger price of $21 per share. Four business days later, on March 6, the six non-Signal UOP (D) directors (the seven common Signal-UOP directors abstained from the voting) voted to approve the merger at $21 per share. The vote was largely due to the fact that at the time, UOP's (D) market price was only $14.50 per share, and also there was a "fairness opinion letter" from UOP's (D) investment banker stating that the $21 per share was a fair price. The merger was then approved by a majority (51.9 percent) of the minority, i.e., remaining 49.5 percent, UOP (D) shareholders. Weinberger (P), a former minority shareholder of UOP (D), then brought a class action to have the merger rescinded, claiming it was unfair to UOP's (D) former shareholders. The Court of Chancery held for UOP (D) and Signal (D). Weinberger (P) appealed.

ISSUE: May a minority shareholder successfully challenge the approval of a cash-out merger that was approved by the majority of the minority shareholders?

HOLDING AND DECISION: (Moore, J.) Yes. A minority shareholder may successfully challenge the approval of a cash-out merger that was approved by the majority of the minority shareholders if he can demonstrate that the corporations involved failed to comply with the fairness test in securing the approval. The fairness test consists of two basic interrelated aspects. The first aspect is "fair dealings," which imposes a duty on the corporations involved to completely disclose to the minority shareholders all information germane to the merger. Here Signal (D) failed to disclose, to the non-Signal UOP (D) directors and the minority shareholders of UOP (D), the Arledge-Chitiea feasibility study that reported it would be a "good investment" for Signal (D) to acquire the minority shares up to a price of $24 per share. In addition, UOP's (D) minority was given the impression that the "fairness opinion letter" from UOP's (D) investment banker had been drafted only after the banker had made a careful study, when, in fact, the investment banker had drafted the letter in three days with the price left blank. Consequently, Signal (D) did not meet the "fair dealing" aspect of the test. The second aspect of the fairness test is "fair price," which requires that the price being offered for the outstanding stock be equivalent to an appraisal where "all relevant nonspeculative factors" were considered. In this case, the Court of Chancery tested the fairness of Signal's (D) $21 per share price against the Delaware weighted average method of valuation. That method shall no longer exclusively control the determination of "fair price." Rather, a new method that considers "all relevant nonspeculative factors" shall now be used for determining fair price. This new method is consistent with the method used in determining a shareholder's appraisal remedy. Here, the Court of Chancery did not consider the $24 per share price determined by the Arledge-Chitiea study. Nor did the court consider Weinberger's (P) discounted cash flow analysis, which concluded that the UOP (D) stock was worth $26 per share on the date of merger. Therefore, since these factors were not considered, it cannot be said that the $21 per share price paid by Signal (D) meets the new method of determining fair price. Finally, in view of the new, more liberal test for determining fair price, together with the Chancery Court's broad remedial discretion, it is concluded that the business purpose requirement for

Continued on next page.

mergers, as required by the trilogy of *Singer* [*v. Singer*, 634 P.2d 766 (1981)], *Tanzer* [*v. International General Industries, Inc.*, 379 A.2d 1121 (Del. 1979)], and [*Roland International Corp. v.*] *Najjar*, 407 A.2d 1032 (Del. Sup. Ct. 1979), adds no further protection to minority shareholders. Accordingly, the business purpose requirement is no longer law. Reversed and remanded.

▶ ANALYSIS

This case demonstrates the use of a cash-out merger to eliminate or "freeze out" the minority interest. A footnote in the case suggests that Signal's (D) freeze out of UOP's (D) minority interest would have met the court's fairness test if UOP (D) had appointed an independent negotiating committee of its non-Signal directors to deal with Signal (D) at arm's length.

■■■■

Quicknotes

CASH-OUT MERGER Occurs when a merging company prematurely redeems the securities of a holder as part of the merger.

DUTY OF CANDOR/DUTY OF FAIRNESS The ethical duty to turn over an instrumentality of crime once it has been used to aid a client's case, owed to the tribunal and opposing counsel to prevent the frustration of justice.

MERGER The acquisition of one company by another, after which the acquired company ceases to exist as an independent entity.

MINORITY STOCKHOLDER A stockholder in a corporation controlling such a small portion of those shares outstanding that its votes have no influence in the management of the corporation.

■■■■

Northeast Harbor Golf Club, Inc. v. Harris

Corporation (P) v. President (D)

Me. Sup. Jud. Ct., 661 A.2d 1146 (1995).

NATURE OF CASE: Appeal from judgment denying an injunction and imposition of a constructive trust.

FACT SUMMARY: Northeast Harbor Golf Club (the "Club") (P) claimed Harris (D) breached her duty of loyalty as president of the Club (P) by purchasing and developing adjacent real estate.

🏛 RULE OF LAW
Prior to availing herself of an opportunity properly belonging to the corporation, an officer or director must first fully disclose the opportunity to the corporation, and allow the board of directors the opportunity to reject it by a majority vote of the disinterested directors.

FACTS: Harris (D), president of Northeast Harbor Golf Club (the "Club") (P), was approached by a listing broker seeking to sell three parcels of land to the Club (P). The Club's (P) board of directors had previously discussed the possibility of developing some of the Club's (P) real estate in an effort to raise funds. Harris (D) purchased the land in her own name in 1979. Harris (D) later disclosed this purchase to the Club (P), assuring the board she would not develop the property. In 1984, Harris (D) purchased another parcel of land adjacent to the Club (P). In 1988, she divided the parcels into 41 smaller lots, and commenced obtaining approval for the development of a subdivision. Several directors formed a separate organization in order to oppose the development. Collectively, however, the board took no action in respect to Harris's (D) actions. In 1990, the board asked Harris (D) to resign as president. Following a change in membership, the board initiated suit against Harris (D), alleging that she breached her fiduciary duty to the Club (P), and seeking an injunction on development and the imposition of a constructive trust on the property. The trial court found that Harris (D) had not violated her duty of loyalty to the Club (P) by seizing a corporate opportunity, since the Club (P) was not in the business of developing real estate. Furthermore, it found that the Club (P) was financially incapable of accepting such opportunity. The Club (P) appealed.

ISSUE: Prior to availing herself of an opportunity properly belonging to the corporation, must an officer or director first fully disclose the opportunity to the corporation, and provide the board with a chance to reject it?

HOLDING AND DECISION: (Roberts, J.) Yes. Prior to availing herself of an opportunity properly belonging to the corporation, an officer or director must first fully disclose the opportunity to the corporation, and allow the

board of directors the opportunity to reject it by a majority vote of the disinterested directors. The directors and officers of a corporation owe a duty of loyalty to the company requiring them to act in good faith and in the best interests of the corporation. This involves a concomitant duty to disclose any information regarding a potential conflict of interest with the corporation, and the duty to refrain from capitalizing on their position in the corporation. The court adopts the American Law Institute's (ALI) approach of determining whether a director has seized a corporate opportunity for her own benefit. The distinguishing feature of this test is the mandatory disclosure of the opportunity to the corporation, providing it with the opportunity to accept or reject the offer, prior to the director's usurpation of it. The ALI's definition of what constitutes a corporate opportunity encompasses not only those related to the company's line of business, but also opportunities that inure to the officer as a result of her position. Thus, the Club (P) must demonstrate that the opportunity seized by Harris (D) was in fact an opportunity in which the Club (P) had a reasonable expectancy, and that Harris (D) neglected to disclose the opportunity to the Club (P), or that it failed to reject the offer by a majority vote of disinterested directors. If the Club (P) fails to make this demonstration, then Harris (D) may avail herself of the fairness defense that her actions were consistent with the best interests of the corporation. Vacated and remanded.

▶ ANALYSIS

In adopting the ALI approach of determining whether or not an officer or director has usurped a corporate opportunity, the court rejects the "line of business" standard applied by the trial court. The line of business test states that a director violates her duty of loyalty to her corporation where she seizes an opportunity that is in the corporation's line of business, that the corporation reasonably expects to be available, and which the corporation is financially capable of accepting. Likewise, the court rejects the "fairness test" in which a court must determine whether the officer's usurpation of the corporate opportunity was just and equitable under the circumstances.

◼◼◼

Quicknotes

ALI § 505 Rule regarding directors or senior executives taking advantage of corporate opportunities.

CONSTRUCTIVE TRUST A trust that arises by operation of law whereby the court imposes a trust upon property

Continued on next page.

lawfully held by one party for the benefit of another, as a result of some wrongdoing by the party in possession so as to avoid unjust enrichment.

CORPORATE OPPORTUNITY An opportunity that a fiduciary to a corporation has to take advantage of information acquired by virtue of his or her position for the individual's benefit.

DUTY OF LOYALTY A director's duty to refrain from self-dealing or to take a position that is adverse to the corporation's best interests.

■■■

CHAPTER 12

Shareholder Derivative Lawsuits

Quick Reference Rules of Law

Gall v. Exxon Corp.

Shareholder (P) v. Corporation (D)

418 F. Supp. 508 (S.D.N.Y. 1976).

NATURE OF CASE: Motion for summary judgment by defendants in shareholder derivative suit.

FACT SUMMARY: At trial of Gall's (P) shareholder derivative suit against Exxon Corp. (D), claiming illegal bribes by the corporation, Exxon (D) motioned for summary judgment, claiming it was in the corporation's sound business judgment to refuse to sue on Gall's (P) complaint.

🏛 RULE OF LAW
The decision of corporate directors, whether or not to assert a cause of action held by the corporation, rests within the sound business judgment of management.

FACTS: Gall's (P) derivative suit arose out of the alleged payment by Exxon Corp. (D) of corporate funds as bribes or political payments, which were improperly contributed to Italian political parties to secure favors. Gall (P), inter alia, claimed a violation of Securities and Exchange Commission (SEC) rules 13(a) and 14(a), misuse of corporate assets, and breach of fiduciary duties by the officers. Exxon (D) had formed a Special Committee on Litigation to study Gall's (P) complaint, and the committee refused to institute suit against the corporation's officers involved in the bribes. At Gall's (P) derivative suit, Exxon (D) motioned for summary judgment, claiming the committee's decision was within the sound business judgment rule and, therefore, proper.

ISSUE: Does the decision of corporate directors, whether or not to assert a cause of action held by the corporation, rest within the sound business judgment of management?

HOLDING AND DECISION: (Carter, J.) Yes. The decision of corporate directors, whether or not to assert a cause of action held by the corporation, rests within the sound business judgment of management. There is no question that the rights sought to be vindicated in the lawsuit are those of the corporation and not those of the plaintiff suing derivatively on the corporation's behalf. Since it is the interests of the corporation that are at stake, it is the responsibility of the directors of the corporation to determine, in the first instance, whether an action should be brought on the corporation's behalf. Courts seldom interfere to control discretion of the board of directors to determine whether or not the corporation shall seek to enforce in courts a cause of action, except when directors are guilty of misconduct equivalent to a breach of trust or where they stand in a dual relationship which prevents an unprejudiced exercise of judgment. Here, the issue for decision is not whether the payments made by Esso Italiana to Italian political parties were improper or proper. Rather, the issue here is whether the Special Committee, acting as Exxon's (D) board of directors and in the sound exercise of their business judgment, may determine that a suit against any present or former director or officer would be contrary to the best interests of the corporation. However, Gall (P) must be given an opportunity to test the bona fides and independence of the Special Committee through discovery and, if necessary, at a special hearing. Issues of intent, motivation, and good faith are particularly inappropriate for summary disposition. Motion denied without prejudice.

▶ ANALYSIS

According to Henn, *Law of Corporations*, 2nd edition (1970), "The 'business judgment' rule sustains corporate transactions and immunizes management from liability where the transaction is within the powers of the corporation (*intra vires*) and the authority of management, and involves the exercise of due care and compliance with applicable fiduciary duties. ... If in the course of management, directors arrive at a decision, within the corporation's powers and their authority, for which there is a reasonable basis, and they act in good faith, as the result of their independent discretion and judgment, and uninfluenced by any consideration other than what they honestly believe to be the best interests of the corporation, a court will not interfere with internal management and substitute its judgment for that of the directors to enjoin or set aside the transaction or to surcharge the directors for any resulting loss."

Quicknotes

BUSINESS JUDGMENT RULE Doctrine relieving corporate directors and/or officers from liability for decisions honestly and rationally made in the corporation's best interests.

DERIVATIVE SUIT Action asserted by a shareholder in order to enforce a cause of action on behalf of the corporation.

INTRA VIRES "Within the power;" refers to powers that are within the scope of authority of an individual or corporation.

Zapata Corp. v. Maldonado

Corporation (D) v. Shareholder (P)

Del. Sup. Ct., 430 A.2d 779 (1981).

NATURE OF CASE: Interlocutory appeal in a stockholder's derivative suit.

FACT SUMMARY: Maldonado (P) initiated a derivative suit charging officers and directors of Zapata (D) with breaches of fiduciary duty, but four years later an "Independent Investigation Committee" of two disinterested directors recommended dismissing the action.

🏛 RULE OF LAW
Where the making of a prior demand upon the directors of a corporation to sue is excused and a stockholder initiates a derivative suit on behalf of the corporation, the board of directors or an independent committee appointed by the board can move to dismiss the derivative suit as detrimental to the corporation's best interests, and the court should apply a two-step test to the motion: (1) Has the corporation proved independence, good faith, and a reasonable investigation, and (2) Does the court feel, applying its own independent business judgment, that the motion should be granted?

FACTS: At the time Maldonado (P) instituted a derivative suit against Zapata (D), he was excused from making a prior demand on the board of directors because they were all defendants (Maldonado [P] asserting a breach of fiduciary duty on the part of officers and directors of Zapata [D]). The board had changed membership when, four years later, it appointed an "Independent Investigation Committee," composed of two new directors, to investigate the litigation. The committee recommended dismissing the action, calling its continued maintenance "inimical to the Company's best interests . . . ." In an interlocutory appeal before the Supreme Court of Delaware, the primary focus was on whether or not the aforementioned Committee had the power to dismiss the action.

ISSUE: In a case in which a stockholder acted properly in instituting a derivative suit on behalf of the corporation without first making a demand on the board of directors to sue, can the board of directors or an independent committee they appoint move to dismiss the suit as detrimental to the best interests of the corporation?

HOLDING AND DECISION: (Quillen, J.) Yes. Where, as in this case, a stockholder acted properly in bringing a derivative suit without first demanding the directors file suit (i.e., where such a demand is "excused"), the board of directors or an independent committee they appoint has the power to choose not to pursue the litigation because such would not be in the best interests of the corporation. The fact that a majority of the board may have been tainted by self-interest is not per se a legal bar to the delegation of the board's power to an independent committee composed of disinterested board members. Thus, a committee, such as that involved in this case, can properly act for the corporation to move to dismiss derivative litigation that is believed to be detrimental to the corporation's best interests. When faced with such a motion, the court should give each side an opportunity to make a record on the motion. The moving party should be prepared to meet the normal burden of showing that there is no genuine issue as to any material fact and that it is entitled to dismiss as a matter of law. The court should apply a two-step test to the motion. First, it should inquire into the independence and good faith of the committee and the bases supporting its conclusions. To aid in such inquiries, limited discovery may be ordered. If the court determines either that the committee is not independent or has not shown reasonable bases for its conclusions, or if the court is not satisfied for other reasons relating to the process, including but not limited to the good faith of the committee, the court shall deny the corporation's motion. It must be remembered, the corporation has the burden of proving independence, good faith, and reasonableness. If the court is satisfied that the committee was independent and showed reasonable bases for good faith findings and recommendations, the court may proceed, in its discretion, to the second step. This second step provides the essential key in striking the balance between legitimate corporate claims as expressed in a derivative stockholder suit and a corporation's best interests as expressed by an independent investigating committee. The court should determine, applying its own independent business judgment, whether the motion should be granted. This second stop is intended to thwart instances where corporation actions meet the criteria of step one, but the result does not appear to satisfy the spirit, or where corporate actions would simply prematurely terminate a stockholder grievance deserving of further consideration in the corporation's interest. Of course, the court must carefully consider and weigh how compelling the corporate interest in dismissal is when faced with a nonfrivolous lawsuit. It should, when appropriate, give special consideration to matters of law and public policy in addition to the corporation's best interests. If, after all of this, the court's independent business judgment is satisfied, it may proceed to grant the motion, subject, of course, to any equitable terms or conditions it finds necessary or desirable. Reversed and remanded for further proceedings.

Continued on next page.

▶ ANALYSIS

Other courts have chosen to treat this type of situation as one where the "business judgment" rule is applicable. They look to see if the committee to whom the board of directors delegated the responsibility of determining if the litigation at issue should be continued was composed of independent and disinterested members and if it conducted a proper review of the matters before it to reach a good faith business judgment concerning whether or not to continue the litigation. If it did, the committee's decision stands. This court found that approach too one-sided, as tending to wrest bona fide derivative actions away from well-meaning derivative plaintiffs and robbing the shareholders of an effective intra-corporate means of policing boards of directors.

■■■■

Quicknotes

8 DEL. C. § 141(a) Businesses shall be managed by a board of directors.

BUSINESS JUDGMENT RULE Doctrine relieving corporate directors and/or officers from liability for decisions honestly and rationally made in the corporation's best interests.

INTERLOCUTORY APPEAL The appeal of an issue that does not resolve the disposition of the case, but is essential to a determination of the parties' legal rights.

SHAREHOLDER DERIVATIVE ACTION Action asserted by a shareholder in order to enforce a cause of action on behalf of the corporation.

■■■■

Aronson v. Lewis

[Parties not identified.]

Del. Sup. Ct., 473 A.2d 805 (1984).

NATURE OF CASE: Appeal from dismissal of shareholder derivative action.

FACT SUMMARY: The trial court dismissed this derivative suit for failure to meet the prerequisite of making a demand on the board of directors to bring the suit.

🏛 RULE OF LAW
A prior demand can be excused only where facts are alleged with particularity that creates a reasonable doubt that the director's action was entitled to the protections of the business judgment rule.

FACTS: Aronson (P) and others brought a shareholder's derivative action contesting an employment contract granted by the corporation to a longtime employee. The contract provided for large lifetime compensation and other benefits. The contract was approved by the board, most of whom were controlled by the principal actors in executing the contract. No prior demand was made on the board to bring the suit on the basis of impartiality. The trial court dismissed the suit, and the appellate court reversed, holding there was a reasonable inference that the actions were not protected by the business judgment rule. Aronson (P) appealed.

ISSUE: Will prior demand be excused where it appears the actions are not protected by the business judgment rule?

HOLDING AND DECISION: (Moore, J.) No. A prior demand can be excused only where facts are alleged with particularity that creates a reasonable doubt that the director's action was entitled to protection under the business judgment rule. In this case, no such facts were alleged. Merely alleging the prior loyalties of the individual board members does not indicate that the business judgment rule may not apply. As a result, the case was properly dismissed. Reversed and remanded.

▶ ANALYSIS

The facts called for which must be alleged to excuse prior demand can include conflict of interest or taking action contrary to the corporate interest. Because derivative suits are brought on behalf of the corporate entity, facts giving rise to a cause of action should be brought to the corporation's attention. The corporation, through its board of directors, will then decide whether it will bring suit. If it declines, the shareholders may then sue.

■==■

Quicknotes

8 DEL. C. § 141(e) Allows directors to rely on reports from officers and other experts.

BUSINESS JUDGMENT RULE Doctrine relieving corporate directors and/or officers from liability for decisions honestly and rationally made in the corporation's best interests.

■==■

Gordon v. Goodyear

Shareholder (P) v. Director (D)

2012 WL2885695 (N.D. Ill. 2012).

NATURE OF CASE: Derivative action asserting claims for breach of the fiduciary duty of loyalty and unjust enrichment.

FACT SUMMARY: Gordon (P), a Navigant company shareholder, brought a derivative action against the company and its directors (D), claiming that the directors (D) breached their fiduciary duty of loyalty, and that its top executives were unjustly enriched, when they approved an executive compensation package that she alleged was excessive. Gordon (P), who did not make pre-suit demand, asserted that such demand would have been futile.

🏛 **RULE OF LAW**

Pre-suit demand in a derivative action is not excused where a plaintiff, through the particularized facts alleged, cannot create a reasonable doubt (1) the directors approving a challenged transaction were disinterested and independent and (2) the challenged transaction was otherwise the product of a valid exercise of business judgment.

FACTS: Between 2006 and 2010, Navigant's (D) stock price fell from $21 per share to $9.20 per share. In 2010, Navigant (D) posted a negative 38 percent shareholder return. Navigant's (D) Compensation Committee Charter (the "Charter") set forth the duties and responsibilities of the Compensation Committee, which, inter alia, was directed to consider a number of factors when setting executive compensation, including Navigant's (D) performance and relative shareholder return, the value of similar incentive awards to chief executive officers at comparable companies, and the awards given to the company's CEO in past years. The Charter's purpose was to attract, retain and appropriately reward employees in order to motivate their performance in the achievement of the company's business objectives and align their interests with the long-term interest of Navigant's (D) shareholders. In 2010 based on the Compensation Committee's recommendations, Navigant's (D) board approved pay increases and cash bonuses to its top executives. In early 2011, Navigant (D) issued and filed a proxy statement with the Securities and Exchange Commission (SEC), in which the board recommended that the shareholders approve the compensation that Navigant (D) paid to its executive officers in 2010. The proxy informed the shareholders that their vote on the compensation package was non-binding on both Navigant (D) and its board. The proxy also informed shareholders that in settling upon the compensation package the Compensation Committee had considered several other factors, including net income

and earnings per share, strategic investment in core growth practice areas, senior level recruitment, and management's timely and effective response to changes in the competitive landscape, individual performance in the area of the company over which an executive had direct responsibility, and his or her individual contributions to the company's financial and strategic performance for the year in question. The board was comprised of eight directors. Other than Goodyear (D), the remaining seven members were outside directors. Notwithstanding that over half of the company's shareholders voted to reject the 2010 compensation package, the board approved it. Gordon (P), a Navigant (D) shareholder, brought a derivative suit on behalf of the company, asserting claims that the directors breached their fiduciary duty of loyalty, and that top executives, including Navigant's (D) CEO and Chairman Goodyear (D), had been unjustly enriched. Gordon (P) alleged that the 2010 compensation package was excessive in light of the company's poor performance and negative returns for its shareholders, and that by awarding the package, the directors failed to act in the shareholders' best interests. However, Gordon (P) failed to make litigation demand on the board, claiming that pre-suit demand would have been futile, as the entire board would have been incapable of evaluating such demand in a disinterested and independent manner because the entire board faced a substantial likelihood of liability for a breach of their fiduciary duty of loyalty. In this regard, she pointed out a majority of the board were members of the Compensation Committee, and that Goodyear (D) employment as CEO excused pre-suit demand as to him, since he received substantial monetary compensation and, therefore, would be unable to impartially consider demand. The directors (D) and Navigant (D) moved to dismiss for failure to make a demand. The district court considered the motion.

ISSUE: Is pre-suit demand in a derivative action excused where a plaintiff, through the particularized facts alleged, cannot create a reasonable doubt (1) the directors approving a challenged transaction were disinterested and independent and (2) the challenged transaction was otherwise the product of a valid exercise of business judgment?

HOLDING AND DECISION: (St. Eve, J.) No. Pre-suit demand in a derivative action is not excused where a plaintiff, through the particularized facts alleged, cannot create a reasonable doubt (1) the directors approving a challenged transaction were disinterested and independent and (2) the challenged transaction was other-

Continued on next page.

wise the product of a valid exercise of business judgment. These two tests are two prongs of the test developed in *Aronson v. Lewis,* 473 A.2d 805 (Del. 1984) for determining demand futility. As to the first prong, Gordon (P) has failed to allege with particularity that any of the executives who personally benefited from the pay package served on the Compensation Committee that recommended the pay package, or that any of the company's seven outside directors benefitted therefrom. Gordon (P) has also failed to show that Goodyear dominated or otherwise influenced the board, or that any board member was double dealing or acting in bad faith with respect to the board's executive pay package decision. Further, even if the directors face liability for approving the package, it is well-established law that the mere threat of personal liability for approving a questioned transaction, standing alone, is insufficient to challenge either the independence or disinterestedness of directors. In any event, Gordon's (P) allegations are insufficient to establish a substantial likelihood of liability for breach of a duty of loyalty on the part of the directors (D). Accordingly, Gordon (P) has failed to satisfy the first prong of the *Aronson* test. As to the second prong, Gordon (P) has failed to rebut the presumption of the business judgment rule. That presumption is that in making a business decision, the directors of a corporation acted on an informed basis, in good faith and in the honest belief that the action taken was in the best interest of the company. Thus, to prevail under this prong, a plaintiff must allege particularized facts sufficient to raise (1) a reason to doubt that the action was taken honestly and in good faith or (2) a reason to doubt that the board was adequately informed in making the decision. Here, Gordon (P) has failed to allege such particularized facts. Her argument that the shareholders' vote against the executive compensation package was evidence that the board either acted in bad faith or was inadequately informed is not persuasive, especially since that vote was expressly non-binding on the board or the company and does not create or imply any additional fiduciary duties imposed on board members. Other courts have similarly held that negative say-on-pay votes alone do not provide a basis to permit a breach of fiduciary duty claim to survive a motion to dismiss. Gordon (P) also failed to allege particularized facts that the board violated company policy in approving the compensation package. Gordon (P) maintains that they violated the Charter's mandate to link pay to performance, but a close reading of the Charter requires consideration of other factors, and the proxy disclosed that the Compensation Committee considered those, as well as several additional, factors. Contrary to the focus of Gordon's (P) argument, the Charter does not focus exclusively on company performance and shareholder return; these are just part of the equation. Thus, this argument also fails to rebut the business judgment presumption. Finally, the decline in Navigant's (D) stock price alone does not justify demand excusal. Such a decrease does not provide the kind of extreme situation necessary to override the great deference given to the board in making executive compensation decisions. For all these reasons, Gordon (P) failed to establish that demand would have been futile. Motion to dismiss is granted.

▶ ANALYSIS

The say-on-pay vote that occurred in this case arose under § 951 of the Dodd-Frank Wall Street Reform and Consumer Protection Act, which became law in 2010. The Act requires issuers with a class of equity securities registered under § 12 of the Securities Exchange Act of 1934 to include a separate shareholder resolution to approve executive compensation in their annual proxy statements at least once every three years. As the court in this case emphasized, a say-on-pay vote is non-binding, but, notwithstanding clear statutory language that the results of the vote may not be construed to create or imply any change to the fiduciary duties of boards or impose any additional fiduciary duties, a number of companies whose shareholders have voted to reject compensation packages have nevertheless been the subject of derivative actions alleging that the directors breached their fiduciary duties. As Gordon (P) did here, to establish demand futility, plaintiffs in those cases have typically alleged that the result of the say-on-pay vote is evidence that the shareholders did not approve of the compensation decisions and that, combined with the company's poor performance, there are sufficient particularized facts to raise a reason to doubt that the board's compensation decisions were the product of valid exercises of business judgment. However, as with this case, most of these claims have not advanced past the demand futility stage, since courts have been ruling that a negative say-on-pay vote is by itself insufficient to rebut the business judgment rule presumption.

■■■■

Quicknotes

BREACH OF FIDUCIARY DUTY The failure of a fiduciary to observe the standard of care exercised by professionals of similar education and experience.

BUSINESS JUDGMENT RULE Doctrine relieving corporate directors and/or officers from liability for decisions honestly and rationally made in the corporation's best interests.

DEMAND REQUIREMENT Requirement that a shareholder make a demand for corrective action by the board of directors before commencing a derivative suit.

UNJUST ENRICHMENT Principle that one should not be unjustly enriched at the expense of another.

■■■■

In re Oracle Corp. Derivative Litigation

Shareholders (P) v. Directors (D)

Del. Ch. Ct., 824 A.2d 917 (2003).

NATURE OF CASE: Motion to terminate a derivative action.

FACT SUMMARY: Oracle Corp.'s special litigation committee moved to terminate a derivative action brought on Oracle's behalf, claiming it was independent.

🏛 RULE OF LAW

A special litigation committee does not meet its burden of demonstrating the absence of a material dispute of fact about its independence where its members are professors at a university that has ties to the corporation and to the defendants that are the subject of a derivative action that the committee is investigating.

FACTS: Shareholders (P) of Oracle Corp. (Oracle) brought a derivative action asserting insider trading by four members (D) of Oracle's board of directors—Ellison (D), Henley (D), Lucas (D), and Boskin (D). Ellison (D) was Oracle's Chairman and one of the wealthiest men in the world. The suit alleged breaches of fiduciary duty by those directors (D) as well as by the non-trading directors (D), whose indifference according to the plaintiff shareholders (P) amounted to subjective bad faith. Oracle formed a special litigation committee (SLC) to investigate the charges in the derivative action and to determine whether to press the claims raised, terminate the action, or settle. Two Oracle board members, who joined the board after the alleged breaches, were named to the SLC. Both were professors at Stanford University. Both agreed to give up any SLC-related compensation if their compensation was deemed to impair their impartiality. The independence of the SLC's legal and analytic advisors was not challenged. The SLC's investigation was extensive, and the committee produced an extremely lengthy report that concluded that Oracle should not pursue any of the derivative action claims. The SLC based its opinion on Oracle's quarterly earnings cycle, and determined that none of the accused directors had possessed material, non-public information. In its report, the SLC took the position that its members were independent. In this regard, the report pointed out that the SLC members received no compensation from Oracle other than as directors, that neither were on the board at the time of the alleged wrongdoing, that they were willing to return their compensation, and that there were no other material ties between the defendants and the SLC members. However, the report failed to indicate that there were significant ties between Oracle, the trading defendants (D), and Stanford University (Stanford)—namely, in the form of very large donations, or

potential donations, of which the SLC members were aware. In addition, one of the SLC members had been taught by one of the trading defendants (D), and the two were both senior fellows and steering committee members of a Stanford research institute. The SLC contended that even together, these facts regarding the ties among Oracle, the trading defendants (D), Stanford, and the SLC members did not impair the SLC's independence. In so arguing, the SLC placed great weight on the fact that none of the trading defendants (D) had the practical ability to deprive either SLC member of their current positions at Stanford. Nor, given their tenure, did Stanford itself have any practical ability to punish them for taking action adverse to Oracle or any of the defendants.

ISSUE: Does a special litigation committee meet its burden of demonstrating the absence of a material dispute of fact about its independence where its members are professors at a university that has ties to the corporation and to the defendants that are the subject of a derivative action that the committee is investigating?

HOLDING AND DECISION: (Strine, V. Chan.) No. A special litigation committee does not meet its burden of demonstrating the absence of a material dispute of fact about its independence where its members are professors at a university that has ties to the corporation and to the defendants that are the subject of a derivative action that the committee is investigating. In analyzing whether the SLC was independent, emphasis should not be placed exclusively on domination and control. Instead, the law should take into account human nature, human motivations, and the social nature of humans. Thus, a court would not only consider greed or avarice, but would also take into account envy, love, friendship, collegiality, and other like motivators. At bottom, the question of independence turns on whether a director is, for any substantial reason, incapable of making a decision with only the best interests of the corporation in mind. Thus, here, the issue is whether the SLC can independently make the difficult decision entrusted to it. In the context of human nature, the SLC has not met its burden to show the absence of a material factual question about its independence. This is the case because the ties among the SLC, the trading defendants (D), and Stanford are so substantial that they cause reasonable doubt about the SLC's ability to impartially consider whether the trading defendants (D) should face suit. The SLC members were already being asked to consider whether the company should level extremely seri-

Continued on next page.

ous accusations of wrongdoing against fellow board members. As to one of the trading defendants (D), Boskin (D), the SLC members faced the additional task of having to determine whether to press serious charges against a fellow professor at their university. Even more daunting was that one of the SLC members had a long history with Boskin (D) and served together with him on a university research institute. That SLC member would find it difficult to assess the Boskin's (D) conduct without pondering his own associations and mutual affiliations with him. This would likewise be true with regard to those trading defendants (D) who were significant university benefactors. In addition, the SLC has not made a convincing argument that tenured faculty are indifferent to large contributors to their institutions, such that a tenured faculty member would not be worried about writing a report finding that a suit by the corporation should proceed against a large contributor and that there was credible evidence that he had engaged in illegal insider trading. To conclude otherwise, would rest on a narrow-minded understanding of the way that collegiality works in institutional settings. Finally, Ellison (D) had publicly indicated that he would make very large contributions to Stanford, and it is implausible that the SLC members were not aware of his intentions. Motion to terminate denied.

▶ ANALYSIS

The Delaware Supreme Court has reaffirmed that the SLC has the burden of establishing its own independence by a yardstick that must be "like Caesar's wife"—"above reproach." Moreover, unlike the pre-suit demand context, the SLC analysis contemplates not only a shift in the burden of persuasion, but also the availability of discovery into various issues, including independence. Moreover, because the members of an SLC are vested with enormous power to seek dismissal of a derivative suit brought against their director-colleagues in a setting where pre-suit demand is already excused, the Court of Chancery must exercise careful oversight of the members of the SLC and the SLC's process.

■■■

Quicknotes

BAD FAITH Conduct that is intentionally misleading or deceptive.

BONA FIDE In good faith.

SHAREHOLDER An individual who owns shares of stock in a corporation.

SHAREHOLDER'S DERIVATIVE ACTION Action asserted by a shareholder in order to enforce a cause of action on behalf of the corporation.

■■■

Cuker v. Mikalauskas

[Parties not identified.]

Pa. Sup. Ct., 692 A.2d 1042 (1997).

NATURE OF CASE: Petition for extraordinary relief from denial of motion for summary judgment in action to terminate derivative actions.

FACT SUMMARY: PECO Energy Company's board of directors (D) sought to quash two derivative actions initiated by its minority shareholders (P).

🏛 RULE OF LAW
Under Pennsylvania law, application of the business judgment rule permits a corporation's board of directors to terminate a derivative suit initiated by the company's minority shareholders.

FACTS: PECO Energy Company (PECO) (D), a publicly regulated utility company, underwent an audit in accordance with state regulations. The report issued from the audit recommended changes in PECO's (D) credit and collection policies. A group of minority shareholders initiated suit alleging mismanagement of funds by PECO's directors (D) and officers (D). The shareholders demanded that PECO (D) allow them to bring suit on its behalf to recover damages done to PECO (D) by the mismanagement. The board of directors established a committee to investigate the claims. A second group of shareholders (P) led by Cuker (P) then brought suit against the officers (D) and directors (D) on the same basis, prior to the establishment of the special committee. The committee investigated both complaints. After many months of investigation aided by outside counsel and an outside auditor, the committee determined there was no evidence of any breach of duty of loyalty on the part of the directors (D) or officers (D). Rather, they concluded that the directors (D) and officers (D) exercised proper business judgment and acted in the best interests of PECO (D). Moreover, they resolved that a derivative suit would be adverse to PECO's (D) interests. The disinterested members of the board voted unanimously to terminate the shareholders' (P) derivative suits. The court of common pleas denied PECO's (D) motion for summary judgment, and PECO (D) petitioned for extraordinary relief.

ISSUE: Under Pennsylvania law, does the business judgment rule permit a board of directors to terminate derivative suits initiated by minority shareholders?

HOLDING AND DECISION: (Flaherty, C.J.) Yes. Under Pennsylvania law, application of the business judgment rule permits a corporation's board of directors to terminate a derivative suit initiated by the company's minority shareholders. On summary judgment, the court may dismiss the action if it is satisfied that the board of direc-

tors' decision was valid. The court must look to the surrounding circumstances to determine whether the business judgment rule applies, and not to the results of the directors' decision. The court must consider such factors as whether the board or committee was comprised of disinterested members, whether it was advised by counsel, the comprehensiveness of the investigation, and whether or not the board acted under the reasonable belief that its decision was in the company's best interests. If these requirements are met, then the court should dismiss the action whether or not the decision ultimately resulted in harm to the corporation. The court adopts the American Law Institute's Principles in order to provide procedural guidelines for judicial review of such business decisions. Reversed and remanded.

▶ *ANALYSIS*

The business judgment rule shields directors from personal liability for decisions made in the management of the corporation's business. The rule creates a rebuttable presumption in favor of the defendant directors that they made an informed decision which they believed to be in the best interests of the corporation. In the absence of contrary evidence, the court will not review the business decision of the directors on the rationale that directors are not insurers of the corporation's success.

■═■

Quicknotes

BUSINESS JUDGMENT RULE Doctrine relieving corporate directors and/or officers from liability for decisions honestly and rationally made in the corporation's best interests.

MINORITY SHAREHOLDER A stockholder in a corporation controlling such a small portion of those shares outstanding that its votes have no influence in the management of the corporation.

STOCKHOLDER DERIVATIVE SUIT Action asserted by a shareholder in order to enforce a cause of action on behalf of the corporation.

■═■

Dissension in the Closely Held Corporation

Quick Reference Rules of Law

Gearing v. Kelly

Shareholder (P) v. Director (D)

N.Y. Ct. App., 182 N.E.2d 391 (1962).

NATURE OF CASE: Action to set aside election of director and hold new election.

FACT SUMMARY: When Mrs. Meacham (P) refused to attend a directors' meeting, the Kellys (D) elected Hemphill, and the Meacham-Gearing (P) faction objected.

🏛 **RULE OF LAW**
Where a shareholder-director deliberately causes a lack of quorum required for a directors' meeting by refusing to attend, equity will refuse to set aside a board decision held at such a meeting for lack of quorum.

FACTS: Radium Chemical Co. bylaws provided for a board of four directors. A majority (three) constituted a quorum for transacting corporate business. In 1955, the board consisted of Mrs. Meacham (P), Mr. Kelly Sr. (D), and Margaret Lee. That same year, Kelly Jr. (D) was elected to the vacant directorship. On March 6, 1961, Margaret Lee resigned at a board meeting at which she and the Kellys (D) were present. Mrs. Meacham (P) chose to stay away from the March 6 meeting. Consequently, the Kellys (D) elected Julian Hemphill to replace Margaret Lee. Mrs. Meacham's (P) mother, Mrs. Gearing (P), a large stockholder in Radium Chemical, condoned the voluntary absence of her daughter and brought this action to set aside the election of Julian Hemphill on grounds that the Kellys (D) were not sufficient to constitute a quorum. The appellate division held that Mrs. Gearing (P) and Mrs. Meacham (P) failed to show that justice required a new election.

ISSUE: May a shareholder-director who deliberately causes a lack of quorum at a directors' meeting in order to frustrate the other directors from carrying on corporate business be successful in equity in overturning any business conducted at such a meeting on grounds that there was a lack of quorum?

HOLDING AND DECISION: (Per curiam) No. Mrs. Meacham (P) did not lack notice of the board meeting, and her absence was deliberate. Even though Mrs. Meacham (P) and Mrs. Gearing (P) desired to protect their equal ownership interests in the corporation through equal representation on the board, this balance was voluntarily surrendered in 1955 when Kelly Jr. (D) was elected. And the ordering of a new election would not help Meacham (P) and Gearing (P), since Mrs. Meacham (P) would then be required, in good faith, to attend the directors' meeting. It is probable that she would still be out-voted by the Kellys (D). A court of equity will not permit directors to refuse to attend meetings in an attempt to force their demands upon other stockholders. Failure to attend directors' meetings, where there is adequate notice, bars a director from invoking exercise of equitable powers. Affirmed.

DISSENT: (Froessel, J.) A quorum did not exist; thus, the March 6 election was a nullity precluding estoppel.

▶ *ANALYSIS*

The common-law rule concerning the requisite quorum for a directors' meeting is that only a majority is needed.

◼◼◼

Quicknotes

GEN. CORP. LAW, § 25 Provides for alternatives where board members vote with an insufficient quorum.

QUORUM The minimum number of persons who must be present in order to conduct business.

◼◼◼

In re Radom & Neidorff, Inc.

[Parties not identified.]

N.Y. Ct. App., 119 N.E.2d 563 (1954).

NATURE OF CASE: Petition by stockholder for voluntary dissolution of a close corporation.

FACT SUMMARY: Radom (P) and his sister Neidorff (D) were the sole shareholders in a music publishing corporation. Due to a mutual dislike and distrust, they were deadlocked as to the election of directors and the declaration of dividends.

🏛 RULE OF LAW
Where corporate dissolution is authorized by statute in the case of deadlock or by other specified circumstances, the existence of the specified circumstances does not mandate the dissolution. The court will exercise its discretion, taking into account benefits to the shareholders as well as injury to the public.

FACTS: David Radom (P) and his brother-in-law Henry Neidorff were the sole shareholders in a corporation engaged in music publication. They operated the business successfully and amicably for over 30 years. Upon Henry Neidorff's death, Anna Neidorff (D), his wife, succeeded to his shares. Although David Radom (P) and Anna Neidorff (D) were brother and sister, their relationship had been strained for many years. Because of their mutual dislike and distrust, they were unable to agree upon a board of directors or the declaration of dividends. In addition, Anna Neidorff (D) had refused to cosign David Radom's (P) salary checks. This deadlock continued over a three-year period, and, despite the antagonism, the corporation continued to prosper. David Radom (P) made several proposals for resolution of the conflict, including an offer to purchase Anna Neidorff's (D) shares. She refused to agree to any proposals but counterproposed the appointment of an outside director, which he refused. To finally resolve the dispute, David Radom (P) petitioned the court for dissolution.

ISSUE: Where the principals in a close corporation have deadlocked on important issues, particularly the election of directors, will a petition for dissolution, statutorily authorized under such circumstances, mandate the dissolution?

HOLDING AND DECISION: (Desmond, J.) No. The granting of a petition for dissolution of a close corporation is discretionary with the forum court. In exercising this discretion, the court will examine whether the conflict among the shareholders has come to the point where the competing interests are so discordant as to prevent efficient management or the attainment of the corporation's object. Further, the court will determine whether dissolution

would be beneficial to the shareholders and not injurious to the public. In this instance, the conflict has not interfered with the management and operation of the corporation. On the contrary, the corporation has continued to prosper. Since the value of a going concern is usually far greater than its liquidating value, the most beneficial course for the shareholders would be to continue the corporation and not dissolve it. David Radom (P) has other less drastic remedies available to recover his unpaid salary. The petition is ordered dismissed without a hearing on the merits of the contentions of the parties. Affirmed.

DISSENT: (Fuld, J.) While the granting of a petition for dissolution is discretionary with the court, that discretion should only be exercised after a full hearing of facts of the situation. The petition sets forth sufficient contentions to make at least a prima facie case for dissolution which should be explored. The denial of the petition will not put the issues to rest but will most probably result in further acrimonious litigation. David Radom (P) is entitled to a full hearing on the merits of his petition.

▶ ANALYSIS

The majority opinion represents the attitude of most courts in jealously guarding that which they have created. Since the corporation is a creation of the law, its proposed demise will be strictly scrutinized. The majority did not deal with the problem of the deadlock over the election of directors or the declaration of dividends. Underlying the decision appears to be the fact that one of the major assets of the corporation was the business acumen of David Radom (P). If dissolution were granted, this asset would go with him along with one-half of all the other assets. This would shortchange Anna Neidorff (D). One solution to this apparent inequity would be to condition the dissolution upon David Radom's (P) buying out Anna Neidorff (D) at a fair price, taking into account the value of the corporation as a going concern.

■■■■

Quicknotes

DISSOLUTION Annulment or termination of a formal or legal bond, tie or contract.

GEN. CORP. LAW, § 103 If directors are evenly divided on management or stockholders are unable to elect directors, majority votes may present petition for dissolution.

■■■■

Donahue v. Rodd Electrotype Co.

Minority shareholder (P) v. Corporation (D)

Mass. Sup. Jud. Ct., 328 N.E.2d 505 (1975).

NATURE OF CASE: Action to rescind a corporate purchase of shares and recover the purchase price.

FACT SUMMARY: Donahue (P), a minority stockholder in a close corporation, sought to rescind a corporate purchase of shares of the controlling shareholder.

🏛 RULE OF LAW

A controlling stockholder (or group) in a close corporation who causes the corporation to purchase his stock breaches his fiduciary duty to the minority stockholders if he does not cause the corporation to offer each stockholder an equal opportunity to sell a ratable number of shares to the corporation at an identical price.

FACTS: As a controlling stockholder of Rodd Electrotype Co. (D), a close corporation, Harry Rodd (D) caused the corporation to reacquire 45 of his shares for $800 each ($36,000 total). He then divested the rest of his holding by making gifts and sales to his children. Donahue (P), a minority stockholder who had refused to ratify this action, offered to sell her shares on the same terms but was refused. A suit followed in which Donahue (P) sought to rescind the purchase of Harry Rodd's (D) stock and make him repay to Rodd Electrotype (D) the $36,000 purchase price with interest. Finding the purchase had been without prejudice to Donahue (P), the trial court dismissed the bill and the appellate court affirmed.

ISSUE: Must a controlling stockholder in a close corporation who has caused the corporation to purchase some of his shares see to it that an equal offer is made to the other stockholders?

HOLDING AND DECISION: (Tauro, C.J.) Yes. Stemming from the fiduciary duty owed by a controlling stockholder of a close corporation to the minority stockholders, a controlling stockholder who causes such a corporation to purchase some of his shares must cause the corporation to offer each stockholder an equal opportunity to sell a ratable number of shares to the corporation at an identical price. Close corporations are somewhat different in that they are very much like partnerships and require the utmost trust, confidence, and loyalty among the members for success. This means a partnership-type fiduciary duty arises between stockholders. It is the basis for the rule herein announced, under which Donahue (P) must be given an equal opportunity to sell her shares. Reversed and remanded.

CONCURRENCE: (Wilkins, J.) I do not join in any implication that this rule applies to other activities of the corporation, like salaries and dividend policy, as they affect minority stockholders.

▶ ANALYSIS

A problem that exists with close corporations is that there is no ready market to which a minority stockholder can turn when he or she wishes to liquidate his or her holdings. Knowing that fact, the controlling stockholder has a very powerful weapon that he or she would not have in a regular corporate setup. This is one of the reasons the controlling stockholder is held to a higher degree of fiduciary duty in this case.

■=■

Quicknotes

FIDUCIARY DUTY A legal obligation to act for the benefit of another, including subordinating one's personal interests to that of the other person.

MINORITY STOCKHOLDER A stockholder in a corporation controlling such a small portion of those shares outstanding that its votes have no influence in the management of the corporation.

■=■

Wilkes v. Springside Nursing Home, Inc.

Director/shareholder (P) v. Close corporation (D)

Mass. Sup. Jud. Ct., 370 Mass. 842, 353 N.E.2d 657 (1976).

NATURE OF CASE: Appeal from a ruling dismissing the complaint in an action for declaratory judgment.

FACT SUMMARY: Wilkes (P) was a director, employee, and shareholder in Springside Nursing Home, Inc., a close corporation. The other directors attempted to freeze him out of the corporation.

🏛 RULE OF LAW
Stockholders in a close corporation are in a fiduciary relationship with each other.

FACTS: Wilkes (P), Quinn, Richie, and Conner formed a corporation to establish and operate a nursing home in 1951. Each of the men invested $1,000 and subscribed to ten shares of $100 par value stock. Over the years the parties each bought more stock. At the time of incorporation, it was understood that each would be a director of the corporation and participate in the management and operation thereof. It was further understood that each of the parties would receive money from the corporation in equal amounts for as long as they participated in the operation of the corporation. By 1955, each party was receiving $100 a week. In 1965, the relationship between the parties began to deteriorate. In February 1967, a directors' meeting was held, and a schedule of payments was set up in which Wilkes (P) was not included. In March 1967, the annual meeting was held. Wilkes (P) was not reelected a director and was not reemployed. Wilkes (P) brought suit, arguing that the agreement of the parties was breached when he was forced out of the corporation. A master dismissed the complaint. Wilkes (P) appealed, contending that he was entitled to damages for breach of contract or breach of fiduciary duties owed to him.

ISSUE: May shareholders in a close corporation act, without a business purpose, to the detriment of other shareholders?

HOLDING AND DECISION: (Hennessey, C.J.) No. Stockholders in a close corporation are in a fiduciary relationship with each other. The standard of duty owed is one of utmost good faith and loyalty. The standard, however, cannot be used to impose limitations on legitimate action by a controlling group. The majority has certain rights that must be balanced against the fiduciary obligation owed to the minority. Thus, where there is a legitimate business purpose for the action, it may be valid. Here, it is apparent that the majority had no legitimate purpose for their action. There is no evidence of misconduct on the part of Wilkes (P) for the performance of his duties as a director or employee. The inescapable conclusion from this is that the action was designed to freeze Wilkes (P) out of the corporation in violation of the parties' original agreement. Reversed and remanded for further proceedings on the issue of damages.

▶ ANALYSIS

Controlling shareholders are given a large amount of discretion in establishing corporate policy. It is only where their actions cannot be justified by a business purpose and do injury to others that the court will interfere. *Schwartz v. Marien*, 37 N.Y. 2d 487 (1975). In many older cases and in some jurisdictions, no business purpose is required so long as the majority acts within the permissible limits imposed by statute and their bylaws.

■══■

Quicknotes

BREACH OF CONTRACT The unlawful failure by a party to perform its obligations pursuant to contract.

BYLAWS Rules promulgated by a corporation regulating its governance.

DECLARATORY JUDGMENT An adjudication by the courts which grants not relief but is binding over the legal status of the parties involved in the dispute.

FIDUCIARY DUTY A legal obligation to act for the benefit of another, including subordinating one's personal interests to that of the other person.

■══■

Merola v. Exergen Corp.

Minority shareholder (P) v. Closely held corporation (D)

Mass. Sup. Jud. Ct., 668 N.E.2d 351 (1996).

NATURE OF CASE: Appeal from affirmance of judgment for plaintiff in action for breach of fiduciary duty.

FACT SUMMARY: Pompei (D), the majority shareholder of Exergen Corp. (D), a close corporation, contended that he did not breach fiduciary duties by failing to give Merola (P), a minority shareholder and employee, an opportunity to become a major stockholder and by terminating Merola's (P) employment.

🏛 RULE OF LAW
The majority shareholder of a close corporation does not breach the fiduciary duty of utmost good faith and loyalty owed to a minority shareholder by terminating the minority shareholder's employment where the company has no policy tying the ownership of stock to continued employment.

FACTS: Pompei (D) was Exergen Corp.'s (D) majority shareholder, owning over 60 percent of its stock. Exergen (D) was a close corporation. Pompei (D) hired Merola (P) to work for Exergen (D), and Merola (P) understood that if he came to work there and invested in Exergen (D) stock, he would have the opportunity to become a major shareholder of Exergen (D) and for continuing employment with Exergen (D). However, there was no general policy regarding stock ownership and employment at the company, and there was no evidence that any other stockholders had expectations of continuing employment because they purchased stock. The investment in the stock was an investment in the equity of the corporation that was not tied to employment in any formal way. Merola (P) became a minority shareholder, but after several years of working at Exergen (D), Merola's (P) employment was terminated. When Merola (P) redeemed his stock, he obtained a price that exceeded his initial investments. Merola (P) brought suit for breach of fiduciary duty against Pompei (D) and Exergen (D), and, based on jury findings that there was no legitimate business purpose for the termination of Merola's (P) employment, and that Merola (P) suffered damages as a result of the termination, the trial court ruled that, as a matter of law, Pompei (D) breached his fiduciary duties to Merola (P) by failing to honor Merola's (P) reasonable expectations concerning investments of time and resources in Exergen (D). The state's intermediate appellate court affirmed, and the state's highest court granted review.

ISSUE: Does the majority shareholder of a close corporation breach the fiduciary duty of utmost good faith and loyalty owed to a minority shareholder by terminating the minority shareholder's employment where the company

has no policy tying the ownership of stock to continued employment?

HOLDING AND DECISION: (Lynch, J.) No. The majority shareholder of a close corporation does not breach the fiduciary duty of utmost good faith and loyalty owed to a minority shareholder by terminating the minority shareholder's employment where the company has no policy tying the ownership of stock to continued employment. Majority shareholders in a close corporation owe a duty of utmost good faith and loyalty to minority shareholders. Nevertheless, even in close corporations, majority shareholders must have a large degree of discretion. Where a close corporation has a policy tying ownership to employment and salaries, a majority shareholder may breach fiduciary duties owed to a minority shareholder by freezing out the minority shareholder through the termination of the minority shareholder's employment. However, that is not the case here. Exergen (D) did not have such a policy, and a shareholder's employment was not tied to ownership in the company. Nor did the company distribute profits in the form of salaries. Further, Merola (D) received a significant return on his investment in Exergen's (D) stock, which indicated that there was some increase in value to the investment independent of any employment expectation. Although there was no legitimate business purpose for Merola's (P) termination, neither was the termination for the financial gain of Pompei (D) nor contrary to established public policy. Not every discharge of an at-will employee of a close corporation who happens to own stock in the corporation gives rise to a successful breach of fiduciary duty claim. Merola (D) was terminated in accordance with his employment contract and fairly compensated for his stock. Reversed.

▶ ANALYSIS

This case demonstrates the principle that employment in a close corporation will be protected by corporate law when a job is proved to be part of a shareholder-employee's investment. In such a situation, the employment is protected not because of the individual's status as an employee, but rather because of harms suffered as a shareholder.

■■■

Quicknotes

AT-WILL EMPLOYEE An employee who is subject to termination at any time, or for any cause, by an employer, or

Continued on next page.

who may terminate his own employment at any time or for any cause, in the absence of a specific agreement otherwise.

DUTY OF GOOD FAITH OF FAIR DEALINGS   An implied duty in a contract that the parties will deal honestly in the satisfaction of their obligations and without an intent to defraud.

■=■

In re Kemp & Beatley, Inc.

Close corporation (D) v. Minority stockholders (P)

N.Y. Ct. App., 64 N.Y.2d 63, 473 N.E.2d 1173 (1984).

NATURE OF CASE: Appeal from an order dissolving a corporation.

FACT SUMMARY: Gardstein (P) contended the corporation's refusal to make distributions to him in contrast to prior policy constituted oppressiveness justifying dissolution.

🏛 **RULE OF LAW**
Actions by majority shareholders to restrict distributions to the prejudice of minority shareholders may constitute oppression and justify dissolution.

FACTS: Gardstein (P) and Dissin (P), two longtime employees of Kemp and Beatley (D), owned approximately 20 percent of the corporation's outstanding stock. While employed by the close corporation, they regularly received distributions as shareholders, yet after leaving the corporation's employ on less than friendly terms, they stopped receiving such distributions, while the other shareholders still did. They sued to dissolve the corporation, contending such action constituted oppression. The trial court ordered the dissolution, and Kemp and Beatley (D) appealed.

ISSUE: May actions by majority shareholders in close corporations to restrict distributions to minority shareholders constitute oppression and justify dissolution?

HOLDING AND DECISION: (Cooke, C.J.) Yes. Actions by majority shareholders of a close corporation to restrict distributions to the prejudice of minority shareholders may constitute oppression and justify dissolution. The action of the majority in this case defeated the expectation of the minority concerning the worth of their stock. Because this was a close corporation, there was little hope of establishing a market for the stock. Thus, dissolution was the only viable remedy. Affirmed as modified.

▶ *ANALYSIS*

Dissolution is an extraordinary remedy that is granted in very selective cases. Only where the actions constitute fraud, illegality, or oppression will dissolution be ordered. Oppression contemplates action significantly infringing on minority shareholder rights.

■■■

Quicknotes

CLOSE CORPORATION A corporation whose shares (or at least voting shares) are held by a closely knit group of shareholders or a single person.

DISSOLUTION Annulment or termination of a formal or legal bond, tie or contract.

OPPRESSION The abuse of one's authority resulting in the infliction of injury on another.

■■■

Nixon v. Blackwell

[Parties not identified.]

Del. Sup. Ct., 626 A.2d 1366 (1993).

NATURE OF CASE: Appeal from award of monetary damages for breach of fiduciary duties.

FACT SUMMARY: Shareholders (P) of a class of corporate stock contended that the directors (D) breached their fiduciary obligations by offering certain liquidity devices to corporate employees but not to minority shareholders. When corporate directors are on both sides of a transaction, they have the burden of establishing the transaction's "entire fairness," sufficient to pass the test of careful scrutiny by the courts.

🏛 RULE OF LAW
There should not be special judicially created rules to protect minority stockholders of closely held corporations that are not statutory "close corporations."

FACTS: Barton incorporated E.C. Barton & Co. in 1928. The articles of incorporation provided for two classes of stock, voting (Class A) and nonvoting (Class B). The corporation, after Barton's death, obtained key man life insurance policies to cover its officers and key employees, who were, for the most part, owners of Class A stock. The corporation also began an employee stock ownership plan (ESOP) program for employees owning Class A stock. Beneficiaries of the program had the option of taking cash instead of stock. The net result of the life insurance policies and the ESOP was to provide a vehicle for holders of Class A stock to cash in their shares. These opportunities were not available to Class B shareholders, although the corporation had at times instituted repurchase programs. Eventually, certain holders of Class B stock (P) filed an action against the directors (D) of the company, contending that the key man life insurance and ESOP programs unfairly benefited the directors (D), who were Class A shareholders, but not those holding Class B. The Chancery Court held the programs inequitable and ordered the directors (D) to discontinue the programs unless all shareholders could participate. The directors (D) appealed.

ISSUE: Should there be special judicially created rules to protect minority stockholders of closely held corporations that are not statutory "close corporations"?

HOLDING AND DECISION: (Veasey, C.J.) No. There should not be special judicially created rules to protect minority stockholders of closely held corporations that are not statutory "close corporations." Although at first blush it is easy to be sympathetic to a minority shareholder of a closely held corporation who wishes to receive fair value for his or her stock as to which there is no market and no market valuation, such a stockholder can make a business judgment whether to buy into such a position and on what terms, through various stockholders agreements bargained for before the stockholder parts with any consideration. It would disrupt normal corporate practice and the corporation law to fashion a judicially created, ad hoc rule that would result in a court-imposed stockholder buy-out for which the parties had not bargained. Moreover, Delaware's General Corporation Law contains provisions governing "Close Corporations," which provisions are applicable only to certain qualifying corporations that elect to be regulated as statutory close corporations. Because the corporation involved here did not elect to be a statutory close corporation, it is not governed by the close corporation provisions. Therefore, there is no special relief that may be granted to the shareholders of this closely held, but not statutory close, corporation, given that the Close Corporation provisions preempt the field in this area.

▶ ANALYSIS

This case provides an illustration of a problem often faced by minority shareholders in a nonpublic corporation. A disgruntled shareholder in a publically traded company can vote with his feet by selling. A shareholder in a nonpublic corporation has no such option. Often, a lawsuit is the only remedy, but success in changing company policy through litigation is unlikely at best.

■═■

Quicknotes

BUSINESS JUDGMENT RULE Doctrine relieving corporate directors and/or officers from liability for decisions honestly and rationally made in the corporation's best interests.

CLOSELY HELD CORPORATION A corporation whose shares (or at least voting shares) are held by a closely knit group of shareholders or a single person.

MINORITY SHAREHOLDER A stockholder in a corporation controlling such a small portion of those shares which are outstanding that its votes have no influence in the management of the corporation.

TENDER OFFER An offer made by one corporation to the shareholders of a target corporation to purchase their shares subject to number, time, and price specifications.

■═■

Gallagher v. Lambert

Employee/shareholder (P) v. Close corporation (D)

N.Y. Ct. App., 74 N.Y.2d 562, 549 N.E.2d 136 (1989).

NATURE OF CASE: Appeal from summary judgment in action for breach of fiduciary duty.

FACT SUMMARY: After Gallagher (P) was fired by the close corporation that had employed him on an at-will basis, he refused to abide by the price terms of a negotiated agreement for a mandatory buy-back of the shares he held as a minority stockholder in the corporation.

🏛 RULE OF LAW
An at-will employee of a close corporation who becomes a minority stockholder in that corporation and who contractually agrees to the repurchase of his shares upon termination of his employment for any reason is bound by the terms of that agreement.

FACTS: During his employment by Eastdil Realty (Eastdil) (D), Gallagher (P) was at all times an employee at will. Gallagher (P) accepted an offer to purchase stock of the close corporation subject to a mandatory buy-back provision at book value if his employment was terminated voluntarily or otherwise prior to January 31, 1985. After that date, the buy-back price would be keyed to the company's earnings. When Gallagher (P) was fired by Eastdil (D) on January 10, 1985, he demanded payment for his shares based on Eastdil's (D) earnings. Eastdil (D) refused, and Gallagher (P) filed this action. The trial court denied Eastdil's (D) motion for summary judgment; the appellate division reversed and certified to the court of appeals the question of whether the appellate division's order was proper.

ISSUE: Is an at-will employee of a close corporation who becomes a minority stockholder in that corporation and who contractually agrees to the repurchase of his shares upon termination of his employment for any reason bound by the terms of that agreement?

HOLDING AND DECISION: (Bellacosa, J.) Yes. An at-will employee of a close corporation who becomes a minority stockholder in that corporation and who contractually agrees to the repurchase of his shares upon termination of his employment for any reason is bound by the terms of that agreement. Gallagher (P) not only agreed to the particular buy-back formula, but he helped write it, and he reviewed it with his attorney during the negotiation process. The buy-back price formula was designed for the benefit of both parties precisely so that they would know their respective rights on certain dates and avoid costly and lengthy litigation on the fair value

issue. The order of the appellate division should be affirmed.

DISSENT: (Kaye, J.) This case is significantly different from *Ingle v. Glamore Motor Sales*, 73 N.Y.2d 183 (1989), where this court reached only the corporation's duty to plaintiff as an employee. Here, Gallagher (P) questions only the duty Eastdil (D) owes him as a shareholder, the question left open in *Ingle*. However, the majority finds that the same rationale applied in *Ingle* is wholly dispositive here, with no analysis of the fiduciary duty owed to Gallagher (P).

▶ ANALYSIS

The court noted that provisions like the one discussed in the instant case are designed to ensure that ownership of all of the stock of a close corporation stays within the control of the remaining corporate owners-employees. They should not be undone simply upon an allegation of unfairness. The question of the fiduciary duty of fair dealing here cannot be considered separately from the employment issue because the buy-back provision links them together as to timing and consequences.

Quicknotes

AT-WILL EMPLOYEE An employee who is subject to termination at any time, or for any cause, by an employer, or who may terminate his own employment at any time or for any cause, in the absence of a specific agreement otherwise.

BUY-BACK PROVISION An agreement between partners or shareholders of a closely held corporation that surviving partners or shareholders will purchase the shares of deceased or withdrawing partners or shareholders.

CLOSE CORPORATION A corporation whose shares (or at least voting shares) are held by a closely knit group of shareholders or a single person.

FIDUCIARY DUTY A legal obligation to act for the benefit of another, including subordinating one's personal interests to that of the other person.

SUMMARY JUDGMENT Judgment rendered by a court in response to a motion by one of the parties, claiming that the lack of a question of material fact in respect to an issue warrants disposition of the issue without consideration by the jury.

Davis v. Sheerin

Director (D) v. Director (P)

Tex. Ct. App., 754 S.W.2d 375, (1988).

NATURE OF CASE: Appeal from forced buy-out of corporate stock.

FACT SUMMARY: Davis (D) contended that the trial court erred in imposing a forced buy-out of Sheerin's (P) shares in the corporation for Davis's (D) oppressive conduct toward the minority shareholder.

> 🏛 **RULE OF LAW**
> Courts, in appropriate cases, may order a buy-out of stock as a remedy for oppressive conduct on the part of majority shareholders.

FACTS: Sheerin (P) and Davis (D) formed a corporation, whereby Davis would be employed and be responsible for the day-to-day operations. Sheerin (P) received 45 percent of the corporate stock with Davis (D) receiving 55 percent. Subsequently, Sheerin (P) demanded to review the corporate books; however, such was refused unless he produced his stock certificate. Davis (D) contended that Sheerin (P) had made a gift of his 45 percent interest in the corporation years before. Sheerin (P) brought suit to enforce his right to inspect the corporate books and alleged oppression on the part of Davis (D) in not allowing him access to the day-to-day operations of the corporation. The trial court found Davis (D) liable for oppressive conduct and ordered a forced buy-out of Sheerin's (P) stock. Davis (D) appealed, contending the remedy of buy-out was not available in Texas, and if such was available, it was not appropriate in this case.

ISSUE: Is the remedy of buy-out appropriate in cases of oppressive conduct by majority shareholders?

HOLDING AND DECISION: (Dunn, J.) Yes. In appropriate cases, a court may order the forced buy-out of a minority shareholder's stock due to the oppressive behavior of the majority shareholder. In this case, Davis (D), as majority shareholder, used his position as possessor of the corporate books to deny Sheerin (P) access to the corporate books. This act of oppression rendered him liable for the dissolution of the corporation. A forced buy-out of Sheerin's (P) stock was appropriate to remedy this oppressive conduct. Oppression has long been recognized as a solid basis for the imposition of the drastic remedy of buy-out. Affirmed.

▶ **ANALYSIS**

The court entered into an analysis whereby it attempted to determine whether a less harsh remedy would have made Sheerin (P) whole in this case. A forced buy-out is an extremely drastic remedy in that it affects the basic corporate structure involved. The court determined, however, that the level of oppressive conduct, which was not spelled out in the casebook excerpt, was sufficiently high that buy-out was necessary. The key in applying the buy-out remedy apparently was the probability that the oppressive conduct would continue in the future and would not be limited to the past acts of oppression. Thus by forcing the buy-out of the stock, the future harm would be avoided.

■■

Quicknotes

FIDUCIARY DUTY A legal obligation to act for the benefit of another, including subordinating one's personal interests to that of the other person.

TEX. BUS. CORP. ACT, ART. 7.05 Provides for appointment of a receiver for aggrieved shareholders who can establish wrongful conduct.

■■

Transactions in Shares: Securities Fraud and Sales of Control

Quick Reference Rules of Law

10. *Perlman v. Feldmann.* A corporate director who is also a dominant shareholder stands, in both situations, in a fiduciary relationship to both the corporation and the minority stockholders if selling controlling interest in the corporation is accountable to it (and the minority shareholders) to the extent that the sales price represents payment for the right to control.   *148*

In re Enron Corporation Securities, Derivative & ERISA Litigation

[Parties not identified.]

235 F. Supp. 2d 549 (S.D. Texas 2002).

NATURE OF CASE: Motions to dismiss in class action for securities law violations.

FACT SUMMARY: A class action brought on behalf of purchasers of Enron Corp. securities alleged that banks, lawyers, and accountant/auditors violated securities laws by making false statements or failing to disclose adverse facts while selling Enron securities, and/or that they participated in a scheme to defraud and/or a course of business, that operated as a fraud. These secondary-actor defendants moved to dismiss.

🏛 RULE OF LAW
A claim brought under § 10(b) of the Securities Exchange Act of 1934 against secondary actors alleged to have participated in a scheme to defraud survives dismissal where a primary violation of § 10(b) is alleged against each individual actor.

FACTS: A class action brought on behalf of purchasers of Enron Corp. securities alleged that numerous banks, lawyers, and accountant/auditors violated securities laws by making false statements or failing to disclose adverse facts while selling Enron securities, and/or that they participated in a scheme to defraud and/or a course of business that operated as a fraud. The scheme that these secondary actors were allegedly involved in was claimed to be "an enormous Ponzi scheme, the largest in history" involving illusory profits generated by phony, non-arm's-length transactions with Enron-controlled entities and improper accounting for the purpose of inflating Enron's reported revenues and profits, concealing its mounting debt, maintaining its artificially high stock prices and credit ratings, as well as allowing the secondary actor defendants to personally enrich themselves by looting the corporation, while continuing to raise money from public offerings of Enron or related securities. The scheme allegedly involved an elaborate network of off-the-books illicit partnerships, secretly controlled by Enron, and established to hide Enron's actual financial status. Typically, these entities would buy troubled assets from Enron by means of sham swaps, hedges, and transfers so that debt would not be reflected on Enron's balance sheet. All of the secondary actor defendants were alleged to have been "rubber stamps" for these deceitful transactions because they were all beneficiaries of enormous fees and increasing business. The defendants allegedly violated GAAP (Generally Accepted Accounting Principles) and SEC rules, and caused Enron to present materially misleading statements in Enron's financial statements, press releases, and SEC filings, such as Form 10-Qs and 10-Ks. Enron also allegedly made misrepresentations

about the second party defendants' manipulations, all concealed by numerous accounting ploys.

(III.B.1) The Banks—Most of the allegations applied, with few exceptions, to all the banks: Canadian Imperial Bank of Commerce (CIBC), CitiGroup Inc., J.P. Morgan Chase & Co., Barclays PLC, Credit Suisse First Boston, Bank of America Corp., Merrill Lynch & Co., Lehman Bros. Holdings Inc., and Deutsche Bank AG. The general claims were that the banks participated in the scheme to enrich themselves through enormous fees and continuing business, as well as to protect their interests once involved. The banks allegedly advanced funds to SPEs (Special Purpose Entities) at key times to allow them and Enron to complete bogus transactions to create fake profits and hid billions of dollars of Enron debt. Supposedly aware of Enron's true dire financial state, the banks further made loans to Enron to ensure its liquidity, while simultaneously helping Enron sell its securities and keep the scheme going. Also, the banks allegedly supported the inflated price of these securities through glowing research reports that contained misleading information about Enron. Some of the banks also allegedly disguised billions of dollars in loans to Enron as sales transactions.

(III.B.1.b) CitiGroup—CitiGroup, like the other banks, allegedly enjoyed spectacular underwriting, advisory, and transactional fees, interest, and commitment charges, and some of its executives participated in the illicit partnerships for lucrative returns. It loaned over $4 billion to Enron, helped Enron raise $2 billion in securities sales, and helped Enron structure and finance the illicit partnerships and SPEs that Enron used to inflate earnings and hide debt. Its executives were in daily contact with Enron executives and discussed its business in detail. CitiGroup also purportedly made false and misleading statements in registration statements and prospectuses, as well as issued numerous analysts' reports that contained false and misleading statements about Enron's financial condition.

(III.B.2) Law Firms—Vinson & Elkins (V & E), Enron's outside counsel, participated in writing, reviewing, and approving Enron's SEC filings, shareholder reports, and financial press releases, and in creating various SPEs and handling related transactions. Allegedly, V & E knew that Enron insiders were on both sides of some of these transactions, to virtually ensure lucrative returns for the entities' partners, and that the illicit entities were manipulative devices. V & E allegedly provided "true sales" and other opinions that were false and that were indispensable for the sham deals. Given V & E's intimate involvement in

Continued on next page.

the formation of and transaction with these blatantly fraudulent entities, V & E allegedly had to know that they were created solely to "cook Enron's books." Although Sherron Watkins, an Enron employee and whistle-blower, warned Enron's CEO, Ken Lay, that V & E was involved in the fraud and had a clear conflict of interest, Lay still turned to top V & E partners to find out how to cover up the allegations. Despite this obvious conflict, V & E agreed to conduct an investigation into the charges of its own misconduct, and issued a letter dismissing the allegations. V & E also agreed not to review the accounting work or judgment of Arthur Andersen (Enron's auditor). Allegedly, during its investigation, V & E interviewed only top level executives that it knew were involved in the fraud and would deny it. Additionally, V & E advised that Watkins should not be fired, for fear that a wrongful termination suit would disclose her allegations, and she was shifted to another position where she would have less exposure to information damaging to Enron.

(III.B.3) The Accountant/Auditor: Arthur Andersen LLP—Allegedly Arthur Andersen abandoned its responsibilities to Enron investors and violated professional standards in perpetrating a massive accounting fraud. Enron was Arthur Andersen's second largest client and the auditing firm was economically dependent on Enron, which provided it with $50 million in annual fees. Partners at the accounting firm were pressured to generate more fees, which created a conflict of interest for auditors and caused them to abandon their independence and integrity. Even though Arthur Andersen was aware that the critical factor to increasing its fees was to maintain Enron's high credit rating, it decided that the possibility of doubling the fees it received from Enron to $100 million was worth maintaining Enron as a client, despite the risk this would entail. When partner Bass opposed the improper accounting practices used at Enron, he was removed from his oversight role on the Enron audits. Arthur Andersen allegedly helped structure hundreds of complicated partnerships, many with no purpose other than to conceal debt and losses. In many of the transactions, Enron maintained control of the entities and deliberately and improperly did not consolidate them. Andersen knew that Enron used at least 600 offshore tax shelters to shift income, minimize taxation, circumvent laws, and maintain secrecy. Even Andersen's tax and consulting departments knew that Enron's use of such entities was excessive and without business justification. Andersen documents revealed that it knew, was concerned about, yet covered up or ignored fraudulent accounting practices by Enron. Minutes of a teleconference meeting of Andersen partners revealed that they knew of the accounting issues that ultimately caused Enron's collapse. Despite such knowledge, they decided to retain Enron as a client and then issued a "clean" audit opinion on Enron's financial statements. In its audits of Enron's financial statements in 1997, Andersen identified $51 million of adjustments where the accounting was improper, and that these accounted for almost 50 percent of Enron's net income for that year. Nevertheless, Andersen acquiesced in Enron's request not to make those adjustments—which would radically reduce the net income that would be reported.

ISSUE: Does a claim brought under § 10(b) of the Securities Exchange Act of 1934 against secondary actors alleged to have participated in a scheme to defraud survive dismissal where a primary violation of § 10(b) is alleged against each individual actor?

HOLDING AND DECISION: (Harmon, J.) Yes. A claim brought under § 10(b) of the Securities Exchange Act of 1934 against secondary actors alleged to have participated in a scheme to defraud survives dismissal where a primary violation of § 10(b) is alleged against each individual actor. Secondary actors, such as lawyers, accountants, bank, and underwriters, are not shielded from § 10(b) and Rule 10b-5 liability as primary violators where they create a misrepresentation that is relied on by investors and they do so with scienter. Moreover, as long as the secondary actor is acting with scienter, it is not necessary for them to be the initiator of the misrepresentation in order to be treated as a primary violator. This rule, as construed by the SEC, is deferred to because it is not arbitrary, capricious, or manifestly contrary to the statute. Thus, to survive a motion to dismiss, a complaint alleging that more than one defendant participated in a scheme to defraud must allege a primary violation of § 10(b) by each defendant.

The defendants argue that the argument that they would pour millions of dollars into a Ponzi scheme and risk their reputations for huge fees, payments and profits, is irrational, implausible, and/or illogical. However, in light of revelations of vast corporate corruption and fraud by auditors and banks, these allegations are not implausible. The secondary-actor defendants are justified in objecting to boilerplate allegations made against them. However, their objections that claims of misconduct based on what are common, legitimate business actions or practices that are not inherently improper must be viewed within the totality of the circumstances to determine if indeed such practices were legitimate and ordinary, or if they were contrivances and deceptive devices used to defraud. The court, therefore will ignore the boilerplate, and focus on specific allegations against each defendant.

As a factor common to all defendants, the scienter pleading requirement is partially met by allegations of a regular pattern of related and repeated conduct involving the creation of unlawful SPEs, the sale of unwanted Enron assets to those entities in non-arm's-length transactions to shift debt off Enron's balance sheet and sham profits onto its books—from which all those involved profited exorbitantly. This pattern undermines claims of unintentional or negligent behavior and supports allegations of intent to

Continued on next page.

defraud. The common motive of extreme monetary gain has also been adequately pleaded. Similarly, conclusory allegations asserted against almost all the secondary actor defendants, such as long-term, continuous, intimate and extensive relationships with Enron and daily interactions with top Enron executives, raises the specter of opportunities to learn about and take an active role in Enron's financial affairs, access to nonpublic information, "intimacy blending into complicity fueled by financial interest." The provision by banks of both commercial and investment banking services raised the possibility of conflicts of interest and the standard mandatory in-depth credit analyses, which should have raised red flags.

All these are background factors that must be considered to determine if the secondary actors' actions were within the bounds of the law, or were outside the boundary of legitimate and professionally acceptable activities in performing material acts to defraud the public.

(1) Attorneys—V & E: With regard to attorneys, there is a tension between the need to provide a remedy to those suffering a loss as a result of attorney conduct and the need to preserve confidentiality, loyalty, and zealous representation. A lawyer may not knowingly assist a client in criminal or fraudulent conduct. Thus, professionals, including lawyers and accountants, when they affirmatively speak out about a client's financial condition, whether individually or as a silent co-author in a statement or report, have a duty to third parties not to knowingly or with severe recklessness issue materially misleading statements on which they intend or have reason to believe that those third parties will rely. Here, the situation alleged is one where V & E was not merely representing Enron, but was in league with Enron and others where each participant made material misrepresentations or omissions or employed a device, scheme, or artifice to defraud. There were specific allegations of acts in furtherance of the scheme and that V & E violated its professional and ethical principles by not resigning in return for lucrative fees. Had it remained silent, the attorney/client relationship may have protected it from liability. The complaint, however, adduces many instances where V & E frequently chose to make public statements about Enron's business and financial condition. It was essentially a co-author of the reports and releases relied on by investors and others, and deliberately, or with severe recklessness, directed those public statements to them in order to influence them to purchase more securities, or to keep Enron's credit rating high, or to keep providing loans to Enron. V & E had a duty to be truthful, and numerous allegations have been made that it breached that duty. As to the "white-wash" investigation it conducted in the wake of Watkins' allegations, the investigation and report can serve as the basis of § 10(b) and Rule 10b 5(a) or (c) claim alleging use of a device, scheme, or artifice to defraud. For these reasons, claims have been stated under § 10(b) against V & E.

(2) Accountant/Auditors—Arthur Andersen: There is no accountant/client privilege such as that accorded to lawyers. Accountants owe ultimate allegiance to the corporation's stockholders and creditors, as well as to the investing public. Here, specific facts were alleged to give rise to a strong inference that Andersen had scienter. Its comprehensive services to Enron necessarily made it intimately privy to the smallest details of Enron's alleged fraudulent activity. Also established was a pattern of such conduct, based on similar prior fraudulent audits of other companies. It was pleaded that despite being aware of accounting improprieties, Andersen decided to retain Enron as its client because of extremely lucrative fees. Because numerous violations of GAAP and GAAS have been pled, giving rise to a strong inference of scienter, a securities fraud claim has been pleaded against Andersen.

(3) The Banks: Viewing the specific allegations together, a claim has been stated against CitiGroup (and other banks) as a primary violator because it knowingly, or with severe recklessness, made a material representation or engaged in an act, practice, or course of business that operated as a fraud of deceit on Enron investors. CitiGroup, through its offshore Cayman Island subsidiary, was also able to disguise $2.4 billion of loans to Enron so that they never appeared on its balance sheet, at double the going interest rate, netting CitiGroup with $70 million annually for its participation in the scheme.

▶ ANALYSIS

The court reviews the Supreme Court's holding in *Central Bank of Denver, N.A. v. First Interstate Bank of Denver, N.A.*, 511 U.S. 164 (1994) and concludes that under that decision, a private plaintiff may not bring an aiding and abetting claim under § 10(b) or Rule 10b-5, since the statute is concerned only with prohibiting the making of a material misstatement or a material omission or the commission of a manipulative act. Thus, liability under the statute may be imposed on secondary actors not as aiders or abettors, but as actors who themselves have made misstatements, or material omissions, or commissions of manipulative acts. Here, the court permits the use of circumstantial evidence to create an inference that the secondary actors acted with scienter. However, it is arguable that by allowing such circumstantial evidence to prove scienter, it can always be possible to infer that a primary actor's advisers had knowledge of the wrongdoing of the primary actor, thus eviscerating the *Central Bank* holding.

■■■

Quicknotes

SCIENTER Knowledge of certain facts; often refers to "guilty knowledge," which implicates liability.

SECURITIES EXCHANGE ACT, § 10(b) Prohibits use of any "manipulative or deceptive device or contrivance" in con-

Continued on next page.

nection with the purchase or sale of a security and in violation of any regulation adopted by the Securities and Exchange Commission.

SECURITIES EXCHANGE ACT OF 1934 Federal statute regulating stock exchanges and trading and requiring the disclosure of certain information in relation to securities traded.

■≡■

Securities and Exchange Commn. v. Texas Gulf Sulphur Co.

Federal government agency (P) v. Corporation (D)

401 F.2d 833 (2d Cir. 1968), *cert. denied*, 394 U.S. 976 (1969).

NATURE OF CASE: Suit by the Securities and Exchange Commission (SEC) against individuals and a corporation for Rule 10b-5 violations.

FACT SUMMARY: Texas Gulf Sulphur Co. (TGS) (D) made a significantly large discovery of mineral deposits. While concealing the magnitude of the find, certain corporate employees purchased large amounts of TGS (D) stock. A misleading press release was issued to suppress the effect of rumors of the large discovery. Some nonemployees bought TGS (D) stock just prior to public release of the discovery based on their advance knowledge of the release.

RULE OF LAW

(1) Where corporate employees come into possession of material information, they are under no duty to disclose that information if there is a valid business reason for nondisclosure, but they may not benefit from transactions in the corporation's securities by reason of that nondisclosure.

(2) A corporation that issues public statements concerning a matter which could affect the corporation's securities in the marketplace must fully and fairly state facts upon which investors can reasonably rely. Any departure from that standard subjects the corporations to liability for violation of the Security Exchange Commission Act of 1939 Rule 10b-5.

FACTS: Texas Gulf Sulphur Co. (TGS) (D) was a corporation engaged in, among other things, exploration for and mining of certain minerals. Pursuant to this activity, TGS (D) conducted aerial and ground surface surveys of an area near Timmins, Ontario, Canada. A particular tract, known as Kidd 55, looked very promising as a source of desired minerals. The procedure to determine if commercially feasible quantities and qualities were present involved drilling a hole to a specified depth and examining and analyzing the contents of the core of the hole. TGS (D) did not have ownership or mineral rights to Kidd 55. In order to determine if acquisition was warranted, a test hole was drilled on November 8, 1963, and was designated Kidd 55-1. Present at the drilling site were various employees and consultants of TGS (D). Included in that group was the TGS (D) employees Clayton (D) and Holyk (D). An on-the-spot analysis of the core sample of Kidd 55-1 revealed a rich deposit of copper, zinc, and silver. In order to conceal the find, a second hole was drilled in an adjacent area that showed no signs of minerals. Kidd 55-1 was covered over.

On the basis of the content of the Kidd 55-1 TGS (D) commenced acquisition of the entire Kidd tract and surrounding tracts. The president of TGS (D), Stephens (D), instructed all on-site personnel to keep absolute secrecy of the find to facilitate the acquisitions. A laboratory analysis revealed the on-site estimate of quality to be slightly conservative and that the find was of amazing quality. Commencing March 31, 1964, TGS (D) drilled three additional holes, Kidd 55-3, Kidd 55-4, and Kidd 55-5, to determine the depth and lateral extent of the deposits. The results of these three core samples indicated the real possibility of a substantial commercially feasible deposit of copper and zinc. The results of the latter three core samplings were communicated daily to TGS (D) by Stephens (D). The last drilling in this series, Kidd 55-5, was completed April 10, 1964.

The amount of activity surrounding the drilling of these core sample holes had resulted in a number of rumors as to the size and quality of the find. On April 11, Stephens (D) read stories in two New York newspapers based, apparently, on these rumors. To counteract the rumors, Stephens (D) determined that a press release should be prepared stating the company's position. Two TGS (D) employees, Fogarty (D) and Carroll (D), prepared the release. The press release was issued on April 12, 1964. The release was attributed to Fogarty (D), describing him as executive vice president of TGS (D). The release denied the validity of the rumors and described them as excessively optimistic. It described various unsuccessful ventures in Canada in general and stated that as to the core drilling near Timmins, Ontario, insufficient data or information was available to evaluate the company's prospects there. The only indication that was available to date was that further drilling was necessary before any conclusions could be reached. The release ended by stating that when sufficient data was available to reach any conclusions a public statement would be issued. The release was stated to be the company's position based on information in its possession through April 12.

Drilling of core samples continued through April 15, by which time five additional holes were drilled and the analysis was completed by April 16. Based on this additional information, a reporter for a widely read Canadian mining journal was invited to this site to report on the discovery. The report was prepared April 13 and submitted to Mollison (D), Holyk (D), and Darke (D), the three TGS (D) employees interviewed. They made no changes in the report, which stated that a 10-million-ton strike had been made, and the article was published April 16, 1964. A

Continued on next page.

report prepared by the three was also submitted to Ontario government officials for their release on April 15. It was, in fact, not released until April 16, for unknown reasons. At 10:00 A.M., a 10- to 15-minute statement was read to representatives of the American financial press detailing the discovery and announcing its size as 25 million tons. The first release was over a brokerage house wire service at 10:29 A.M. Dow Jones reported it at 10:54 A.M. A review of the market price of TGS (D) stock as quoted on the New York Stock Exchange was made for the period from November 8, 1963, when drilling of Kidd 55-1 was begun, to May 15, 1964. On November 8, the stock sold for about $17.50. When Kidd 55-1 had been completed, the stock was selling for $18. When the results of the chemical tests of the Kidd 55-1 core were completed in December, the shares were quoted at almost $21. On February 21, 1964, the shares were selling at $24. By March 31, 1964, the price had risen to $26. On April 10, it was traded at $30. As a result of the press release of April 12, the stock rose temporarily to $32, but by April 15 had dropped back to just over $29. On April 16, 1964, the date of the official announcement of the size of the strike, sales were around $37. By May 15, 1964, TGS (D) stock was selling at just over $58 per share.

What gave rise to the action by the Securities and Exchange Commission (P) against the individual defendants and Texas Gulf Sulphur (D) was that during the period from November 8, 1963, through April 16, 1964, the named defendants had purchased either shares in TGS (D) or had been granted options by the company to buy shares at 95 percent of the current market value. In addition, certain earlier named individuals who were not connected with TGS (D) were also named as defendants due to their purchases of shares or calls to buy shares as a result of learning of the strike prior to complete dissemination of the news to the public. One of the directors of TGS (D), Coates (D), made purchases through his son-in-law, a broker, of 2,000 shares at 10:20 A.M., April 16, for certain family trusts for which he was trustee but not beneficiary. As a result of the call from Coates (D), the son-in-law also made substantial other purchases for his customers at the same time. Many of the people buying shares during this period, including several employees, had not previously been buyers of any stock of any corporation or had ever engaged in the somewhat speculative practice of buying calls.

Of the named defendants, prior to November 12, 1963, they collectively owned 1,135 shares of TGS (D) stock and no calls. By March 31, 1964, they owned 8,235 shares and calls on 12,300 more shares. The aggregate investment of four employees alone was in excess of $100,000. The stock options to five employee-defendants were granted by the TGS (D) board of directors on February 20, 1964. The facts of the discovery had been concealed from the members of the board. The recipients of the options did not notify the New York Stock Exchange as required. The SEC filed charges against all named defendants and the corporation alleging their actions violated § 10(b) and Rule 10b-5 of the Securities Exchange Act of 1934. Specifically, they charged that by simultaneously concealing the information about the size of the find while purchasing shares and calls and accepting options, the defendant-employees violated the provisions; that others acting on inside information purchased shares; and that TGS (D) violated the provisions by the press release of April 12, 1964.

Trial was held in United States District Court for the Southern District of New York. The judge, in a lengthy opinion, declared all defendants, save two individuals, were not guilty of violations for any offenses charged. The two defendants found to have committed illegal acts had traded in TSG (D) stock between April 9, 1964, and April 16, 1964. The trial judge determined that prior to April 9, no material information had been concealed and, therefore, any trading prior to that date did not violate the act and that the press release was not misleading in that there were no material facts to misstate at that time.

ISSUE:

(1) May individual employees and directors of a corporation be held to have violated § 10(b) and Rule 10b-5 by purchasing securities and accepting options to purchase securities in their corporation while in possession of information that could affect the price of those securities, which is not available to the public? May persons they communicate this information to privately, who then purchase those securities, be similarly held liable?

(2) Can a corporation be held liable to the investing public for issuing a report that misstates a material fact about an activity of the corporation?

HOLDING AND DECISION: (Waterman, J.)

(1) Yes. Individual employees and directors of a corporation may be held to have violated § 10(b) and Rule 10b-5 by purchasing securities and accepting options to purchase securities in their corporation while in possession of information that could affect the price of those securities, which is not available to the public. Persons to whom they communicate this information to privately, who then purchase those securities may be held similarly liable. The court laid a foundation for its decision by examining the purpose and intent of Congress and the Securities Exchange Commission in enacting the Securities Exchange Act of 1934 and the promulgation of Rule 10b 5 pursuant to the Act. The basic thrust of the Act was to promote fairness in securities transactions generally and to prevent specific unfair and inequitable practices in securities transactions. The regulations and controls so imposed were to apply to all transactions, whether face-to-face or in the impersonal markets of the organized exchanges and the over-the-counter market. Rule 10b-5 was designed to

Continued on next page.

insure that all investors trading in the impersonal securities markets should have relatively equal access to material information relating to their transactions. The court found that the essence of Rule 10b-5 was to prevent a person who has direct or indirect access to internal corporate information that is not, nor intended to be, publicly known from making use of that information for his personal benefit by trading in corporate securities.

As to the individual defendants, the court examined their individual conduct as it related to the circumstances as they developed over the period involved. Since the major thrust of the trial court's dismissal of most charges was a finding that no material information existed prior to April 9, 1964, this court first dealt with that issue. The court stated that the test for a determination of materiality is whether a reasonable man would consider the information important in forming a decision in relation to transacting in the security involved. Implicit in this definition is the existence of any fact that objectively and reasonably could be expected to influence the price or value of the security involved. Rule 10b-5 does not require a corporate insider to make public any information within his knowledge that would be expected to affect the shares of his corporation. There are many circumstances in which such information may rightfully be withheld. But, if a legitimate decision to withhold is made, the insider may not transact in the securities of the corporation unless and until it is effectively disclosed to the public. An insider is not to be expected to make public disclosure of his predictions or educated guesses derived from his expert analytical abilities or superior financial acumen. What must be disclosed is the factual basis for his analysis results. In determining whether facts are material, there must be a balancing of the indicated probability of the occurrence against the magnitude of the occurrence in relation to the size of the corporate enterprise.

Applying this principle to the results of the analysis of the core sample obtained from Kidd 55-1 indicates that this was material information. The results of that core sample analysis were described by various experts as "most impressive" and "beyond your wildest expectation." But perhaps the most significant objective indicator of the material nature of the initial core sample was that four employees who had direct knowledge invested over $100,000 in the stock of TGS (D). Some of these individuals had never invested before. It should be clearly evident that outside investors, had they been in possession of the core analysis information, would have taken that information to be a significant factor in determining their investment course. This is not to say that the information must have been made public, only that the insiders could not trade on that information for their benefit without disclosing it. TGS (D) and the individuals had a valid

reason for withholding the information, since they had yet to acquire the Kidd tract or the surrounding tracts which they desired. Yet, they chose to purchase the stock and, in Darke's (D) case, pass along tips to associates who purchased while the information was suppressed. In addition, the corporate employee who directed the land acquisition program while also buying TGS (D) stock must be considered to have had sufficient knowledge that the find was valuable to subject him to liability as well.

A different situation is presented by the purchases of Crawford (D) and Coates (D). Crawford's (D) purchases were ordered on April 15 and April 16. Coates's (D) purchases were made on April 16 immediately after the reading of the complete public statement issued by TGS (D). Both contend that their purchases occurred after the public disclosure of the material information. But public disclosure means effective public disclosure, not just technical disclosure. At the time of their purchases, there had not been any wide dissemination of the TGS (D) statement. Both purchases were made before even the Dow Jones wire service had published the contents of the statement. Both defendants assert, however, that they honestly believed the information had been effectively disclosed. A finding of liability under the federal securities laws and, in particular, Rule 10b-5 does not require proof of a specific intent to defraud. While the standard to be applied must contain some measure of scienter, this requirement will be satisfied by a showing of negligent conduct, lack of diligence, or unreasonable conduct. We find that it cannot be said that either Crawford (D) or Coates (D) could have reasonably believed that the material information had been fully and effectively disseminated to the public at the time of their purchases.

The third type of conduct that must be examined was the acceptance of the stock options by the corporate officers and directors. There can be no reasonable distinction made between this type of transaction and a transaction involving an actual purchase or sale. When the board of directors granted the options in February 1964, the defendants had withheld from the granting directors the information about the Timmins discovery that has already been determined to have been material. Before accepting the proffered options, the defendants were under a duty to disclose the material information. The fact that they did not disclose subjects the options to a remedy of rescission under Rule 10b-5. Since the trial court determined that no liability attached to the acceptance of the options by two employees who were not considered top management personnel and the SEC (P) did not see fit to appeal that judgment, we need not render an opinion as to their liability.

Continued on next page.

(2) Yes. A corporation can be held liable to the investing public for issuing a report that misstates a material fact about an activity of the corporation. The court's decision then moved to a determination of the liability, if any, of TGS (D) itself for violation of Rule 10b-5. The determination of liability would be made on the basis of an examination of the statement issued, in the form of a press release, on April 12, 1964.

TGS (D) contended that no liability could be found based on four defenses. First, there was no showing that the statement produced any significant market action, and therefore, second, there was no showing of intent to affect the market price for the benefit of TGS (D) or to TGS (D) insiders. Third, the lack of a showing of intent to benefit TGS (D) or insiders established that the release was not issued in connection with any purchases or sales by TGS (D) or the insiders. Finally, the company contended that even if the statement were found to be issued in connection with the security transactions, there was no showing that it was false, misleading, or deceptive.

In determining the proper meaning and application of the term "in connection with the purchase or sale of any security" clause of § 10b and Rule 10b-5 the court made an extensive examination of the legislative history of the statute. Their conclusion was that the thrust of the legislation was to prevent false, misleading, or deceptive devices or information from affecting the securities market. By examining other legislation (e.g., the Securities Act of 1933), the court found that if Congress intended to limit 10b and Rule 10b-5 to transactions made by the parties charged, different, more specific language to that effect would have been employed. The court determined the legislative intent to be the protection of the investing public and that the broad language of § 10b did not limit its application to situations in which the perpetrator had engaged in transactions. To find liability, therefore, the SEC need only establish that the statement was false or misleading and that the issuer knew, or should have known, that the statement was of such a nature. There need not be a finding that the statement was issued with a wrongful purpose, that is, to benefit the corporation or the insiders. To apply that standard could conceivably allow the wrongdoer to gamble a little in the issuance of the statement. If the statement is issued but does not have the desired effect, then no liability would be found. But, if the desired effect does result, then the wrongdoer can hope he is not found out and escape liability. The fact that the April 12 release did not produce any significant market activity is only indicative that its desired purpose may not have been achieved. This interpretation imposes a duty on corporate management to ascertain that any proposed public statement fairly and accurately represents the whole truth in regard to the subject matter of the release. Where statements are made that are calculated to influence the market in a

corporate security, if those statements are false or misleading, then Rule 10b-5 has been violated if the officers of the corporation cannot establish that every reasonable effort was made to ascertain the accuracy and completeness of the statement. By application of these standards, the court considered the effect of the April 19 release. It found that the statements in the release were less than candid and complete and certainly did not describe the actual state of the facts, which were apparently known to its authors. If the company felt compelled to make a statement on April 12, then that statement should have consisted of the details of what was actually known at that time, thus allowing the individual investor to form his own conclusions. Since the point was not fully developed by the trial court, this court remanded the case back to the trial court for a determination of whether the statement was, in fact, misleading and whether discretion should be exercised in the favor of the SEC's request for an injunction against future violations. Affirmed in part, reversed in part, and remanded.

▎ANALYSIS

The *Texas Gulf Sulphur* case is one of the most important decisions to date on judicial interpretation of Rule 10b-5. It provided some indication of the all-inclusive nature of the rule. Corporate officers may not take advantage of undisclosed material information to trade in the securities of their corporation. Even if the insiders do not transact, they cannot reveal the information to outsiders who may then trade to their advantage. A person who learns of inside information, even though an outsider, may not trade if he knows or has reason to know the information has not been effectively disseminated to the public. In *Texas Gulf Sulphur* alone, the remedies granted included money damages, rescission (of the options), and injunction. While the plaintiff in *Texas Gulf Sulphur* was the SEC, previous decisions have found an implied right of private action under 10b-5. The scope of 10b-5 is, therefore, enormous. Both the government and private plaintiffs may hold liable corporate insiders, persons they tip, persons who independently learn of inside information, and the corporation itself. The concept of privity is abandoned and the requirement of scienter greatly limited. And, based on the opinion of a New York State court, violations of 10b-5 can be asserted in a state action. Many authorities have expressed alarm at the potential scope of Rule 10b-5. They fear that the evils of the marketplace sought to be corrected may be replaced by another equally damaging evil—that is, that conduct by individuals and corporations that would not have gotten by the complaint stage in a traditional lawsuit will subject the individuals and corporations to staggering penalties.

■■■■

Continued on next page.

Quicknotes

INSIDER Any person within a corporation who has access to information not available to the public.

MATERIALITY Importance; the degree of relevance or necessity to the particular matter.

RULE 10b-5 Unlawful to defend or make untrue statements in connection with purchase or sale of securities.

SECURITIES EXCHANGE ACT, § 10(b) Makes it unlawful for any person to use manipulation or deception in the buying or selling of securities.

■═■

Chiarella v. United States

Printer (D) v. Federal government (P)

445 U.S. 222 (1980).

NATURE OF CASE: Appeal from conviction for violating federal securities law.

FACT SUMMARY: While employed as a printer, Chiarella (D) saw information that one corporation was planning to attempt to secure control of another, and he used this information by going out and trading stock.

🏛 RULE OF LAW
A purchaser of stock who has no duty to a prospective seller because he is neither an insider nor a fiduciary has no obligation to disclose material information he has acquired, and his failure to disclose such information does not, therefore, constitute a violation of § 10(b) of the Securities Exchange Act of 1934.

FACTS: In the course of his job as a printer at Pandick Press, Chiarella (D) was exposed to documents of one corporation revealing its plan to attempt to secure control of a second corporation. Although the identities of the corporations were concealed by blank spaces or false names until the true names were sent over on the night of the final printing, Chiarella (D) had deduced the names of the target companies beforehand from other information contained in the documents. Without revealing any of this information to the prospective sellers, he went about purchasing shares in the target corporations. He sold them after the takeover attempts were made public, thus realizing a gain of more than $30,000 in the course of 14 months. The SEC began an investigation, which culminated in Chiarella's (D) entering into a consent decree agreeing to return his profits to the sellers of the shares. He was, that same day, fired by Pandick Press. Eight months later, he was indicted on 17 counts of violating § 10(b) of the Securities Exchange Act of 1934 and SEC Rule 19b-5. Chiarella (D) argued that his silence about the information he had obtained did not constitute a violation of § 10(b) because he was under no duty to disclose the information to the prospective sellers, inasmuch as he was neither an insider nor a fiduciary. The district court charged the jury that Chiarella (D) should be convicted if it found he had willfully failed to inform sellers of target companies securities that he knew of a forthcoming takeover bid that would make their shares more valuable. In affirming the resulting conviction, the court of appeals held that "(a)nyone—corporate insider or not—who regularly receives material non-public information may not use that information to trade in securities without incurring an affirmative duty to disclose." The Supreme Court granted certiorari.

ISSUE: If a stockholder owed no duty of disclosure to the party from whom he purchased securities, does his failure to disclose to the seller material information he has acquired constitute a violation of § 10(b) of the Securities Exchange Act of 1934?

HOLDING AND DECISION: (Powell, J.) No. If one who purchases stock is neither an insider nor a fiduciary, and thus owes no duty to the prospective seller, his failure to disclose inside material information he has acquired does not constitute a fraud in violation of § 10(b) of the Securities Exchange Act of 1934. Administrative and judicial interpretations have established that silence in connection with the purchase or sale of securities may operate as a fraud actionable under § 10(b) despite the absence of statutory language or legislative history specifically addressing the legality of nondisclosures. However, such liability is premised upon a duty to disclose arising from a relationship of trust and confidence between parties to a transaction. In this case, the charges of the lower courts did not reflect his duty requirement adequately. Furthermore, both courts failed to identify a relationship between Chiarella (D) and the sellers that could give rise to a duty and thus provide a basis for his conviction under § 10(b) for failure to disclose the information he had. It may well be that he breached a duty to the acquiring corporation when he acted upon information he obtained by virtue of his position as an employee of the printer employed by the corporation. Whether this breach of duty would support a conviction under § 10(b) for fraud need not be decided, for this theory was not presented to the jury. Reversed.

DISSENT: (Burger, C.J.) I would read § 10(b) and Rule 10b-5 to mean that a person who has misappropriated nonpublic information has an absolute duty to disclose that information or to refrain from trading. The broad language of the statute and Congress's intent to use it as an elastic "catchall" provision to protect the uninitiated investor from misbehavior evidences the propriety of such an interpretation.

DISSENT: (Blackmun, J.) Chiarella (D) was guilty of fraud because he knowingly "stole" the information concerning the pending tender offers. His conduct was also fraudulent within the meaning of § 10(b) and Rule 10b-5, as this type of manipulative trading lies at the heart of what the security laws are intended to prohibit, regardless of whether his employer's principals had approved his conduct. The majority's requirement of a "special relationship" akin to fiduciary duty undermines the flexible, purposefully catchall nature of § 10(b). Such a requirement, on which the duty to disclose or to abstain from trading on material

Continued on next page.

nonpublic information is now conditioned, finds no support in the language of the statute or its legislative history. It is also not consistent with the principle that the securities laws should be construed flexibly rather than with narrow technicality. Because Chiarella's (D) misuse of confidential information was "inherently unfair," his conviction should be upheld.

▶ ANALYSIS

The SEC has not made a practice of challenging trading by noninsiders on the basis of undisclosed market information. In fact, it has generally pointed to some fiduciary duty or special relationship between the purchase or seller and the outsider trader as a basis for such challenges. For example, in *SEC v. Campbell*, [1972–1973 Transfer Binder] Fed. Sec. L. Rep. (CCH) P93, 580 (C.D. Cal. July 24, 1972), the writer of a financial column engaged in "scalping," i.e., purchasing stocks shortly before recommending them in his column and then selling them when the price rose after the recommendation was published. The SEC went to great lengths to equate his relationship with his readers to that of an adviser's relationship with his clients.

Quicknotes

RULE 10b-5 Unlawful to defend or make untrue statements in connection with purchase or sale of securities.

SECURITIES EXCHANGE ACT, § 10(b) Makes it unlawful for any person to use manipulation or deception in the buying or selling of securities.

United States v. O'Hagan

Federal government (P) v. Alleged insider trader (D)

521 U.S. 642 (1997).

NATURE OF CASE: Writ of certiorari reviewing reversal of convictions for mail and securities fraud, fraudulent trading, and money laundering.

FACT SUMMARY: O'Hagan (D), an attorney, was indicted for trading securities in Pillsbury based on confidential information he obtained by virtue of his association with the corporation's law firm.

> 🏛 **RULE OF LAW**
> (1) When a person misappropriates confidential information in violation of a fiduciary duty, and trades on that information for his own personal benefit, he is in violation of SEC § 10(b) and Rule 10b-5.
> (2) The SEC did not exceed its rulemaking authority by promulgating Rule 14e-3(a), which prohibits trading on undisclosed information in a tender offer situation, even where the person has no fiduciary duty to disclose the information.

FACTS: Dorsey & Whitney, a law firm, was retained by Grand Metropolitan PLC (Grand Met) as counsel in a proposed tender offer for the stock of Pillsbury. O'Hagan (D), a partner in Dorsey & Whitney, was not assigned to the case. However, during the course of the representation, O'Hagan (D) purchased a total of 2,500 Pillsbury call options and 5,000 shares of common stock. Following the announcement of the tender offer, he sold his interests, at a profit of more than $4.3 million. The Securities and Exchange Commission (SEC) (P) commenced an investigation of O'Hagan (D), and indicted him on fifty-seven counts of mail and securities fraud, fraudulent trading, and money laundering. He was convicted on all fifty-seven counts and sentenced to forty-one months imprisonment. The Court of Appeals for the Eighth Circuit reversed all of the convictions on the basis that Rule 10b-5 liability may not be based on a misappropriation theory. Furthermore, the court held that SEC Rule 14e-3(a) was beyond the scope of the SEC's (P) rulemaking power. As a result, none of the convictions could stand since they were based on the underlying securities fraud violations. The Supreme Court granted certiorari to determine the propriety of the misappropriation theory, and the authority of the SEC (P) to promulgate Rule 14e-3(a).

ISSUE:
(1) When a person misappropriates confidential information in violation of a fiduciary duty, and trades on that information for his own personal benefit, is he in violation of SEC § 10(b) and Rule 10b-5 of the Securities Exchange Act?
(2) Did the SEC exceed its rulemaking authority by promulgating Rule 14e-3(a), which prohibits trading on undisclosed information in a tender offer situation, even where the person has no fiduciary duty to disclose the information?

HOLDING AND DECISION: (Ginsburg, J.)
(1) Yes. When a person misappropriates confidential information in violation of a fiduciary duty, and trades on that information for his own personal benefit, he is in violation of SEC § 10(b) and Rule 10b-5. Section 10(b) prohibits the use of any deceptive device in conjunction with the purchase or sale of securities. The "traditional" theory holds an insider liable for trading in securities of his corporation based on relevant, nonpublic information. Such trading satisfies the requirement of deception due to the relationship of trust and confidence reposed in the insider by virtue of his position. Such entrustment requires the insider to disclose or abstain from trading in the securities of the corporation in order to protect nonsuspecting shareholders. This duty applies to officers and directors, as well as to anyone else who acts in a fiduciary capacity toward the corporation, including attorneys, accountants, and consultants. In contrast, the "misappropriation" theory holds a person liable for the misappropriation of material, nonpublic information for the purpose of trading thereon, in breach of a fiduciary duty due to the provider of the information. The misappropriation theory extends liability to include corporate outsiders who owe no duty to the shareholders of the corporation, but who nonetheless have access to the confidential information by virtue of their fiduciary position. Here, O'Hagan (D) did not owe a duty to the shareholders of Pillsbury since he was not an attorney involved in the case. However, O'Hagan (D) owed a fiduciary duty to his law firm, Dorsey & Whitney, to refrain from trading on the basis of material, nonpublic information he may have acquired by virtue of his position in the firm.
(2) No. The SEC (P) did not exceed its rulemaking authority in promulgating Rule 14e-3(a), which prohibits trading on undisclosed information in a tender offer situation, even where the person has no fiduciary duty to disclose the information. Under § 14(e) of the Exchange Act, the SEC (P) is granted the authority to pass such rules and regulations as are necessary to

Continued on next page.

prevent the commission of fraud or deception in connection with the sale of securities. The rationale supporting the rule is the protection of uninformed shareholders involved in a potential tender offer situation. The rule imposes a duty on the trader to disclose the confidential information, or abstain from trading on it. This rule is consistent with the legislative goal of proscribing fraudulent or deceptive acts in the purchase or sale of securities. In reviewing the propriety of SEC (P) regulations, the Court must give great deference to the SEC's (P) judgment absent a patently contrary intent. Reversed and remanded.

CONCURRENCE AND DISSENT: (Scalia, J.) The broad statutory language of § 10(b) and Rule 10b-5 prohibiting the use of any deceptive device in conjunction with the purchase or sale of any security must be narrowly construed to apply only to the deception of a party involved in a securities transaction.

CONCURRENCE AND DISSENT: (Thomas, J.) The application of the misappropriation theory ratified by the majority of the Court results in an inconsistent application of § 10(b). Furthermore, the imposition of liability, regardless of the existence of a fiduciary duty, fails to comport with the purpose of § 14(e) in the prevention of fraudulent acts in connection with the sale of securities.

▶ ANALYSIS

The validity of the misappropriation theory turned on whether it satisfied the requirement of a "deceptive device" under § 10(b). The Court holds that a misappropriator of confidential information necessarily effectuates a deception on the source of that information through his nondisclosure of his intent to trade on it. Such deception involves illusory loyalty to the company that has the exclusive right to use of the information, and is equivalent to an act of embezzlement.

■══■

Quicknotes

RULE 10b-5 Unlawful to defend or make untrue statements in connection with purchase or sale of securities.

RULE 14a-3 Imposes a duty of disclosure on person who trades securities that are being sought in a tender offer.

SECURITIES EXCHANGE ACT, § 10(b) Makes it unlawful for any person to use manipulation or deception in the buying or selling of securities.

■══■

Dirks v. SEC

Brokerage firm officer (D) v. Federal government agency (P)

463 U.S. 646 (1983).

NATURE OF CASE: Securities and Exchange Commission (SEC) action for violation of § 10(b).

FACT SUMMARY: Dirks (D), based on some nonpublic information he received and a subsequent investigation, aided the SEC (P) in convicting Equity Funding of America (EFA) for corporate fraud and was then sued by the SEC (P) for violating § 10(b) because he openly disclosed the nonpublic information to investors.

🏛 RULE OF LAW
Before a tippee will be held liable for openly disclosing nonpublic information received from an insider, the tippee must derivatively assume and breach the insider's fiduciary duty and the tippee will be deemed to have derivatively assumed and breached such a duty only when he knows or should know that the insider will benefit in some fashion for disclosing the information to the tippee.

FACTS: Dirks (D), the tippee and officer of a brokerage firm, was told by Secrist, the insider, Equity Funding of America (EFA) was engaging in corporate fraud. Dirks (D) then investigated EFA to verify Secrist's information. Neither Dirks (D) nor his firm owned or traded EFA stock. However, during Dirks's (D) investigation he openly revealed the information to investors and caused many of them to sell their EFA stock. Consequently, the price of EFA stock dropped from $26 to $15. However, largely due to Dirks's (D) investigation, the SEC (P) was able to convict the officers of EFA for corporate fraud. Still, the SEC (P) sued and reprimanded Dirks (D) for his disclosure of the nonpublic information to the investors. The court of appeals affirmed; and Dirks (D) applied for and was granted certiorari by the United States Supreme Court.

ISSUE: Will a tippee automatically be liable for openly disclosing nonpublic information received from an insider?

HOLDING AND DECISION: (Powell, J.) No. Before a tippee will be held liable for openly disclosing nonpublic information received from an insider, the tippee must derivatively assume and breach the insider's fiduciary duty to the shareholders of not trading on nonpublic information. The tippee will be deemed to have derivatively assumed and breached such a duty only when he knows or should know that the insider will benefit in some fashion for disclosing the information to the tippee. Mere receipt for nonpublic information by a tippee from an insider does not automatically carry with it the fiduciary duty of an insider. In this case, Secrist, the insider, did not receive a benefit for his disclosure. He disclosed the information to Dirks (D), the tippee, solely to help expose the fraud being perpetrated by the officers of EFA. Therefore, since Secrist, the insider, did not receive a benefit for his disclosure of nonpublic information to Dirks (D), the tippee, Secrist did not breach his fiduciary duty to the shareholders. Consequently, since Secrist, the insider, did not breach his duty to the shareholders, there was no derivative breach by Dirks (D) when he passed on the nonpublic information to investors. Reversed.

▶ ANALYSIS

This case is consistent with the Court's decision in *Chiarella v. U.S.*, 445 U.S. 222 (1980), where the Court found that there is no general duty to disclose before trading on material nonpublic information and held that a duty to disclose under § 10(b) does not arise from mere possession of nonpublic market information. Rather, such a duty, the Court found, arises from the existence of a fiduciary relationship.

■≡■

Quicknotes

INSIDER A person who obtains material nonpublic information from another who is standing in a fiduciary relationship to the corporation that is the subject of such information.

TIPPEE A person who obtains material nonpublic information from another standing in a fiduciary relationship to the corporation that is the subject of such information.

■≡■

United States v. Chestman

Federal government (P) v. Stockbroker (D)

947 F.2d 551 (2d Cir. 1991), *on rehearing en banc.*

NATURE OF CASE: Appeal from reversal of a conviction for insider trading.

FACT SUMMARY: After stockbroker Chestman (D) purchased shares of a corporation when he acquired nonpublic inside information, he was indicted and convicted of violating the Securities Exchange Act of 1934.

RULE OF LAW
One who misappropriates material nonpublic information in breach of a fiduciary duty or similar relationship of trust and confidence and uses that information in a securities trade violates Rule 10b-5.

FACTS: Waldbaum, the controlling shareholder of Waldbaum's, Inc., told some members of the family that he was going to sell the corporation. Chestman (D) learned from Loeb, who was married to Waldbaum's niece, Waldbaum was to be sold to A & P for substantially more than the market price. Chestman (D) was a broker for the junior members of the Waldbaum family. After receiving the information but before public announcement of the sale, Chestman (D) purchased Waldbaum stock for himself and several of his customers, including Loeb. Loeb cooperated with the Securities and Exchange Commission (SEC) (P) during its investigation, disgorging his profits and paying a fine. Chestman (D) was indicted and convicted for violating Rules 10b-5 and 14e-3(a), for mail fraud, and for perjury. On Chestman's (D) appeal, a panel of the Second Circuit set aside his conviction in its entirety. The United States (P) appealed, resulting in this *en banc* rehearing by the Second Circuit.

ISSUE: Does one who misappropriates material nonpublic information in breach of a fiduciary duty or similar relationship of trust and confidence and uses that information in a securities trade violate Rule 10b-5?

HOLDING AND DECISION: (Meskill, J.) Yes. One who misappropriates material nonpublic information in breach of a fiduciary duty or similar relationship of trust and confidence and uses that information in a securities trade violates Rule 10b-5. However, a fiduciary duty cannot be imposed unilaterally by entrusting a person with confidential information, and mere kinship does not of itself establish a confidential relation. Moreover, a similar relationship of trust and confidence is the functional equivalent of a fiduciary relationship. The evidence in this case is insufficient to establish a fiduciary relationship or its functional equivalent between Loeb and the Waldbaum family. Absent an act of fraud by Loeb, Chestman (D) cannot be derivatively liable as Loeb's tippee or as an aider and abettor. Thus, Chestman's (D) mail fraud convictions, based on the same theory as his 10b-5 convictions, cannot stand. Reversed as to the Rule 10b-5 and mail fraud convictions, and affirmed as to the Rule 14e-3(a) convictions.

CONCURRENCE AND DISSENT: (Winter, J.) Chestman's (D) convictions under both Rule 14e-3 and Rule 10b-5 should be affirmed. When members of a family have benefited from the family's control of a corporation and are in a position to acquire such information in the ordinary course of family interactions, that position carries with it a duty not to disclose.

CONCURRENCE: (Miner, J.) I agree with the majority opinion. As for J. Winter's "family relationship" rule, family discourse would be inhibited rather than promoted by a rule that would automatically assure confidentiality on the part of a family member receiving nonpublic corporate information.

▶ ANALYSIS

The excerpt omits the majority's discussion of *Chestman's* (D) Rule 14e-3(a) convictions. The traditional theory of insider trader liability derives principally from the Supreme Court's holdings in *Chiarella v. U.S.*, 445 U.S. 222 (1980), and in *Dirks v. SEC*, 463 U.S. 646 (1983). The misappropriation theory has not yet been the subject of a Supreme Court holding but has been adopted in the Second, Third, Seventh, and Ninth Circuits. In contrast to *Chiarella* and *Dirks*, the misappropriation theory does not require that the buyer or seller of securities be defrauded.

■■■■

Quicknotes

FIDUCIARY DUTY A legal obligation to act for the benefit of another, including subordinating one's personal interests to that of the other person.

RULE 14e-3(a) Makes it unlawful to make false statements in connection with tender offers.

■■■■

Securities and Exchange Commn. v. Cuban

Federal government agency (P) v. Shareholder-investor (D)

634 F. Supp. 2d 713 (N.D. Tex. 2009).

NATURE OF CASE: Insider trading action.

FACT SUMMARY: The Securities and Exchange Commission (SEC) (P) contended that Cuban (D) undertook a non-use of information duty before selling his 6.3 percent stake in Mamma.com Inc. on the basis of material, confidential information, and that Cuban (D) was therefore liable under the misappropriation theory of insider trading.

🏛 **RULE OF LAW**
A shareholder does not undertake a duty of non-use of information sufficient to support a claim of insider trading under the misappropriation theory where the shareholder agrees to keep nonpublic material information confidential, but does not agree to not trade on that information.

FACTS: Cuban (D), the largest shareholder of Mamma.com Inc., with a 6.3 percent interest, was contacted and informed by Mamma.com's CEO that the company was planning to raise capital through a private investment in public equity (PIPE) offering. Before revealing this information to Cuban (D), the CEO informed Cuban (D) that the CEO was about to reveal confidential information, and Cuban (D) agreed that he would keep whatever information the CEO intended to share with him confidential. The CEO, in reliance on Cuban's (D) agreement to keep the information confidential, proceeded to tell Cuban (D) about the PIPE offering. At the end of the call Cuban (D) said: "Well, now I'm screwed. I can't sell." Immediately after receiving more nonpublic information from the investment bank handling the transaction, Cuban (D) sold all his Mamma.com stock. Cuban (D) did not inform Mamma.com of his intention to trade on the information that he had been given. The next day, after the markets had closed, Mamma.com publicly announced the PIPE offering. Trading in the company's stock opened substantially lower the next day and continued to decline in the days following. Cuban (D) avoided losses in excess of $750,000 by selling his shares prior to the public announcement of the PIPE. After the sale, Cuban (D) filed the required disclosure statement with the SEC and "publicly stated that he had sold his Mamma.com shares because the company was conducting a PIPE[.]" Based on these events, the Securities and Exchange Commission (SEC) (P) brought suit against Cuban (D) under the misappropriation theory of insider trading, claiming violations of § 17(a) of the Securities Act of 1933 (Securities Act), § 10(b) of the Securities Exchange Act of 1934 (Exchange Act), and Rule 10b-5 promulgated thereunder. Cuban (D) moved to dismiss, asserting that, to establish liability for insider trading, the SEC (P) had to demonstrate that his conduct was deceptive under § 10(b), which he asserted the SEC (P) had not done. Specifically, he contended that the SEC (D) had alleged merely that he entered into a confidentiality agreement, which is in itself insufficient to establish misappropriation theory liability because the agreement must arise in the context of a pre-existing fiduciary or fiduciary-like relationship, or create a relationship that bears all the hallmarks of a traditional fiduciary relationship. Moreover, he maintained that the existence of a fiduciary or fiduciary-like relationship is governed exclusively by state law, under which the facts pleaded did not demonstrate that he had such a relationship with Mamma.com, and that even under federal common law, the facts pleaded still failed to show such a relationship. Finally, he argued that the SEC (P) could not rely on Rule 10b5-2(b)(1) to supply the requisite duty because the Rule applies only in the context of family or personal relationships, and, if the Rule does create liability in the absence of a preexisting fiduciary or fiduciary-like relationship, it exceeds the SEC's § 10(b) rulemaking authority and could not be applied against him.

ISSUE: Does a shareholder undertake a duty of non-use of information sufficient to support a claim of insider trading under the misappropriation theory where the shareholder agrees to keep nonpublic material information confidential, but does not agree to not trade on that information?

HOLDING AND DECISION: (Fitzwater, C.J.) No. A shareholder does not undertake a duty of non-use of information sufficient to support a claim of insider trading under the misappropriation theory where the shareholder agrees to keep nonpublic material information confidential, but does not agree to not trade on that information. The law of insider trading is not based on a federal statute expressly prohibiting the practice, but has instead developed through SEC and judicial interpretations of § 10(b)'s prohibition of "deceptive" conduct and Rule 10b-5's antifraud provisions. The misappropriation theory of insider trading holds that a person commits fraud in connection with a securities transaction, and thereby violates § 10(b) and Rule 10b-5, when he misappropriates confidential information for securities trading purposes, in breach of a duty owed to the source of the information. The fraud arises because the undisclosed, self-serving use of a principal's information to purchase or sell securities, in breach of a duty of loyalty and confidentiality, defrauds the

Continued on next page.

principal of the exclusive use of that information. Thus, instead of premising liability on a fiduciary relationship of a company insider who, the misappropriation theory premises liability on a fiduciary-turned-trader's deception of those who entrusted him with access to confidential information. Under the SEC's (P) Rule 10b5-2, a "duty of trust or confidence" exists whenever a person agrees to maintain information in confidence. The SEC (P) argues that, under Rule 10b5-2(b)(1) and the facts pleaded in the complaint, it has stated a claim on which relief can be granted. According to the SEC (P), Cuban (D) is liable under the misappropriation theory based on a duty created by his agreement to keep confidential the information that Mamma.com's CEO provided him and his breach of that duty when, without disclosing to Mamma.com his intent to trade in its stock based on the information, he sold his shares in the company. Cuban (D) counters that the SEC (P) must demonstrate that his conduct was deceptive under § 10(b) and that it has not done so. Cuban (D) contends that his liability under the misappropriation theory depends on the existence of a preexisting fiduciary or fiduciary-like relationship, which he asserts must be determined exclusively under state law. While state law can supply the requisite duty, it is not the exclusive source of the duty, and the source of the duty may be located elsewhere without violating the general rule against creating federal common law. For example, the SEC (P) can promulgate such a rule, provided the rule conforms to the SEC's (P) rulemaking authority. In addition, liability under the misappropriation theory does not depend on the existence of a preexisting fiduciary or fiduciary-like relationship. This raises the issue of whether breach of a legal duty arising by agreement can be the basis for misappropriation theory liability, and, if so, what are the essential components of the agreement. As previously noted, the misappropriation theory requires deception, where the misappropriator acts deceptively, not merely because he uses the source's material, nonpublic information for personal benefit, in breach of a duty not to do so, but because he does not disclose to the source that he intends to trade on or otherwise use the information. Therefore, trading on the basis of material, nonpublic information cannot be deceptive unless the trader is under a legal duty to refrain from trading on or otherwise using it for personal benefit. Where the trader and the information source are in a fiduciary relationship, this obligation arises by operation of law upon the creation of the relationship, because based on the fiduciary's duty of loyalty, the principal has a right to expect that the fiduciary is not trading on or otherwise using the principal's confidential information. There is no reason why such a duty cannot be created contractually, as the duty would arise out of a relationship between specific parties, albeit a contractual relationship, and not the mere possession of the confidential information. Indeed, the case for misappropriation liability is even stronger where the trader has expressly agreed to refrain from trading on the information. The agreement, however, must consist of

more than an express or implied promise to keep information confidential; it must also impose on the party who receives the information the legal duty to refrain from trading on or otherwise using the information for personal gain. That is because with respect to confidential information, nondisclosure and non-use are distinct concepts. A person may use information for his benefit without disclosing the information to others. Absent a duty not to use the information for personal benefit, there is no deception in doing so. Moreover, the duty cannot depend on one party's unilateral expectation that the other party will not use the information where the other party has not expressly agreed to not use it. Instead, the duty must rest on the other party's undertaking of a duty to refrain from doing so. Thus, while Cuban (D) is correct in asserting that an agreement must contain more than a promise of confidentiality, he is incorrect that the agreement must create a fiduciary-like relationship. Additionally, the enforcement of duties of nondisclosure and non-use that arise by agreement would promote the purpose of the misappropriation theory to protect the integrity of the securities markets and encourage investor confidence. The next issue is whether Cuban (D) entered into an agreement, whether express or implied, sufficient to create the duty necessary to establish under this theory. State common law is one source of law that can provide the answer. Under state common law, Cuban (D) can at best be determined to have agreed to not divulge the confidential information given him by Mamma.com's CEO. In this crucial regard, therefore, the SEC's (P) complaint is deficient, since it cannot show that Cuban (D) agreed to refrain from trading on or otherwise using for his own benefit the information the CEO shared with him. Cuban's (D) statement that he was "screwed" and "I can't sell" seem to express his belief, at least at the time, that it would be illegal for him to trade on the information he had received, but this belief by itself does not constitute an agreement to refrain from trading on the information. Nor is it sufficient that there was evidence that the company's executives or board members unilaterally expected that Cuban (D) would not sell until the PIPE was publicly announced. Outside a fiduciary or fiduciary-like relationship, a mere unilateral expectation on the part of the information source cannot create the predicate duty for misappropriation theory liability. For these reasons, the SEC (P) has failed to plead a duty arising by agreement. However, the SEC (P) also claims that such a duty may arise from Rule 10b5-2. Because the SEC's (P) rulemaking authority is bounded by the statute's proscription of conduct that is manipulative or deceptive, the SEC (P) cannot by rule predicate misappropriation liability on an agreement's breach of which lacks the necessary manipulation or deception. Here, Cuban's (D) agreement lacked the necessary component of an obligation not to trade on or otherwise use confidential information for his personal

Continued on next page.

benefit. His failure to disclose that he was doing so, therefore, is not deceptive under § 10(b) and Rule 10b-5. By its plain terms, Rule 10b5-2(b)(1) attempts to base misappropriation theory liability on an agreement that lacks an obligation not to trade on or otherwise use confidential information. The agreement specified in the Rule—"to maintain information in confidence"—relates merely to preserving the confidentiality of the information. There is nothing in the Rule's language or purpose that indicates it relates to anything in addition to a confidentiality agreement, as it is concerned with maintaining trust and confidentiality. Because Rule 10b5-2(b)(1) attempts to predicate misappropriation theory liability on a mere confidentiality agreement lacking a non-use component, the SEC (P) cannot rely on it to establish Cuban's (D) liability under the misappropriation theory. To permit liability based on Rule 10b5-2(b)(1) would exceed the SEC's § 10 (b) authority to proscribe conduct that is deceptive. Accordingly, Cuban's (D) motion to dismiss is granted, but the SEC (P) may replead its case.

MEMORANDUM OPINION AND ORDER:

In the court's prior ruling, the SEC (P) was given 30 days to file an amended complaint that included a well-pleaded claim that Cuban (D) undertook a duty, expressly or implicitly, not to trade on or otherwise use material, nonpublic information about the PIPE offering. The SEC (P) has notified the court that it does not intend to file an amended complaint. Consequently, the action against Cuban (D) is dismissed with prejudice.

▶ ANALYSIS

The Fifth Circuit accepted the SEC's (P) appeal and ruled that the case should not have been dismissed but should have been permitted to proceed. The SEC (P) argued before the appellate court that a confidentiality agreement creates a duty to disclose or abstain and that, regardless, the confidentiality agreement alleged in the complaint also contained an agreement not to trade on the information. The court of appeals based its decision exclusively on its interpretation of the complaint, and, accordingly, did not reach the issue of whether the SEC (P) overstepped its authority under section 10(b) in issuing Rule 10b5-2(b)(1). The court concluded that the allegations, taken in their entirety, provided more than a plausible basis to find that the understanding between the CEO and Cuban (D) was that he was not to trade, that it was more than a simple confidentiality agreement. By contacting the investment bank's sales representative to obtain the pricing information, Cuban (D) was able to evaluate his potential losses or gains from his decision to either participate or refrain from participating in the PIPE offering. Therefore, it was at least plausible that each of the parties understood, if only implicitly, that Mamma.com would only provide the terms and conditions of the offering to Cuban (D) for the purpose of evaluating whether he would participate in the offering,

and that Cuban (D) could not use the information for his own personal benefit. The court observed that it would require additional facts that had not been put before it to conclude that the parties could not plausibly have reached this shared understanding. Accordingly, it vacated and remanded the case to the district court.

Quicknotes

CONFIDENTIAL COMMUNICATIONS A communication made between specified classes of persons which is privileged.

FIDUCIARY DUTY A legal obligation to act for the benefit of another, including subordinating one's personal interests to that of the other person.

INSIDER INFORMATION Information regarding a corporation that is available only to insiders

Basic Inc. v. Levinson

Corporation (D) v. Shareholder (P)

485 U.S. 224 (1988).

NATURE OF CASE: Action brought under § 10(b) of the Securities and Exchange Act.

FACT SUMMARY: Levinson (P), representing a class of shareholders, brought an action against Basic Inc. (D) and its directors, asserting that Basic (D) issued three false or misleading public statements and thereby was in violation of § 10(b) of the Securities and Exchange Act.

🏛 RULE OF LAW
A public statement issued by a corporation violates § 10(b) of the Securities and Exchange Act if it is materially misleading.

FACTS: Prior to December 20, 1979, Basic Inc. (D) was a publicly traded company primarily engaged in the business of manufacturing chemical refractors for the steel industry. Beginning in 1976, Combustion Engineering, Inc., a company producing aluminum refractors, sought a merger with Basic (D). During 1977 and 1978, Basic (D) made three public statements denying it was engaged in merger negotiations. On December 18, 1978, Basic (D) asked the New York Stock Exchange to suspend trading in its shares and issued a release stating it had been "approached" by another company concerning a merger. On December 20, 1978, Basic (D) publicly announced its approval of Combustion's tender offer for all outstanding shares of Basic (D). Levinson (P), a shareholder of Basic, then brought a class action against Basic (D) asserting that Basic (D) and its directors had issued three false or misleading public statements and thereby were in violation of § 10(b) of the Securities and Exchange Act. Levinson (P) contended that the class was injured because class members sold Basic (D) shares at artificially depressed prices in a market affected by Basic's (D) misleading statements and in reliance thereon. The district court granted summary judgment for Basic (D), holding that as a matter of law, any misstatements made by Basic (D) were immaterial. The court of appeals reversed, holding that Basic's (D) statements were misleading. Basic (D) appealed.

ISSUE: Does a public statement issued by a corporation violate § 10(b) of the Securities and Exchange Act if it is materially misleading?

HOLDING AND DECISION: (Blackmun, J.) Yes. A public statement issued by a corporation violates § 10(b) of the Securities and Exchange Act if it is materially misleading. Whether merger discussions in any particular case are material will depend on the facts. To assess the magnitude of the transaction to the issuer of the securities allegedly manipulated, a fact-finder will need to consider such facts as the size of the two corporate entities and of potential premiums over market value. No particular event or factor short of closing the transaction need be either necessary or sufficient by itself to render merger discussions material. Materiality depends on the significance the reasonable investor would place on the misrepresented information. Here, in the merger context, materiality depended upon the probability that the transaction would be consummated and its significance to the issuer of securities, Basic Inc. (D). The court of appeals adopted the argument, with respect to materiality, that once Basic (D) made a statement denying the existence of merger discussions, even discussions that might not have been material in the absence of the denial were material because they made the statements untrue. This Court rejects the proposition that information becomes material by virtue of a public statement denying it, and thus remands the matter to that court to decide the issue of materiality consistent with this opinion. Vacated and remanded.

CONCURRENCE AND DISSENT: (White, J.) A congressional policy that the majority's opinion ignores is the strong preference the securities laws display for widespread public disclosure and distribution to investors of material information concerning securities. This congressionally adopted policy is expressed in the numerous and varied disclosure requirements found in the federal securities law scheme. This Court should limit its role in interpreting § 10(b) and Rule 10b-5 to one of giving effect to such policy decisions by Congress.

▌ ANALYSIS

The determination of an appropriate remedy is a private action under § 10(b) and Rule 10b-5 is a difficult problem whose solution depends on a number of variables. These include whether the corporation is closely or publicly held, whether the plaintiff is a buyer or a seller and whether the wrong is a misrepresentation or a wrongful disclosure. Often, as in many Rule 10b-5 problems, rules governing analogous torts provide a good framework of analysis, especially since Rule 10b-5 cases often rely upon tort concepts in the area of remedies.

▬■▬

Quicknotes

TENDER OFFER An offer made by one corporation to the shareholders of a target corporation to purchase their shares subject to number, time, and price specifications.

▬■▬

DeBaun v. First Western Bank and Trust Co.

Director (P) v. Corporation (D)

Cal. Ct. App., 46 Cal. App. 3d 686, 120 Cal. Rptr. 354 (1975).

NATURE OF CASE: Appeal from an award of damages upon a stockholders' derivative action.

FACT SUMMARY: First Western Bank and Trust Co. (D), trustee of a controlling number of shares in Johnson Corporation, sold the shares to the S.O.F. fund of which Mattison was trustee without checking out reports of Mattison's past questionable financial practices.

🏛 RULE OF LAW
A controlling shareholder owes a duty to his corporation, when selling his control in the corporation, of reasonable investigation and due care when possessed of facts establishing a reasonable likelihood that the purchaser of control intends to loot the corporation.

FACTS: Johnson Corporation was a modestly successful photo processor whose 100 outstanding shares were owned by Johnson. Subsequently, Johnson sold some shares including ten each to employees DeBaun (P) and Stephens (P), who became directors. At Johnson's death, his remaining 70 shares went to a testamentary trust of which First Western Bank and Trust Co (First Western) (D) was trustee. Under DeBaun's (P) and Stephen's (P) guidance the corporation became very successful, but First Western (D) secretly decided that it was not an appropriate trust investment and decided to sell the 70 shares. Mattison, the settlor and trustee of S.O.F. fund, made successive offers. Despite a Dun & Bradstreet report showing Mattison to be the principal in a number of bankruptcies, tax liens, and lawsuits and the personal knowledge of First Western's (D) vice-president of an unsatisfied judgment against Mattison acquired from First Western's (D) predecessor in interest, First Western (D) negotiated with Mattison. Mattison explained the unfraudable report by his practice of acquiring failing companies. In accepting Mattison's offer, First Western (D) allowed the corporate assets to secure the balance of the purchase price. First Western (D) failed to check public litigation records after seeing that Mattison was warmly received at the Jonathan Club, an exclusive private club. Los Angeles County public records would have revealed 38 unsatisfied judgments totaling $330,886; 54 pending actions totaling $373,588; 22 recorded abstracts of judgment totaling $285,204; and 18 tax liens amounting to $20,327, all against Mattison. As soon as Mattison acquired control of the corporation, he proceeded to intercept incoming funds, stopped paying creditors, and otherwise looted the corporation for his own benefit. The corporation, its net worth originally $220,000, was $200,000 in debt excluding its liability to First Western (D). First Western (D) sought appointment of a receiver, and after sale of its assets and payment of taxes, the corporation still owed $218,426 to creditors. DeBaun (P) and Stephens (P) brought a derivative action against First Western (D) alleging it breached its duty as majority shareholder. The trial court awarded $473,836 ($200,000, the value at time of sale to Mattison, plus an amount equal to anticipated after-tax earnings for a 10-year period at an 8 percent growth factor). This appeal followed.

ISSUE: When selling his controlling interest, does the controlling shareholder owe a duty to his corporation of reasonable investigation and due care when possessed of facts establishing a reasonable likelihood that the purchaser of control intends to loot the corporation?

HOLDING AND DECISION: (Thompson, J.) Yes. A controlling shareholder, when selling his control in the corporation, owes a duty to his corporation of reasonable investigation and due care when possessed of facts establishing a reasonable likelihood that the purchaser of control intends to loot the corporation. The duty of good faith and fairness of a majority stockholder encompasses an obligation, when in possession of questionable facts such as to awaken suspicion, and put a prudent man on his guard. Here, First Western (D) knew of the bad Dun & Bradstreet report, that Mattison's only source of funds lay in the corporation's assets, and that one of its officers was personally aware of an unsatisfied judgment. It could not rely upon Mattison's friendly reception at the Jonathan Club as an indication of financial stability. Mattison's explanation of the bad reports on him was questionable in light of the fact that he never saved one failing company. By selling its shares to Mattison, First Western (D) placed the corporation and its assets in peril. Its duty ran to both the corporation and the minority shareholders. As for the measure of damages, it was correct. Total damage to the corporation was the sum necessary to restore its net worth, plus the value of its tangible assets, plus its going business value determined with reference to future profits reasonably estimated. Since a derivative action is equitable, it was proper to frame damages in terms of an obligation dependent upon future contingencies rather than a fixed amount. Affirmed and remanded.

▶ ANALYSIS

Early case law held that a controlling shareholder owed no duty to minority shareholders or to the controlled corpora-

Continued on next page.

tion in the sale of his stock. Since then, it has been recognized as a fact of financial life that corporate control by ownership of a majority of shares may be misused. Thus, the applicable proposition now is that "in any transaction where the control of the corporation is material, the controlling majority shareholder must exercise good faith and fairness from the viewpoint of the corporation and those interested therein." It appears that most of the looting cases involve investment companies, i.e., companies whose principal or sole assets constituted cash and readily marketable securities.

■■■■■

Quicknotes

DUTY OF REASONABLE CARE Duty to exercise the degree of care as would a reasonably prudent person under like circumstances.

MAJORITY STOCKHOLDER A stockholder of a corporation who holds in excess of 50 percent of the corporation's shares.

■■■■■

Perlman v. Feldmann

Minority stockholder (P) v. Director (D)

219 F.2d 173 (2d Cir. 1955).

NATURE OF CASE: Stockholder derivative action for an accounting.

FACT SUMMARY: Feldmann (D), a director and dominant stockholder of Newport Steel, sold, along with others, the controlling interest of that steel manufacturer, to steel users, along with the right to control distribution.

🏛 RULE OF LAW
A corporate director who is also a dominant shareholder stands, in both situations, in a fiduciary relationship to both the corporation and the minority stockholders if selling controlling interest in the corporation is accountable to it (and the minority shareholders) to the extent that the sales price represents payment for the right to control.

FACTS: Feldmann (D) was director and dominant stockholder (he and his family owned controlling interest) of Newport Steel Corp. (Newport), a small steel-producing company. Though actually too small to compete with other steel suppliers, Newport was able to survive and thrive because of a severe steel shortage that existed at the time of this case and because of the so-called Feldmann plan. Under this plan, Newport was able to exact from buyers (who were desperate for steel) interest-free advances that permitted it to expand and finance operations without incurring normal financing costs (allowing it to compete with other steel suppliers). To avoid this and be assured of a higher percentage of Newport's steel, several independent steel users formed the Wilport Company. Though Newport stock had never been worth more than $12 per share, Wilport paid Feldmann (D) and his family $20 per share for controlling interest in Newport, which included control over distribution of steel (since Feldmann [D], directors, and officers quickly resigned and were replaced by Wilport nominees). Perlman (P), a minority stockholder in Newport, sued Feldmann (D) for an accounting for all profits gained from his sale of the controlling interest, charging a breach of fiduciary duty in depriving Newport of future Feldmann plan benefits by selling to someone whose purpose in buying was to circumvent the Feldmann plan pressures. From judgment for Feldmann (D), Perlman (P) appealed.

ISSUE: May a controlling shareholder and corporate director be held accountable for profits from sale of controlling interest?

HOLDING AND DECISION: (Clark, C.J.) Yes. A controlling shareholder and corporate director may be held accountable for profits from sale of controlling interest. A corporate director, who is also a dominant shareholder, stands, in both situations, in a fiduciary relationship to both the corporation and the minority stockholders (as beneficiaries of the fiduciary relationship), and, where such a director-shareholder sells controlling interest in the corporation, he is accountable to it and the minority shareholders, thereby, to the extent that the sales price represents payment for the right to control. Directors of a corporation act in a strictly fiduciary capacity. Their office is a trust. They must not in any degree allow their official conduct to be determined by their private interests. This same rule should apply to controlling stockholders as well. In both cases, their actions are subject to strict scrutiny by the courts. The burden is upon them to justify their actions and establish their undivided loyalty to the corporation. Here, Feldmann (D) quite obviously acted in self-interest and to the detriment of the corporation and the minority shareholders. His actions in siphoning off, for personal gain, the value of market advantages sold to Wilport, to the detriment of Newport (they lose Feldmann plan advantages), violate his trust relationship with Newport. The decision below is reversed and remanded to the trial court for determination of damages i.e., the exact increment in the sales price attributable to control. Reversed and remanded.

DISSENT: (Swan, J.) Justice Swan points out that the majority does not clearly delineate what fiduciary duties are owed as directors, and what duties are owed as controlling stockholders. Further, ignoring the loss of Feldmann plan benefits, he sees no detriment to the minority here in permitting the sale to Wilport.

▶ ANALYSIS

This case points out the clear trend of authority that attributes liability to controlling stockholders for sale of corporate control. Note the manner of proof here. The fact that "control" was the object of Wilport is to be inferred from the fact that they obviously bought so as to avoid the Feldmann plan. Minority shareholders, of course, feared worse. Even though it had not yet occurred, it is obvious that minority stockholders feared a *Gerdes v. Reynolds* situation (28 N.Y.S.2d 6221, 650 [N.Y. App. Div. 1941]), in which control is purchased in order to permit waste of corporate assets. To be sure, Wilport companies have little reason to care about Newport progress, and every reason, in the steel shortage, to take Newport for all it's worth, forcing it to operate at little or no profit. As

Continued on next page.

such, this case may be viewed as a further step in protecting minority stockholder interests from abuse.

∎▬∎

Quicknotes

FIDUCIARY DUTY A legal obligation to act for the benefit of another, including subordinating one's personal interests to that of the other person.

MAJORITY STOCKHOLDER A stockholder of a corporation who holds in excess of 50 percent of the corporation's shares.

MINORITY STOCKHOLDER A stockholder in a corporation controlling such a small portion of those shares which are outstanding that its votes have no influence in the management of the corporation.

∎▬∎

Indemnification and Insurance

Quick Reference Rules of Law

Merritt-Chapman & Scott Corp. v. Wolfson

Corporation (D) v. Corporate agents (P)

Del. Super. Ct., 321 A.2d 138 (1974).

NATURE OF CASE: Motion for summary judgment in an action for indemnification.

FACT SUMMARY: Wolfson (P) was criminally charged, tried and sentenced, and sought to be indemnified by Merritt-Chapman & Scott Corporation (MCS) (D) for the costs of legal defense.

🏛 **RULE OF LAW**
Corporate agents, criminally charged for their conduct in regard to their corporation, are entitled to indemnification for the costs of their legal defense only on those indictment counts on which they are successful even if unsuccessful on another related count.

FACTS: Wolfson (P), Gerbert (P), Kosow (P), and Staub (P), agents of Merritt-Chapman & Scott Corporation (MCS) (D), were criminally charged on various counts resulting out of a plan to cause MCS (D) to purchase secretly hundreds of thousands of shares of its own common stock in violation of federal securities laws. The charges were settled as follows: Wolfson (P) pleaded nolo contendere to a count of filing false annual reports and other charges were dropped upon a $10,000 fine and an 18-month suspended sentence; Gerbert (P) agreed not to appeal his conviction for perjury before the Securities and Exchange Commission (SEC) and was fined $2,000 with an 18 month suspended sentence; and all other charges including all charges against Kosow (P) and Staub (P) were dropped. Each sought to be indemnified by MCS (D) for the costs of their legal defense. Both sides moved for summary judgment, MCS (D) arguing that no indemnification should be granted.

ISSUE: Are corporate agents, criminally charged for their conduct in regard to their corporation, entitled to indemnification for the costs of their legal defense on those indictment counts on which they are successful, even if unsuccessful on another related count?

HOLDING AND DECISION: (Balick, J.) Yes. Corporate agents, criminally charged for their conduct in regard to their corporation, are entitled to indemnification for the costs of their legal defense only on those indictment counts on which they are successful, even if unsuccessful on another related count. Success is vindication and any result other than conviction must be considered success. Complete success is not required. Although a corporation may pass a by-law making mandatory a provision for permissive indemnification, MCS (D) was empowered to indemnify except in relation to matters as to which any such director or officer or person shall be found liable for negligence or misconduct in the performance of duty. If an action does not go to judgment, MCS (D) could determine whether the agent has been derelict or negligent. Conviction established Wolfson (P) and Gerbert (P) to be derelict as to those counts that were not dropped. Thus, they are not entitled to indemnification for expenses related to their convictions.

▶ **ANALYSIS**

The invariant policy of Delaware legislation on indemnification is to "promote the desirable end that corporate officials will resist what they consider" unjustified suits and claims, "secure in the knowledge that their reasonable expenses will be borne by the corporation that they have served if they are to be vindicated." Beyond that, its larger purpose is "to encourage capable men to serve as corporate directors, secure in the knowledge that expenses incurred by them in upholding their honesty and integrity as directors will be borne by the corporation they serve." Ernest L. Folk, *The Delaware General Corporation Law*, 98 (1972), Little, Brown & Co.

◼▬◼

Quicknotes

8 DEL. C. § 145(a) A corporation may indemnify director, officer, employer against expenses for defending suits.

8 DEL. C. § 145(c) Requires corporations to indemnify directors, officers, and employers who successfully defend suits.

INDEMNIFICATION The payment by a corporation of expenses incurred by its officers or directors as a result of litigation involving the corporation.

◼▬◼

Aleynikov v. Goldman Sachs Group, Inc.

Former employee (P) v. Corporation (D)

2013 WL 5739137 (D.N.J. 2013).

NATURE OF CASE: Action seeking indemnification and advancement of legal fees pursuant to corporate bylaws.

FACT SUMMARY: Aleynikov (P) contended that under the bylaws of Goldman, Sachs Group, Inc. ("GS Group" or "Goldman") (D), he was entitled to advancement and indemnification of legal fees and expenses because he qualified as an "officer" of Goldman, Sachs & Co. (GSCo), a GS Group (D) subsidiary, and the litigation for which he was seeking indemnification or advancement arose in connection with his being an officer of GSCo.

🏛 RULE OF LAW
Under a bylaw provision that provides for advancement and indemnification of legal fees and expenses for officers under specified circumstances, an employee whose title is "vice president" qualifies as an "officer" for purposes of the provision where no evidence is presented to contradict the plain and commonly understood meaning of that term.

FACTS: Aleynikov (P) was employed by Goldman, Sachs & Co. (GSCo), a subsidiary of Goldman, Sachs Group, Inc. ("GS Group" or "Goldman") (D). His title was "vice president," and he worked as part of a team of computer programmers responsible for developing source code relating to GSCo's high frequency trading system. This proprietary code, alleged to be a trade secret, enhanced the quality of the firm's analysis and decision-making in the trading business. GSCo was a limited liability partnership organized under the laws of New York. After working for GSCo for around two years, Aleynikov (P) accepted an employment offer from Teza Technologies. Before leaving GSCo, Aleynikov (P) allegedly copied and transmitted to his home computer and other devices hundreds of thousands of lines of confidential source code. About a month later, Aleynikov (P) flew to Teva's offices carrying a laptop and flash drive that allegedly contained the stolen source code. Immediately upon his return, he was arrested by the FBI and charged federally in the Southern District of New York (the "Federal Case"). Although the district court convicted Aleynikov (P) of several federal crimes, the court of appeals reversed, concluding that although Aleynikov (P) had breached his confidentiality obligations to Goldman (D), his conduct did not fall within the scope of the charged federal offenses. Accordingly, he was acquitted. Two months later, he was rearrested on the same charges, and indicted in state court (the "State Case"). Aleynikov (P) brought suit against GS Group (D)

seeking indemnification for legal fees and expenses he had already incurred in the Federal Case, and sought advancement of legal fees and expenses for his ongoing defense of the State Case. He based his action on a GS Group (D) bylaw provision, which provided for indemnity and advancement of legal fees and expenses for an "officer" "of a Subsidiary of the Corporation," where the litigation at issue arose by reason of the fact that the individual was an "officer" of the corporation or its subsidiary. The term "officer" for a non-corporate subsidiary entity, such as GSCo, was defined as encompassing "in addition to any officer of such entity, any person serving in a similar capacity or as the manager of such entity." Aleynikov (P) argued that, as a "vice president," he was an officer under the "plain and commonly-understood meaning" of the term. Goldman (D) countered that Aleynikov's (P) job designation reflected title inflation in the financial services industry. Aleynikov (P) moved for summary judgment on both his request for indemnification and for advancement.

ISSUE: Under a bylaw provision that provides for advancement and indemnification of legal fees and expenses for officers under specified circumstances, does an employee whose title is "vice president" qualify as an "officer" for purposes of the provision where no evidence is presented to contradict the plain and commonly understood meaning of that term?

HOLDING AND DECISION: (McNulty, J.) Yes. Under a bylaw provision that provides for advancement and indemnification of legal fees and expenses for officers under specified circumstances, an employee whose title is "vice president" qualifies as an "officer" for purposes of the provision where no evidence is presented to contradict the plain and commonly understood meaning of that term. There is a fundamental distinction between indemnification and advancement. Indemnification is a claim for fees incurred in a case that has already concluded in plaintiff's favor; it is a claim for damages based on events concluded in the past. Advancement of fees, on the other hand, is designed to fund an ongoing case, and the recipient of the funds is required to pay them back should he be unsuccessful in that case. Even if Aleynikov (P) ultimately will be entitled to indemnification, his current request for it must be denied, mostly as a matter of procedural fairness. Advancement is both time-sensitive (the funds are needed in pending legal proceedings now) and provisional (the funds must be paid back if plaintiff is not successful). As to indemnification, however, neither is true. Therefore, sum-

Continued on next page.

mary judgment is denied as to indemnification, and, when both sides' remaining claims are ripe, such motions may be entertained, or tried. The availability of advancement and indemnification depends on whether Aleynikov (P) was an "officer" of GSCo within the meaning of the GS Group (D) bylaws. The bylaws restrict indemnification and advancement to particular persons, including "officers," a defined term. Aleynikov (P) claims he was an officer of a GS Group (D) non-corporate subsidiary entity, since GSCo was a limited liability partnership. The bylaw's phrasing for this category of officer is less than clear, since it states that "the term 'officer' shall include in addition to any officer of such entity. . . ." Thus, for a non-corporate subsidiary, an "officer" is defined as, inter alia, "any officer." In the corporate context, a vice president is typically considered an officer. In a non-corporate partnership entity like GSCo, however, "officer" and "vice president" have no fixed definition. Moreover, it does not appear that Aleynikov (P), a computer programmer, performed functions normally associated with the status of officer or manager. Because the definition of a non-corporate "officer" in GS Group's (D) bylaws is circular and unhelpful, it is ambiguous. Aleynikov (P) argues that this ambiguity should be construed against GS Group (D), which counters that it has a process of appointment that clearly distinguishes between officers and non-officers. However, this policy is not in writing. Under a broad reading of the bylaws, supported by public policy favoring indemnification and advancement, the bylaws' plain language, supplemented by case law interpretations, suggests that a vice president be considered an officer. Because the bylaws grant advancement to the fullest extent of the law, they must be read to implement the strong policy favoring advancement. The statutory policy, and, concomitantly the bylaws, requires immediate assistance, postponing the issue of whether such assistance is deserved. It does not distinguish between "worthy" and "unworthy" recipients, and it does not distinguish between claims brought by the corporate entity and claims brought by outsiders. In contrast to indemnification, which is reserved for persons who prevail in the underlying case, advancement is indifferent as to the underlying merits. Thus, with advancement, the statute almost explicitly prioritizes speed over accuracy. However, the advancement remedy has a backstop, since it is provisional to the extent that a person who receives advancement of fees must furnish an "undertaking" to pay them back if he or she is unsuccessful in the underlying litigation. In sum, advancement is urgent and the applicant's defense must be funded "now," while the action is pending. Here, in light of these considerations, even if it is true as Goldman (D) contends that Aleynikov's (P) job designation reflects title inflation in the financial services industry, where vice president is merely a functional title, because it connotes a level of seniority between associate and managing director, and as distinguished from an officer title, which is somebody who has been appointed through the process, this contention does not help Gold-

man (D). While it may be the case that Goldman (D) (or the industry of which it is a part) has been profligate in conferring the title of vice president, Goldman (D) must bear the consequences of that profligacy. Goldman (D) might easily have chosen to be more sparing with job titles, or to confer them in some other way, and it might easily have drafted its bylaws to restrict indemnification to a well-defined class, but it did none of these things. Accordingly, Aleynikov (P) is entitled to advancement. He is entitled to advancement of (1) reasonable fees and expenses incurred to date for Aleynikov's (P) legal defense in the State Case; (2) reasonable fees and expenses that he incurs for his ongoing defense in the State Case, on a rolling basis until a final judgment is reached; and (3) "fees on fees," i.e., fees and expenses in this action that can reasonably be apportioned and attributed to the issue of advancement. Summary judgment for Aleynikov (P) as to advancement.

▶ *ANALYSIS*

As this case emphasizes, the right to indemnification and the right to advancement are "separate and distinct." Indemnification depends upon whether the officer's defense in underlying litigation has succeeded. Advancement, by contrast, depends on the pendency, not the merits, of the claims asserted against the corporate official. Notwithstanding the rights are distinct and separate, the public policy served by authorizing both the advancement and indemnification of litigation expenses is singular and well-settled. Without these rights, corporations would find it difficult to retain high-quality directors and officers, willing to make socially useful decisions that involve economic risk. By authorizing indemnity and advancement within certain guidelines, the corporation law seeks to encourage well-qualified persons to serve as directors and officers of corporations and, in that capacity, to be willing to commit their corporations, after the exercise of good faith and care, to risky transactions that promise a lucrative economic return. Because of the public policy favoring these rights, and the courts' liberal interpretation of indemnification and advancement provisions to further that public policy, the drafters of these provisions should take great care to precisely define which employees qualify as officers and to tailor the definition of "officer" to include only a "well-defined class."

■=■

Quicknotes

INDEMNIFICATION The payment by a corporation of expenses incurred by its officers or directors as a result of litigation involving the corporation.

■=■

McCullough v. Fidelity & Deposit Co.

[Parties not identified.]

2 F.3d 110 (5th Cir. 1993).

NATURE OF CASE: Appeal from judgment granting the defendant's motion for summary judgment in a declaratory judgment action.

FACT SUMMARY: When Fidelity & Deposit Co. (D) canceled the liability policies covering claims against officers and directors of certain insolvent banks, refusing to defend those officers and directors, the Federal Deposit Insurance Corporation (P) brought this action.

🏛 RULE OF LAW
An insurer must provide coverage for claims made after a policy expires, as long as the insured notifies the insurer of any specified wrongful act, error, or omission that may later give rise to a claim being made against its directors or officers.

FACTS: Fidelity & Deposit Co. (F & D) (D) issued liability policies, covering claims made against insured officers and directors if the required notice was given to the insurer during the policy period, to four affiliate banks and three subsidiaries. Due to increasing loan losses and delinquencies, F & D (D) informed the banks that it intended to cancel their policies. The Office of the Comptroller of the Currency (OCC) issued a cease-and-desist order to one of the subsidiaries by its primary regulator. After the banks were declared insolvent, the Federal Deposit Insurance Corporation (FDIC) (P) sued the directors and officers for improperly making, administering, or collecting loans. F & D (D) denied coverage to the officers and directors under the policies. FDIC (P) then filed this action. The court, finding that FDIC (P) had failed to show that F & D (D) received written notice of a potential claim under the policy, granted summary judgment to F & D (D). FDIC (P) timely appealed.

ISSUE: Will coverage be provided if the insured notifies the insurer of any specified wrongful act, error, or omission that may later give rise to a claim?

HOLDING AND DECISION: (Davis, J.) Yes. An insurer must provide coverage for claims made after a policy expires as long as the insured notifies the insurer of any act, error, or omission which may later give rise to a claim being made against its directors and officers. In this case, the insured banks did not furnish F & D (D) with a copy of the cease-and-desist order and gave F & D (D) no notice of the particular subsidiary involved, the particular agents, officers, or directors involved, the time period during which the events occurred, the identity of potential claimants, or the specific unsound practices that were the basis of the order. Notice of an institution's worsening financial condition, which the banks did give, is not notice of an officer's or director's act, error, or omission. Moreover, rising delinquencies and bad loan portfolios are insufficient to constitute such notice. Affirmed.

▶ ANALYSIS

Claims against an insured covered by "occurrence" policies—i.e., those policies that cover injuries occurring during the policy period, regardless of when the loss is actually reported—may not surface for years. Toxic tort claims covered by such policies may cause financial havoc for an insurer. Therefore, directors' and officers' liability (D&O) policies are limited to "claims made" policies that only cover claims asserted against a company during the policy period.

■═■

Quicknotes

CEASE AND DESIST ORDER An order from a court or administrative agency prohibiting a person or business from continuing a particular course of conduct.

■═■

Takeovers

Quick Reference Rules of Law

CTS Corp. v. Dynamics Corp. of America

Target corporation (D) v. Acquiring corporation (P)

481 U.S. 69 (1987).

NATURE OF CASE: Review of order invalidating the Indiana Business Corporations Law as to tender offers.

FACT SUMMARY: Dynamics Corp. of America (P) contended that the tender offer provisions of the Indiana Business Corporations Law were invalid.

🏛 RULE OF LAW
The tender offer provisions of the Indiana Business Corporations Law are valid.

FACTS: In 1986, Indiana enacted the Indiana Business Corporations Law. Part of the statute concerned tender offers. The law provided that the makers of tender offers to corporations incorporated in Indiana or having their principal place of business there had to comply with certain rules. One rule required the offeree's shareholders to approve a takeover, or the acquired shares would not confer voting rights. Provisions also create a 50-day waiting period from announcement to actual offer. Dynamics Corp. of America (P), which had made a tender offer for control of CTS Corp. (D), an Indiana entity, challenged the law. The district court held the law preempted by the Williams Act and contrary to the dormant Commerce Clause. The Seventh Circuit affirmed. CTS (D) appealed.

ISSUE: Are the tender offer provisions of the Indiana Business Corporations Law valid?

HOLDING AND DECISION: (Powell, J.) Yes. The tender offer provisions of the Indiana Business Corporations Law are valid. The Williams Act, the federal law regulating tender offers, does not specifically preempt state law. Therefore, preemption will occur only if the laws contain inconsistent provisions such that mutual compliance is impossible, or if the state law violates the intention behind the federal law. Here, compliance with both laws is possible. Further, it appears that the intention behind the Williams Act was to protect shareholders by guaranteeing a "level playing field" between the offeror and management. The law here gives power directly to the shareholders, which is a different approach than that of the Williams Act but not inconsistent therewith. As to the dormant Commerce Clause, the law here does not discriminate against interstate commerce. While it may hinder tender offers, nothing in the Commerce Clause prevents states from regulating the procedures used by and concerning its corporations which, after all, are purely creatures of state law. Thus, neither the Williams Act nor the Commerce Clause is violated by the law, and it is therefore valid. Reversed.

CONCURRENCE: (Scalia, J.) The Commerce Clause analysis requires only a finding that no discrimination against interstate regulation exists, or that no likelihood of inconsistent state regulation exists.

DISSENT: (White, J.) The law in question undermines the Williams Act by effectively preventing minority shareholders from selling their stock if the majority does not ratify the offer.

▶ ANALYSIS

The prior Supreme Court ruling regarding antitakeover laws was *Edgar v. Mite Corp.,* 457 U.S. 624 (1982). That action involved a challenge to an Illinois law that required governmental approval of tender offers. The Court, in a plurality opinion, found this to upset the balance between offeror and management struck by the Act.

◼▬◼

Quicknotes

DORMANT COMMERCE CLAUSE The regulatory effect of the Commerce Clause on state activity affecting interstate commerce, where Congress itself has not acted to control the activity; a provision inferred from, but not expressly present in, the language of the Commerce Clause.

INDIANA CONTROL SHARE ACQUISITIONS CHAPTER Provides rules regarding the acquisition of controlling shares in Indiana corporations; majority of preexisting disinterested shareholders must approve.

PREEMPTION Judicial preference recognizing the procedure of federal legislation over state legislation of the same subject matter.

TENDER OFFER An offer made by one corporation to the shareholders of a target corporation to purchase their shares subject to number, time, and price specifications.

WILLIAMS ACT Federal rules for tender offers.

◼▬◼

Moran v. Household Int'l., Inc.

Director (P) v. Corporation (D)

Del. Sup. Ct., 500 A.2d 1346 (1985).

NATURE OF CASE: Appeal from enforcement of a Preferred Share Purchase Rights Plan.

FACT SUMMARY: Moran (P) contended that the Household Int'l. Inc.'s (D) board of directors lacked authority to thwart takeover bids through the use of a Preferred Share Purchase Rights Plan.

🏛 RULE OF LAW

Boards of directors may, under the business judgment rule, validly protect the corporation from hostile takeovers through the use of a Preferred Share Purchase Rights Program.

FACTS: In an attempt to thwart hostile takeover attempts, the board of directors of Household Int'l., Inc. (Household) (D) adopted an amendment to its bylaws which provided that if a tender offer for 30 percent of the corporation's shares were announced, or if any one entity obtained 20 percent or more of the outstanding stock, common stockholders were entitled to the issuance of one Right per common share. Each Right then is entitled to purchase a fractional amount of a new preferred stock. If the Right is not redeemed, following a takeover, the holder can purchase $200 worth of the common stock of the tender offer. A shareholder of Household (D) sued, contending such a plan was beyond the power of the board of directors. The trial court upheld the plan, and Moran (P) appealed.

ISSUE: May boards of directors validly protect the corporation from hostile takeovers through the use of a Preferred Share Purchase Rights Program?

HOLDING AND DECISION: (McNeilly, J.) Yes. Boards of directors may, under the business judgment rule, validly protect the corporation from hostile takeovers through the use of a Preferred Share Purchase Rights Program. The Rights were intended to and will be exercised upon the occurrence of the triggering events. Thus, the plan cannot be considered a sham and was implemented with the best interests of the corporation in mind. This use of such a plan does not alter the structure by which the corporation is controlled, and, therefore, it was a valid defensive mechanism. Affirmed.

▶ ANALYSIS

Hostile takeovers have prompted many potential target corporations to adopt defensive tactics such as that illustrated in the present case. Such mechanisms are aimed at making the target less attractive by making the takeover more expensive. Differing levels of voting power triggered by a threshold level of concentrated ownership is a typical defensive device.

Quicknotes

BUSINESS JUDGMENT RULE Doctrine relieving corporate directors and/or officers from liability for decisions honestly and rationally made in the corporation's best interests.

PROXY CONTEST A solicitation of proxies in order to oppose another proxy solicitation regarding the election or removal of a corporation's directors.

TENDER OFFER An offer made by one corporation to the shareholders of a target corporation to purchase their shares subject to number, time, and price specifications.

Mentor Graphics Corporation v. Quickturn Design Systems, Inc.

Hostile bidder (P) v. Corporation (D)

Del. Ch. Ct., 728 A.2d 25 (1998).

NATURE OF CASE: Challenge of poison pill rights plan.

FACT SUMMARY: Mentor Graphics Corp. (Mentor) (P) challenged the legality of a "no hand" rights plan of limited duration that the target company, Quickturn Design Systems, Inc. (D), adopted in response to Mentor's (P) tender offer and proxy contest.

🏛 RULE OF LAW
Where a board of a Delaware corporation takes action to resist or defend against a hostile bid for control, the defensive actions are subjected to enhanced judicial scrutiny lest the board be acting in its own, rather than the corporation's, interest.

FACTS: Mentor Graphics Corp. (Mentor) (P), an Oregon electronics corporation, launched a hostile tender offer for the acquisition of Quickturn Design Systems, Inc. (Quickturn) (D), a Delaware electronics business. Quickturn (D) decided the offer was inadequate and adopted two defensive measures in response to the hostile takeover bid. First, a new By-Law Amendment was enacted providing for special stockholders meetings to take place 90 to 100 days after the receipt of the shareholders request. Second, Quickturn (D) amended its shareholders rights plan by eliminating the "dead hand" feature and replacing it with a Deferred Redemption Plan (DRP). The effect of these amendments was to delay any special meeting and delay the ability of the new board to redeem the poison pill for six months. Mentor (P) claimed that the DRP violated Delaware law and sought an injunction and declaratory judgment to that effect. Quickturn (D) moved for summary judgment but its motion was denied.

ISSUE: Where a board of a Delaware corporation takes action to resist or defend against a hostile bid for control, are the defensive actions subjected to enhanced judicial scrutiny lest the board be acting in its own, rather than the corporation's, interest?

HOLDING AND DECISION: (Jacobs, V. Chan.) Yes. Where a board of a Delaware corporation takes action to resist or defend against a hostile bid for control, the defensive actions are subjected to enhanced judicial scrutiny lest the board be acting in its own, rather than the corporation's, interest. For a target board's actions to be entitled to business judgment rule protection, the target board must establish that it had reasonable grounds to believe that the hostile bid constituted a threat to corporate policy and that the defensive measures were proportionate or reasonable. The board here reasonably perceived a cog-

nizable threat, but the DRP was disproportionate. The bylaw provision was valid but the DRP was invalid.

▶ ANALYSIS

The court found that the DRP could not pass the proportionality test. The purpose of the DRP was to protract the delay by another six months. The board failed to show why the additional six months delay was necessary to achieve its stated purpose for its adoption.

Quicknotes

HOSTILE TAKEOVER Refers to a situation in which an outside group attempts to seize control of a target corporation against the will of the targeted company's officers, directors, or shareholders.

POISON PILL A tactic employed by a company, which is the target of a takeover attempt, to make the purchase of its shares less attractive to a potential buyer by requiring the issuance of a new series of shares to be redeemed at a substantial premium over their stated value if a party purchases a specified percentage of voting shares of the corporation.

PROXY CONTEST A solicitation of proxies in order to oppose another proxy solicitation regarding the election or removal of a corporation's directors.

TENDER OFFER An offer made by one corporation to the shareholders of a target corporation to purchase their shares subject to number, time, and price specifications.

International Brotherhood of Teamsters v. Fleming Companies

Shareholders (P) v. Corporation (D)

Okla. Sup. Ct., 975 P.2d 907 (1999).

NATURE OF CASE: Certified question regarding shareholder rights plans.

FACT SUMMARY: International Brotherhood of Teamsters General Fund (P) owned 65 shares of Fleming Companies, Inc. (D) and wanted to restrict Fleming's (D) ability to adopt anti-takeover measures without shareholder approval.

> 🏛 **RULE OF LAW**
> Shareholders may, through proper channels of corporate governance, restrict the board of directors' authority to implement shareholder rights plans.

FACTS: International Brotherhood of Teamsters General Fund (Teamsters) (P) owned 65 shares of Fleming Companies, Inc. (D). Fleming (D) implemented a shareholder rights plan as an anti-takeover mechanism. Teamsters (P) alleged that the plan was a means of entrenching the current Fleming (D) board of directors in the event Fleming (D) became the target of a takeover. Teamsters (P) prepared a proxy statement and proposal that any rights plan be put to the shareholders for a majority vote. Fleming (D) refused to include the Teamsters' (P) resolution in its 1997 proxy statement and Teamsters (P) sued in federal court. The district court ruled in favor of Teamsters (P) and Fleming (D) appealed to the Tenth Circuit Court of Appeals, which submitted the certified question to the Oklahoma Supreme Court.

ISSUE: May shareholders, through proper channels of corporate governance, restrict the board of directors' authority to implement shareholder rights plans?

HOLDING AND DECISION: (Simms, J.) Yes. Shareholders may, through proper channels of corporate governance, restrict the board of directors' authority to implement shareholder rights plans. There is no exclusive authority granted boards of directors to create and implement shareholder rights plans, where shareholders' objection passes through official channels. Shareholders may restrict the board authority to implement shareholder rights plans.

> ▶ **ANALYSIS**
>
> The court noted that the Oklahoma legislature had not enacted a share rights plan endorsement statute. At least twenty-four states have enacted such statutes. The court found that a certificate of incorporation that is silent on the issue does not preclude shareholder-enacted bylaws regarding the implementation of rights plans.

Quicknotes

ARTICLES OF INCORPORATION Written instrument that gives rise to the existence of a corporation when filed with the appropriate governmental agency.

BYLAWS Rules promulgated by a corporation regulating its governance.

POISON PILL A tactic employed by a company, which is the target of a takeover attempt, to make the purchase of its shares less attractive to a potential buyer by requiring the issuance of a new series of shares to be redeemed at a substantial premium over their stated value if a party purchases a specified percentage of voting shares of the corporation.

Corporate Books and Records

Quick Reference Rules of Law

Thomas & Betts Corporation v. Leviton Manufacturing Co., Inc.

Acquiring corporation (P) v. Target corporation (D)

Del. Sup. Ct., 681 A.2d 1026 (1996).

NATURE OF CASE: Appeal from decision limiting inspection of corporation's books and records.

FACT SUMMARY: Thomas & Betts Corp. (P) sought to compel inspection of Leviton Manufacturing Co. Inc.'s (D) corporate books and records in order to effectuate its acquisition of Leviton (D).

🏛 RULE OF LAW
When a stockholder seeks to compel inspection of a corporation's books and records, he must demonstrate by a preponderance of the evidence that he is motivated by a proper purpose relevant to the inspection of each document requested.

FACTS: Thomas & Betts (P), a New Jersey electronics corporation, showed an interest in a possible union with Leviton Manufacturing (Leviton) (D), a Delaware corporation and manufacturer of electronic components. Harold Leviton, the company's (D) President and CEO, was also a majority stockholder and controlled a voting trust of 76.45 percent of Leviton's (D) Class A stock. Thomas & Betts (P) sought to acquire a minority of shares in Leviton (D) in order to attempt a merger between the two companies. Thomas & Betts (P) entered into secret negotiations with Thomas Blumberg and his wife, members of the Leviton family, who owned 29.1 percent of Leviton's (D) stock. Thomas & Betts (P) purchased the Blumberg's stock for $50 million, with the potential of their receiving another $20 million if the sale were completed. When Harold Leviton was notified of the sale, he attempted to repurchase the shares sold by Blumberg. Thomas & Betts (P) executed a formal written demand for inspection of Leviton's (D) corporate books and records. A final offer of $250 million for Leviton's (D) remaining shares was extended. Leviton (D) rejected both the offer to purchase the shares and the demand for inspection. Thomas & Betts (P) initiated suit to compel the inspection. The Court of Chancery narrowly limited the scope of Thomas & Betts's (P) inspection of Leviton's (D) records for valuation purposes only. Thomas & Betts (P) appealed.

ISSUE: When a stockholder seeks to compel inspection of a corporation's books and records, must he prove by a preponderance of evidence the existence of a proper purpose permitting him to examine each document requested?

HOLDING AND DECISION: (Veasey, C.J.) Yes. When a stockholder seeks to compel inspection of a corporation's books and records, he must demonstrate by a preponderance of the evidence that he is motivated by a proper purpose relevant to the inspection of each docu-

ment requested. The burden of proof is on the complaining shareholder to show he is motivated by a proper purpose related to his investment in the corporation. In satisfying that burden, the shareholder must present credible evidence substantiating his allegations. The trial court incorrectly stated the shareholder's burden as "greater-than-normal." However, the overstated evidentiary burden was not the reason for the trial court's refusal to allow inspection. Thomas & Betts (P) proffered two purposes for the inspection, the investigation of possible waste and mismanagement of the assets of the corporation, and the valuation of its shares. In determining the propriety of a shareholder's declared purpose, the court reviewing the decision must give great deference to the trial court's factual determinations. Although the investigation of possible waste and mismanagement is a proper purpose to compel shareholder inspection of a company's books and records, here the evidence fails to substantiate Thomas & Betts's (P) allegations. Rather, the court concluded that Thomas & Betts's (P) true motivation was to coerce Leviton (D) into a sale of substantially all its assets. As such, the purpose was improper as adverse to Leviton's (D) best interests. However, the trial court permitted Thomas & Betts's (P) limited inspection of Leviton's (D) records for the specific purpose of appraising the value of its shares as a minority shareholder. Such a decision is consistent with the trial court's broad discretion in prescribing the proper extent of the shareholder's inspection. Affirmed.

▶ ANALYSIS

The definition of a proper purpose warranting a shareholders' inspection of the corporation's books and records is generally stated as a purpose related to the individual's economic interests in the company. Thus, courts generally permit inspection in circumstances where the shareholder seeks to advance either his own interests or those of the corporation. Conversely, a motion to compel inspection will be denied where the shareholder's motivations in seeking inspection are for purposes adverse to the interests of the corporation.

■=■

Quicknotes

DEL. GEN. CORP. LAW, § 220(b) Allows for the inspection of corporate records by shareholders with a proper purpose.

■=■

Paul v. China MediaExpress Holdings, Inc.

Shareholder (P) v. Corporation (D)

Del. Ch. Ct., 2012 WL 28818 (2012)

NATURE OF CASE: Action to inspect books and records of a corporation.

FACT SUMMARY: Paul (P) a shareholder of China MediaExpress Holdings, Inc. (CME) (D), sought to inspect CME's (D) books and records for the purpose of investigating fraud and mismanagement and the ability of the board to act independently and in good faith.

🏛 RULE OF LAW

(1) A shareholder demonstrates a proper purpose for a books and records inspection demand—to investigate fraud and mismanagement and the ability of the board to act independently and in good faith—where there is a credible basis for suspicion of waste and mismanagement based on numerous third-party media reports alleging fraudulent conduct, the halting of trading by a stock exchange, delisting of the company's shares, the resignation of the company's independent auditors, the noisy resignations of board members and executives, as well as the initiation of the company's own internal investigation.

(2) A books and records inspection demand will not be stayed pending the outcome of federal litigation where the risk of the plaintiffs in the federal action obtaining state discovery is minimal; where there is minimal risk of inconsistency between a judgment in the state action and a ruling in the federal action; and where the state action will not create an unreasonable discovery burden for the federal defendant.

FACTS: China MediaExpress Holdings, Inc. (CME or the "Company") (D), a Delaware corporation with its principal place of business in Hong Kong, China, had allegations of fraud and mismanagement leveled against it by the media, as well as shortsellers. The company, which was listed on the NASDAQ Stock Market, denied the allegations. Then, the company's independent auditor, Deloitte Touche Tohmatsu (DTT) formally resigned. In a press release following DTT's resignation, CME (D) acknowledged that DTT had stated in its resignation letter that it was "no longer able to rely on the representations of management," that certain issues raised in the audit should be addressed through an independent investigation, and that the issues may have adverse implications for prior periods' financial reports. That same day, the Company (D) requested that NASDAQ temporarily suspend trading

in its stock. Shortly thereafter, three directors resigned, as did the company's (D) CFO, and NASDAQ halted trading in CME (D), and then delisted it altogether. The Company's (D) audit committee also began an internal investigation. Based on these events, a shareholder brought suit in federal district court alleging violations of state and federal law (Federal Action). In response to these events, and while the Federal Action was pending, Paul (P), a CME (D) shareholder, served CME (D) with a written demand for inspection of the books and records of the Company pursuant to 8 Del. C. § 220. CME (D) did not respond to the demand, and Paul (P) filed suit in Delaware Chancery Court to compel compliance with his demand. Paul (P) asserted two purposes for his request to inspect the books and records of CME (D): (1) to investigate "possible mismanagement and breaches of fiduciary duties by the directors and officers of the Company (D), including, but not limited to, mismanagement and breaches of fiduciary duties in connection with the Company's lack of oversight and possible participation in fraudulent conduct involving the Company's customer contracts, revenues and net income"; and (2) to "determin[e] whether the Company's directors are independent and have acted, and are capable of acting, in good faith with respect to the Company's potential misconduct." CME (D) opposed Paul's (P) inspection demands on the basis that he failed to state a proper purpose. CME (D) also sought to stay the proceedings pending resolution of the Federal Action.

ISSUE:

(1) Does a shareholder demonstrate a proper purpose for a books and records inspection demand—to investigate fraud and mismanagement and the ability of the board to act independently and in good faith—where there is a credible basis for suspicion of waste and mismanagement based on numerous third-party media reports alleging fraudulent conduct, the halting of trading by a stock exchange, delisting of the company's shares, the resignation of the company's independent auditors, the noisy resignations of board members and executives, as well as the initiation of the company's own internal investigation?

(2) Will a books and records inspection demand be stayed pending the outcome of federal litigation where the risk of the plaintiffs in the federal action obtaining state discovery is minimal; where there is minimal risk of inconsistency between a judgment in the state action and a ruling in the federal action; and where the state

Continued on next page.

action will not create an unreasonable discovery burden for the federal defendant?

HOLDING AND DECISION: (Parsons, V. Chan.)

(1) Yes. A shareholder demonstrates a proper purpose for a books and records inspection demand—to investigate fraud and mismanagement and the ability of the board to act independently and in good faith—where there is a credible basis for suspicion of waste and mismanagement based on numerous third-party media reports alleging fraudulent conduct, the halting of trading by a stock exchange, delisting of the company's shares, the resignation of the company's independent auditors, the noisy resignations of board members and executives, as well as the initiation of the company's own internal investigation. Paul (P) has stated a proper purpose for his demand. To meet its burden of proving a proper purpose, a shareholder must make more than mere conclusory statements, and, instead, must present some credible basis "through documents, logic, testimony or otherwise" from which the court can infer wrongdoing. Moreover, although shareholders have the burden of coming forward with specific and credible allegations sufficient to warrant a suspicion of waste and mismanagement, they are "not required to prove by a preponderance of the evidence that waste and [mis]management are actually occurring." Instead, shareholders only need to show a credible basis from which the court can infer that there are reasonable grounds to suspect mismanagement that would warrant further investigation, and such a showing "may ultimately fall well short of demonstrating that anything wrong occurred." Here, the evidence presented by Paul (P)—(1) numerous third-party media reports alleging fraudulent conduct by CME's (D) officers and directors; (2) the NASDAQ Stock Market's halting of trading in, and subsequent delisting of, CME (D) shares; (3) the resignation of the Company's (D) independent auditor; (4) the noisy resignations of three board members, including the Company's (D) CFO, citing concerns about senior management and the Company's (D) accounting practices; and (5) CME's (D) initiation of its own internal investigation—provided a credible basis from which the court could infer that CME's (D) officers and directors may had mismanaged CME (D) or engaged in wrongdoing in breach of their fiduciary duties. CME's (D) argument that hearsay evidence, such as that of shortsellers, cannot form the basis of credible-basis evidence is also rejected. Instead, if such evidence is deemed sufficiently reliable, it may be considered in determining whether there is a credible basis for determining that waste or mismanagement may have occurred. Accordingly, Paul's (P) demand is granted to the extent necessary, essential, and sufficient to further the purposes of his investigation. Accordingly, he is entitled to production of all documents requested that relate to CME's (D) claimed business relationships,

intellectual property, and customer contracts. The existence, or nonexistence, of these contracts and documents would affect directly CME's (D) revenue and net income. Likewise, DTT's resignation letter also directly relates to alleged wrongdoing and fraudulent accounting practices by CME (D). The media kits used by CME (D) relate to representations made by the Company (D) about its business relationships and profitability, and such documents could impact the veracity of CME's (D) financial reporting and would help confirm or repudiate Paul's (P) suspicions of fraud and wrongdoing at CME (D). While Paul (P) is entitled to production of documents constituting any contracts between CME (D) and other entities, he is not entitled to production of documents evidencing any business relationship between the Company (D) and the more than 20 entities listed by Paul (P), as such demand is simply too broad and ill-defined, and Paul (P) has made no showing that such documents are necessary to his purposes. Finally, Paul's (P) request for all memoranda, presentations, reports, correspondence, email, minutes, recordings, consents, agendas, resolutions, summaries, analyses, transcripts, notes, and board or committee packages created by, distributed to, or reviewed by or on behalf of CME's (D) board or any committee thereof, concerning the subjects referenced in Paul's (P) other demands, is simply overbroad, and is rejected in its entirety. This demands is much more like a sweeping discovery request than a narrowly focused § 220 demand. Finally, Paul's (P) right to receive any documents ordered produced is contingent on his entering into a confidentiality agreement with CME (D) as to those documents. Paul's (P) § 220 demand is, therefore, granted in part.

(2) No. A books and records inspection demand will not be stayed pending the outcome of federal litigation where the risk of the plaintiffs in the federal action obtaining state discovery is minimal; where there is minimal risk of inconsistency between a judgment in the state action and a ruling in the federal action; and where the state action will not create an unreasonable discovery burden for the federal defendant. The federal district court may have authority to stay the books and records inspection action if it determines that such inspection would interfere with the automatic stay in the Federal Action. Federal courts generally rely on three factors in deciding whether to stay a state action: (1) whether there is a risk that the federal plaintiffs will obtain the state plaintiff's discovery, and to what extent a confidentiality agreement and/or protective order with defendants can minimize that risk; (2) whether the underlying facts and legal claims in the state and federal actions overlap; and (3) the burden that the state court discovery proceedings will impose on the federal defendants. As to

Continued on next page.

the first factor, Paul (P) is not a party to the Federal Action, and has no relationship with the plaintiffs in that action. He also has agreed to sign a confidentiality agreement that would restrict him from sharing information with the federal plaintiffs. Thus, it is unlikely that further proceedings in this case will result in some form of discovery inadvertently reaching the federal plaintiffs. As to the second factor, although the state and federal claims against CME (D) relate to the same underlying facts, they involve entirely different legal claims. Consequently, there is minimal risk of inconsistency between a judgment here and a ruling on the federal motion to dismiss. Moreover, to the extent this action could be deemed to constitute the incipient stages of a state derivative action, it still is unlikely that any judgment will issue from such a future derivative action before the district court has an opportunity to rule on the motion to dismiss that is before it. Finally, as to the third factor, relevant concerns include (1) whether discovery in the federal and state actions will be duplicative and (2) whether the defendant will be required to litigate and resolve the same discovery disputes in two different courts, wasting judicial resources and imposing substantial costs on the defendant. Here, the court has carefully tailored the production ordered to Paul's (P) proper purposes, and CME (D) will not be required to submit to any deposition discovery, will not have to answer interrogatories, and faces only a minimal risk of further disputes over the scope of production. Accordingly, complying with the production ordered in this action will not be overly burdensome for CME (D). For these reasons, Paul's (P) action should not be stayed. Judgment for Paul (P) as to this issue.

▶ *ANALYSIS*

Where, as here, a shareholder seeks to inspect the books and records of a company other than the stock ledger or list of stockholders, the burden of proof is on the shareholder to demonstrate a proper purpose for inspection by a preponderance of the evidence. "Proper purpose," under Delaware law, means a purpose reasonably related to such person's interest as a stockholder. To plead a proper purpose successfully, the purpose asserted by the shareholder should be intended to further the interest of all stockholders and should increase stockholder return.

■■■

Quicknotes

BREACH OF FIDUCIARY DUTY The failure of a fiduciary to observe the standard of care exercised by professionals of similar education and experience.

■■■

CHAPTER 18

The Limited Partnership

Quick Reference Rules of Law

Gateway Potato Sales v. G.B. Investment Co.

Creditor (P) v. Limited partnership (D)

Ariz. Ct. App., 822 P.2d 490 (1991).

NATURE OF CASE: Appeal from a court order granting summary judgment to a defendant and a denial of plaintiff's motion for reconsideration in a suit to recover payment for goods supplied.

FACT SUMMARY: Gateway Potato Sales (P), a creditor of Sunworth Packing Limited Partnership (Sunworth) (D), brought suit against limited partner G.B. Investment Co. (D) to recover payment for goods it had supplied to Sunworth (D).

🏛 RULE OF LAW
A limited partner may become liable for the obligations of the limited partnership under certain circumstances in which the limited partner has taken part in the control of the business.

FACTS: Gateway Potato Sales (Gateway) (P), a creditor of Sunworth Packing Limited Partnership (Sunworth) (D), brought suit to recover payment for goods it had supplied to Sunworth (D). Gateway (P) also sought recovery from Sunworth (D) as a general partner and from G.B. Investment Co. (D), a limited partner, pursuant to Arizona Revised Statutes Annotated § 29-319, which imposes liability on limited partners who control the business. At trial, G.B. Investment's (D) vice-president, Anderson, testified in his affidavit that G.B. Investment (D) had exerted no control over the daily management and operation of the limited partnership, Sunworth (D). However, this testimony was contradicted by the affidavit testimony of Ellsworth, president of Sunworth (D). According to Ellsworth, G.B. Investment's (D) employees Anderson and McHolm controlled the day-to-day affairs of the limited partnership (D) and made Ellsworth account to them for nearly everything he did. G.B. Investment (D) moved for summary judgment, urging that there was no evidence that the circumstances described in A.R.S. § 29-319 had occurred in this case. It argued that, as a limited partner, it was not liable to the creditors of Sunworth (D) except to the extent of its investment. The trial court agreed, granting G.B. Investment's (D) motion for summary judgment. Gateway (P) appealed from the judgment and the denial of its motion for reconsideration, arguing the existence of conflicting evidence of material facts.

ISSUE: May a limited partner become liable for the obligations of the limited partnership under certain circumstances in which the limited partner has taken part in the control of the business?

HOLDING AND DECISION: (Taylor, J.) Yes. A limited partner may become liable for the obligations of the

limited partnership under certain circumstances in which the limited partner has taken part in the control of the business. In enacting A.R.S. § 29-319(a), the legislature stopped short of expressly stating that if the limited partner's participation in the control of the business is substantially the same as the exercise of the powers of a general partner, he is liable to persons who transact business with a limited partnership even though they have no knowledge of his participation and control. It has made this statement by implication, though, by stating to the opposite effect that if the limited partner's participation in the control of the business is not substantially the same as the exercise of the powers of a general partner, he is liable only to persons who transact business with the limited partnership with actual knowledge of his participation in control. Moreover, in the absence of actual knowledge of the limited partner's participation in the control of the partnership business, there must be evidence from which a trier-of-fact might find not only control, but control that is substantially the same as the exercise of powers of a general partner. The evidence Gateway (P) presented in this case should have allowed it to withstand summary judgment. The affidavit testimony of Ellsworth raises the issue whether he was merely a puppet for the limited partner, G.B. Investment (D). Ellsworth's detailed statement raises substantial issues of material facts. It cannot be said, as a matter of law, that G.B. Investment (D) was entitled to summary judgment. Reversed and remanded.

▶ ANALYSIS

The decision in *Gateway* represents the general rule under the amended version of the Uniform Limited Partnership Act regarding the liability of limited partners who participate in the control of the business. Under this rule, limited partners may be found liable only to individuals engaging in business with the limited partnership reasonably believing, based upon the limited partner's conduct, that the limited partner is actually a general partner. This provision is widely considered to be the Act's most significant method of liability defense.

■▬■

Quicknotes

GENERAL PARTNERSHIP A voluntary agreement entered into by two or more parties to engage in business whereby each of the parties is to share in any profits and losses

Continued on next page.

therefrom equally and each is to participate equally in the management of the enterprise.

LIMITED PARTNERSHIP A voluntary agreement entered into by two or more parties whereby one or more general partners are responsible for the enterprise's liabilities and management and the other partners are liable only to the extent of their investment.

In re USACafes, L.P.

Limited partnership (D) v. Shareholders (P)

Del. Ch. Ct., 600 A.2d 43 (1991).

NATURE OF THE CASE: Consolidated class action seeking imposition of constructive trust.

FACT SUMMARY: The shareholders of a reorganized corporation filed breach of duty claims against the directors of the new corporation based on transactions that took place counter to the interests of the shareholders as reflected in the original prospectus.

🏛 RULE OF LAW
The duty of loyalty in a limited liability corporation extends to directors of the corporation's general partners sufficient to support a breach of duty claim by controlling shareholders.

FACTS: USACafes, L.P. (D) was formed after the reorganization of a Nevada corporation, which included the creation of a general partner that was also named as a defendant in the present case. Metsa Acquisition Corp. (Metsa) moved to purchase substantially all of the assets of USACafes (D), which triggered a breach of the duty of loyalty action against USACafes (D) by the holders (P) of the limited partnership. The holders (P) alleged that the sale of assets took place at a price favorable to Metsa, and that the directors of USACafes' (D) general partner received substantial side payments. In addition, the holders (P) asserted that the directors of USACafes' (D) general partner were not sufficiently informed to make a valid business judgment on the sale. Finally, the holders (P) asserted a breach of duty claim on behalf of the shareholders of the original Nevada corporation based on the original shareholders' belief that a sale of substantially all the assets of the reorganized corporation required an affirmative majority vote by all the shareholders. In amending its complaint to include this assertion, the holders (P) requested judicial recognition of the right to vote on the Metsa transaction, or a rescission of the transaction.

ISSUE: Does the duty of loyalty in a limited liability corporation extend to directors of the corporation's general partners sufficient to support a breach of duty claim by controlling shareholders?

HOLDING AND DECISION: (Allen, Chan.) Yes. The duty of loyalty in a limited liability corporation extends to directors of the corporation's general partners sufficient to support a breach of duty claim by controlling shareholders. The directors of USACafes' (D) general partner concede that a fiduciary duty exists between the general partner and the limited partners of the corporation, but that no such duties are owed by the directors of the general partner toward the limited partners. In the view of the

court, the directors' (D) assertion of the independence of the corporate general partner from its directors is incorrect. No precedents exist to directly address the question that the directors of a corporate general partner owe fiduciary duties to a corporation and its general partners. However, one who controls the property of another may not intentionally use that property to the detriment of the true owner without consent. Corporate directors are thus regarded as fiduciaries for corporate stockholders. Relevant authority extends the fiduciary duty of the general partner to a controlling shareholder. In addition, we recognize this duty in the directors of a general partner who are in control of the partnership's property, more so than a controlling shareholder. The directors (D) have breached a fiduciary duty imposed upon them as directors of the general partner, and the motion by the directors (D) to dismiss the claim is therefore denied.

▶ ANALYSIS

The court likened the role of a director owing fiduciary duties based on the control of property to that of a trustee. The law of trusts requires that a fiduciary may not waste property, even when there is no self-interest involved. In addition, a fiduciary is required to exercise due care when controlling property for the benefit of another. Eventually, courts of equity would extend these duties by analogy to corporate directors controlling the corporate enterprise. Thus, the appropriate remedy imposed by the court in the present case was a constructive trust, requiring the return of the value of the property as held in trust by the directors on the shareholders' behalf.

■ ▬ ■

Quicknotes

CONSTRUCTIVE TRUST A trust that arises by operation of law whereby the court imposes a trust upon property lawfully held by one party for the benefit of another, as a result of some wrongdoing by the party in possession so as to avoid unjust enrichment.

FIDUCIARY DUTY A legal obligation to act for the benefit of another, including subordinating one's personal interests to that of the other person.

GENERAL PARTNERSHIP A voluntary agreement entered into by two or more parties to engage in business whereby each of the parties is to share in any profits and losses therefrom equally and each is to participate equally in the management of the enterprise.

Continued on next page.

LIMITED LIABILITY An advantage of doing business in the corporate form by safeguarding shareholders from liability for the debts or obligations of the corporation.

■━━■

KE Property Management Inc. v. 275 Madison Management Corp.

General partner (P) v. Managing general partners (D)

Del. Ch. Ct., 1993 WL 285900 (1993).

NATURE OF CASE: Action for declaratory judgment and injunction stemming from purported removal by a limited partner of a general partner.

FACT SUMMARY: KE Property Management Inc. (KE Property) (P), one of the general partners of 275 Madison Associates L.P., a limited partnership (the "Partnership"), sought a declaratory judgment that the purported removal of 275 Madison Management Corp. (275 Madison Corp.) (D), the managing general partner of the Partnership, by KJ Capital Management, Inc. (KJ Capital), a limited partner and an affiliate of KE Property (P), was effective. It therefore sought to enjoin 275 Madison Corp. (D) from purporting to act as the managing general partner.

RULE OF LAW
Fraud by the agent of a managing general partner of a limited partnership justifies removal of the managing general partner by a limited partner affiliated with a different general partner where the partnership agreement provides for removal by limited partners of a general partner who has injured the partnership through fraud or willful misconduct.

FACTS: 275 Madison Management Corp. (275 Madison Corp.) (D) was the managing general partner of 275 Madison Associates L.P., a limited partnership (the "Partnership"). KE Property Management Inc. (KE Property) (P) was a general partner, and its affiliate, KJ Capital Management, Inc. (KJ Capital), was a limited partner. The Partnership's original managing general partner, Skydell, who served as the president and part owner of 275 Madison Corp. (D), misappropriated $2 million of Partnership funds by diverting them from the Partnership's bank accounts. Skydell was able to divert the funds because he was an authorized signatory on the accounts in his capacity as a representative of 275 Madison Corp. (D). Prior to Skydell's fraud, the Partnership had borrowed $70 million from Kawasaki Leasing International, Inc. (Kawasaki Lender). KJ Capital and KE Property were affiliated with the Kawasaki Lender. After the fraud, the Partnership experienced financial hardship and its finances were restructured with the Kawasaki Lender. Then, the Kawasaki Lender informed the Partnership that it was in default and risked foreclosure. 275 Madison Corp. (D) urged the Partnership to seek bankruptcy protection, but KE Property (P) refused. 275 Madison Corp. (D) claimed that this refusal was a breach of fiduciary duty to the other partners, based on improper loyalty to the Kawasaki Lender. About a month later, KJ Capital purported to remove

275 Madison Corp. (D) as managing general partner, purportedly under the Partnership Agreement, which provided that limited partners, under certain circumstances (which were met) could expel any general partner if the general partner had injured the partnership as a result of fraud or willful misconduct in the performance of his duties as a general partner. KJ Capital claimed that Skydell's misappropriation of $2 million constituted fraud or willful misconduct on the part of 275 Madison Corp. (D) in its capacity as the managing general partner of the Partnership. 275 Madison Corp. (D), however, claimed that this was a pretext, instituted at the Kawasaki Lender's behest, to prevent 275 Madison Corp. (D) from filing for bankruptcy for the Partnership. Nonetheless, two days after its purported removal, 275 Madison Corp. (D) went ahead with such a filing. KE Property (P) then brought suit for a declaratory judgment that the purported removal of 275 Madison Corp. (D) was effective, and for an injunction to stop 275 Madison Corp. (D) from acting on the Partnership's behalf. KE Property (P) sought summary judgment, which 275 Madison Corp. (D) argued was improper because the Kawasaki affiliates had acted in bad faith to block the foreclosure of their loan by preventing the Partnership from entering bankruptcy.

ISSUE: Does fraud by the agent of a managing general partner of a limited partnership justify removal of the managing general partner by a limited partner affiliated with a different general partner where the partnership agreement provides for removal by limited partners of a general partner who has injured the partnership through fraud or willful misconduct?

HOLDING AND DECISION: (Hartnett, V. Chan.) Yes. Fraud by the agent of a managing general partner of a limited partnership justifies removal of the managing general partner by a limited partner affiliated with a different general partner where the partnership agreement provides for removal by limited partners of a general partner who has injured the partnership through fraud or willful misconduct. First, there is a presumption that the Kawasaki entities acted in "good faith" and 275 Madison Corp. (D) bears the burden of showing "bad faith." Moreover, 275 Madison Corp.'s (D) 275 allegation of "bad faith" is predicated upon KJ Capital having owed a fiduciary duty to it, and although a general partner owes a fiduciary duty to its partner, here it was KJ Capital, a limited partner, that purported to remove 275 Madison Corp. (D). Nonetheless, even though the state's Revised

Continued on next page.

Uniform Limited Partnership Act (RULPA) does not specifically state that a limited partner owes a fiduciary duty to a general partner, it does so by referencing the state's Uniform Partnership Act (UPA), which provides that all partners owe each other fiduciary obligations. Therefore, to the extent that a partnership agreement—as here—empower a limited partner discretion to take actions affecting the governance of the limited partnership, such as removing a general partner, the limited partner must act as a fiduciary, and is obligated to act in "good faith." Here, however, the Partnership Agreement does not give KJ Capital unlimited discretion in this regard. Instead, removal can only occur upon "fraud or willful misconduct" that injures the Partnership. Because Skydell's fraudulent acts may be imputed to 275 Madison Corp. (D), it was guilty of the type of conduct permitting its removal by a limited partner. The issue of "bad faith" is one of fact. Here, because 275 Madison Corp. (D) bears the burden on this issue, and because it has not adduced competent evidence to rebut KJ Capital's or the Kawasaki affiliates' "good faith," summary judgment is granted to KE Property (P).

▶ *ANALYSIS*

Here, the court imposes fiduciary duties on limited partners only in those instances where a partnership agreement empowers limited partners with discretion to take actions affecting the limited partnership's governance, but not where the partnership agreement spells out the conditions under which the limited partners may act. Thus, with respect to KJ Capital, the court determines that KJ Capital owed no fiduciary obligations to 275 Madison Corp. (D). Accordingly, the court reasoned that it did not need to reach the issue of whether KJ Capital owed such fiduciary obligations by virtue of being controlled by the same entity that controlled KE Property (P).

■≡■

Quicknotes

FIDUCIARY DUTY A legal obligation to act for the benefit of another, including subordinating one's personal interests to that of the other person.

GOOD FAITH An honest intention to abstain from taking advantage of another.

LIMITED PARTNERSHIP A voluntary agreement entered into by two or more parties whereby one or more general partners are responsible for the enterprise's liabilities and management and the other partners are liable only to the extent of their investment.

■≡■

CHAPTER 19

The Limited Liability Partnership

Quick Reference Rules of Law

Kus v. Irving

Client (P) v. Law firm partner (D)

Conn. Super. Ct., 736 A.2d 946 (1999).

NATURE OF CASE: Motion for summary judgment in action for negligence, wrongful acts, and misconduct.

FACT SUMMARY: Attorneys Dubicki (D) and Camassar (D), who were partners with Irving (D) in a limited liability partnership law firm, contended that they were not liable to Kus (P), Irving's (D) client, for Irving's (D) misconduct where they had no personal knowledge of the dealings between Irving (D) and Kus (P), where they received no benefit from those dealings, and where they did not supervise or control Irving (D).

> ## 🏛 RULE OF LAW
> Limited liability partners are not personally liable for the misconduct of another partner where they have no personal knowledge of such misconduct, do not benefit from the misconduct, and do not exercise supervision or control over the other partner.

FACTS: Kus (P) was the client of Irving (D), an attorney and a partner in a limited liability partnership law firm that had two other partners, Dubicki (D) and Camassar (D). Kus (P) brought suit against Irving (D), claiming that he had engaged in various acts of misconduct, and also named Dubicki (D) and Camassar (D) in the action. Dubicki (D) and Camassar (D) moved for summary judgment, on the grounds that they had no personal knowledge of the dealings between Irving (D) and Kus (P), did not benefit from Irving's (D) misconduct, did not exercise supervision or control over Irving (D), and otherwise were protected from liability by the state's limited liability partnership statute, which stated that "a partner in a registered limited liability partnership is not liable directly or indirectly . . . for any debts, obligations and liabilities . . . chargeable to the partnership or another partner or partners . . . arising in the course of the partnership business while the partnership is a registered limited liability partnership" unless such liability is based on his own negligence, wrongful acts or misconduct, or that of any person under his direct supervision and control.

ISSUE: Are limited liability partners personally liable for the misconduct of another partner where they have no personal knowledge of such misconduct, do not benefit from the misconduct, and do not exercise supervision or control over the other partner?

HOLDING AND DECISION: (Hurley, J.) No. Limited liability partners are not personally liable for the misconduct of another partner where they have no personal knowledge of such misconduct, do not benefit from the

misconduct, and do not exercise supervision or control over the other partner. While Kus (P) asserted that Dubicki (D) and Camassar (D) were guilty of negligence, wrongful acts and misconduct, she failed to produce evidence in support of this claim. Accordingly, there is no issue of material fact in this regard. Also, because Dubicki (D) and Camassar (D) shared no benefit, did not have direct supervision or control over Irving (D) and did not know about the misconduct until after it occurred, they were protected from liability by the limited liability partnership statute. Summary judgment is granted to Dubicki (D) and Camassar (D).

▶ ANALYSIS

Many law firms use the limited liability partnership form of entity, and such use has been ruled by the American Bar Association's Ethics Committee to be consistent with the Model Rules of Professional Conduct.

■▬■

Quicknotes

LIMITED LIABILITY PARTNERSHIP (LLP) A partnership combining characteristics of corporations and partnerships where the partners have limited liability, usually for the negligence, errors, omissions, misconduct or malpractice of other partners, and usually share equally in the company's management. In some states, LLPs can be formed only for certain professional endeavors, such as accounting or the practice of law.

■▬■

Ederer v. Gursky

Limited liability partner (P) v. Limited liability partner (D)

N.Y. Ct. App., 881 N.E.2d 204 (2007).

NATURE OF CASE: Appeal from denial of dismissal of action for breach of a partnership withdrawal agreement and for monies owed thereunder.

FACT SUMMARY: Ederer (P), a partner in a limited liability partnership (LLP), sued the LLP and its partners (D) for breach of a partnership withdrawal agreement and for monies owed thereunder; the partners (D) moved to dismiss, contending that the state's LLP statute shielded them from personal liability for the LLP's obligations.

🏛 RULE OF LAW

A limited liability partnership does not shield a general partner from personal liability for breaches of the partnership's or partners' obligations to each other.

FACTS: Ederer (P), a partner in a limited liability partnership (LLP), sued the LLP and its partners for breach of a partnership withdrawal agreement and for monies owed thereunder. There was no partnership agreement in place. The individual partners (D) moved to dismiss, contending that the state's LLP statute (Partnership Law § 26(b)) shielded them from personal liability for the LLP's obligations. The lower courts denied the motion.

ISSUE: Does a limited liability partnership shield a general partner from personal liability for breaches of the partnership's or partners' obligations to each other?

HOLDING AND DECISION: (Read, J.) No. A limited liability partnership does not shield a general partner from personal liability for breaches of the partnership's or partners' obligations to each other. The matter is one of statutory construction. Section 26 as originally enacted, and its prototype, section 15 of the Uniform Partnership Act (UPA), made general partners jointly and severally liable to nonpartner creditors for all wrongful acts and breaches of trust committed by their partners in carrying out the partnership's business, and jointly liable for all other debts to third parties. As in many states, this state's legislature enacted limited liability partnership legislation that eliminated such vicarious liability of general partners to nonpartner creditors. This provision is found in Section 26(b). Section 26(c) excludes from § 26(b)'s liability shield "any negligent or wrongful act or misconduct committed by [a partner] or by any person under his or her direct supervision and control while rendering professional services on behalf of [the] registered limited liability partnership." The partners (D) argue that because § 26(b) eliminates "any debts" without distinguishing between debts owed to a third party or to the partnership or each other, debts to Ederer (P) are covered and they are shielded from the debts. This argument ignores, however, that the phrase "any debts" is part of a provision of § 26 that has always governed only a partner's liability to third parties. Thus, absent very clear legislative intent to the contrary, "any debts" refers to debts owed to third parties, but not to other partners or the partnership. Although it is true, as argued by the partners (P), that the LLP form in this state was intended to—and does—offer limited liability partners the same protections as offered to shareholders in professional corporation and members of limited liability companies, such protection comes in the form of enhanced protection from vicarious liability to third parties. It has never been suggested that the LLP statute in this state, or any other state, was ever intended to shield partners from their obligations to the partnership or other partners. Because there was no written partnership agreement in this case, the LLP law governs. Affirmed.

DISSENT: (Smith, J.) The language of § 26(b) is unambiguous, providing that "no partner of a partnership which is a registered limited liability partnership is liable ... for any debts, obligations or liabilities of ... the registered limited liability partnership ... whether arising in tort, contract or otherwise." The only exceptions are contained in § 26(c) and the court should not create exceptions not created by the legislature. While the majority draws a distinction between liability to third parties and liabilities to former partners, it is an illusory distinction because former partners are third parties where the partnership is concerned, and under the statute there is no good reason to treat such former partner third parties more favorably than any other third party. This does not mean that partners are in any way exempted from their fiduciary obligations, but where a former partner claims his partnership share, he should be able to reach the personal assets of partners who are no more blameworthy than he is, and have no more been unjustly enriched that he has. Where, as here, the partnership's business has gone bad through no fault of any partner, there is no reason why a former partner should be allowed to collect his debt when other third-party creditors may not. Where the partnership's business has gone bad as the result of an insolvent partner, it would be even more perverse to enable him to proceed against the other innocent partners. If the partnership here had remained a professional corporation, there would be no question that the individual shareholders would not be liable for the corporation's obligation to a

Continued on next page.

former shareholder; thus, there is no reason that the partners of an LLP should have an obligation that the shareholders of a PC do not.

▶ *ANALYSIS*

As the court itself points out, the LLP law provides default rules that the partners can, in many instances, contract away. For example, partners could agree to limit the right of contribution or indemnification, or exclude it altogether.

■═■

Quicknotes

GENERAL PARTNER A partner, whether an individual or an entity, that assumes unlimited liability for the debts of a partnership and who, in a limited partnership, usually is responsible for the partnership's management.

JOINT AND SEVERAL LIABILITY Liability amongst tortfeasors allowing the injured party to bring suit against any of the defendants, individually or collectively, and to recover from each up to the total amount of damages awarded.

LIMITED LIABILITY PARTNERSHIP (LLP) A partnership combining characteristics of corporations and partnerships where the partners have limited liability, usually for the negligence, errors, omissions, misconduct or malpractice of other partners, and usually share equally in the company's management. In some states, LLPs can be formed only for certain professional endeavors, such as accounting or the practice of law.

VICARIOUS LIABILITY The imputed liability of one party for the unlawful acts of another.

■═■

The Limited Liability Company

Quick Reference Rules of Law

Taghipour v. Jerez

LLC member (P) v. LLC managing member (D)

Utah Sup. Ct., 52 P.3d 1252 (2002).

NATURE OF CASE: Appeal from affirmance of dismissal of action for declaratory judgment, negligence, and partition.

FACT SUMMARY: Members of a limited liability company (LLC), and the LLC (collectively, Taghipour) (P) contended that Mount Olympus Financial, L.C. (Mt. Olympus) (D) negligently dispersed funds to the LLC's managing member, Jerez (D), and that its loan agreement with the LLC, and the foreclosure thereof, were invalid because the LLC's operating agreement provided that no loans could be contracted on behalf of the LLC unless authorized by resolution of the members; Mt. Olympus (D) asserted that the state's LLC Act, which provided that loan and mortgage documents executed by an LLC's manager were binding on the LLC, took precedence over the operating agreement.

🏛 **RULE OF LAW**
Where two provisions of an LLC Act conflict in their operation, the provision more specific in application governs over the more general provision.

FACTS: Jerez (D) was the managing member of an LLC. The LLC's operating agreement provided that no loans could be contracted on behalf of the LLC unless authorized by resolution of the members. Jerez (D), unbeknownst to the other LLC members, entered into a loan agreement on behalf of the LLC with Mount Olympus Financial, L.C. (Mt. Olympus) (D) whereby Mt. Olympus (D) loaned $25,000 to the LLC, the loan being secured by a deed of trust and trust note executed by Jerez (D) permitting the trustee to sell LLC real property in the event of default. Mt. Olympus (D) dispensed the funds net of fees to Jerez (D), who misappropriated and absconded with the funds. Jerez (D) never remitted payment on the loan, and because the other members were unaware of the loan, the LLC eventually defaulted and Mt. Olympus (D) foreclosed on the loan. The LLC members, other than Jerez (D), were never notified of the default or foreclosure proceedings or sale. Prior to making the loan, Mt. Olympus (D) had not investigated Jerez's (D) authority to enter the loan agreement, other than to ascertain that he was an LLC manager. The LLC members and the LLC (collectively "Taghipour") (P) brought suit, claiming, inter alia, that Mt. Olympus (D) had negligently dispersed the funds to Jerez (D) because it had failed to conduct due diligence as to whether Jerez (D) had authority to enter into the loan agreement on behalf of the LLC. They also sought a declaratory judgment that the loan agreement with the LLC, and the foreclosure thereof, were invalid, and sought partition of the property interests

at issue. Mt. Olympus (D) moved to dismiss, asserting that under the state's LLC Act, § 48-2b-127(2), the loan agreement documents were valid and binding on the LLC because they were executed by an LLC manager. That section provides that mortgages on LLC property are valid and binding on an LLC if executed by one or more LLC managers. The trial court granted the motion to dismiss. Taghipour (D) appealed, arguing that the trial court's interpretation of § 48-2b-127(2) was erroneous because the court failed to read it in conjunction with § 48-2b-125(2)(b), which provides that a manager's authority to bind an LLC can be limited in its operating agreement. The state's intermediate appellate court rejected this argument and affirmed. The state's highest court granted review.

ISSUE: Where two provisions of an LLC Act conflict in their operation, does the provision more specific in application govern over the more general provision?

HOLDING AND DECISION: (Russon, J.) Yes. Where two provisions of an LLC Act conflict in their operation, the provision more specific in application governs over the more general provision. Resolution of the issue at bar comes down to which of the conflicting LLC Act provisions govern. When two statutory provisions purport to cover the same subject, the legislature's intent must be considered in determining which provision applies. To determine that intent, rules of statutory construction provide that when two statutory provisions conflict in their operation, the provision more specific in application governs over the more general provision. The appellate court determined that § 48-2b-127(2) was more specific. That ruling was not erroneous because § 48-2b-127(2) is the more specific statute because it applies only to documents explicitly enumerated in the statute, i.e., instruments and documents that provide for the acquisition, mortgage, or disposition of LLC property. Thus, this section is tailored precisely to address the documents and instruments Jerez (D) executed, e.g., the trust deed and trust deed note. Conversely, section 48-2b-125(2)(b) is more general because it addresses every situation in which a manager can bind the LLC. In addition, a statute is more specific according to its content, not according to how restrictive it is in application. Finally, holding that § 48-2b-125(2)(b) is the more specific provision would essentially render § 48-2b-127(2) superfluous and inoperative, because it would then simply restate § 48-2b-125(2)(b), by which it would be subsumed. Because § 48-2b-127(2) is the applicable statute, the loan documents, and their foreclosure,

Continued on next page.

were valid and binding, and Mt. Olympus (D) did all that was required by statute. Affirmed.

▶ *ANALYSIS*

The court's holding produces a perverse result, but one based on a flaw in the LLC Act itself: if, as in this case, there are restrictions in an LLC's organic documents on its managers' ability to unilaterally bind the company, those restrictions will be effective across the range of mundane and comparatively insignificant contracts purportedly entered into by the company, but the restrictions will be ineffective in the case of the company's most important contracts. Thus, if the articles of organization or operating agreement provide that the managers will enter into no contract without the approval of the company's members, as memorialized in an appropriate resolution, the company can escape an unauthorized contract for something like janitorial services, coffee supplies, or photocopying, but is stuck with the sale of its property for less than fair value or a loan on unfavorable terms. Such a result is at odds with the expectations of the business community. Moreover, financial institutions can protect themselves by insisting on seeing articles of incorporation, bylaws, and board resolutions—or the limited liability company equivalents—as part of the mortgage loan process. A cursory review of such documents in this case would have disclosed that Jerez (D) lacked the authority to bind the company to the proposed loan agreement. Section 48-2b-127(2) was subsequently repealed, exactly because of the potential for causing the kind of anomalous result reached by the court here.

■━━■

Quicknotes

DEED OF TRUST A legal document that acts as a mortgage, placing a security interest in the deeded property with a trustee to insure the payment of a debt.

LIMITED LIABILITY COMPANY (LLC) A business entity combining the features of both a corporation and a general partnership; the LLC provides its shareholders and officers with limited liability, but it is treated as a partnership for taxation purposes.

■━━■

Kasten v. Doral Dental USA, LLC

Non-managing member (P) v. Limited liability company (LLC) (D)

Wis. Sup. Ct., 733 N.W.2d 300 (2007).

NATURE OF CASE: Appeal, on certified questions, from judgment in action to compel production of company documents and records.

FACT SUMMARY: Kasten (P), a non-managing member of Doral Dental USA, LLC (Doral Dental) (D), contended that the LLC's operating agreement, which permitted members "upon reasonable request" to inspect company "documents" and "books," required Doral Dental (D), upon her request, to disclose to her company emails and document drafts going back three years.

RULE OF LAW

(1) Where an LLC operating agreement provides for the inspection by members of "company documents," business-related emails and document drafts may be subject to inspection.

(2) Where a state's LLC statute and an LLC operating agreement require that a member will be granted an inspection demand "upon reasonable request," the inquiry as to the reasonableness of the request must weigh the bias in favor of the member's right of inspection against the financial burden a specific request may place upon the LLC.

FACTS: Kasten (P), a non-managing member of Doral Dental USA, LLC (Doral Dental) (D) asserted her rights under the LLC's operating agreement and state statute to inspect and copy company records and documents, including emails and document drafts from three years prior that might be related to the sale of the company and possible mismanagement. The operating agreement provided for a member's right to inspect the company's "books and records" as well as "Company documents" "upon reasonable request." The company (D) complied with some of her requests but not others. Kasten (P) then brought suit to compel the production of documents and records not yet produced. The company (D) opposed her request to inspect emails and other electronically stored files, claiming that the request was unreasonable as it potentially would cover hundreds of thousands of emails. The trial court held that emails and document drafts categorically were not subject to inspection under state statute or the operating agreement. The state's intermediate appellate court then certified the issue to the state's highest court.

ISSUE:

(1) Where an LLC operating agreement provides for the inspection by members of "company documents,"

may business-related emails and document drafts be subject to inspection?

(2) Where a state's LLC statute and an LLC operating agreement require that a member will be granted an inspection demand "upon reasonable request," must the inquiry as to the reasonableness of the request weigh the bias in favor of the member's right of inspection against the financial burden a specific request may place upon the LLC?

HOLDING AND DECISION: (Butler, J.)

(1) Yes. Where an LLC operating agreement provides for the inspection by members of "Company documents," business-related emails and document drafts may be subject to inspection. A purpose of the state's LLC Act is to give maximum effect to the principle of freedom of contract and to the enforceability of operating agreements. The state LLC statute provides for inspection "upon reasonable request" of any LLC "record," unless otherwise provided in the operating agreement, but does not define what constitutes such a record. LLC managers have a corresponding duty to disclose such records where it is reasonable to do so. Doral Dental's (D) operating agreement provided for the inspection of "books and . . . records" and "documents" but was silent on the company managers' duty to disclose information to members. The company (D) asserts that only the types of documents, such as those listed in the LLC statute, such as member lists, tax returns, copies of the operating agreement and the like, qualify as "records," but not emails or document drafts, which are not mentioned in the statute. While the state's corporation and partnership statutes place express limitations on the types of documents that may be inspected by partners or shareholders, or have additional requirements, the LLC statute, by contrast, contains no such restrictions or requirements. Therefore, these other statutes cannot be looked to for guidance as to how to interpret the LLC statute, which is intended to establish a more transparent business form than the other statutes. In fact, the other statutes do not impose on a manager a duty of disclosure of requested records. Accordingly, an LLC member's right of inspection is exceptionally broad, which is consistent with the purposes of simplicity and freedom of contract that are at the heart of the LLC statute. Here, however, Doral Dental's (D) inspection provisions are not identical to those of the LLC statute, and neither the operating agreement nor the

Continued on next page.

statute defines "record" or "Company document." A "record" is an authentic official copy of a document. Thus, a "document" is a broader category of stored information than a "record." Doral Dental's (D) operating agreement, by permitting inspection of "Company documents" as well as the statutorily-provided "records," affords access to more forms of stored information than the default inspection provisions of the LLC statute. The issue then becomes whether emails and document drafts are covered by "Company documents." While it is true, as the trial court found, that email is a form of communication, it can also be a type of business "document." This does not mean that all emails sent and received by a company are a "company document." Only those relating to company business may be deemed a "company document." Accordingly, the trial court's conclusion that email is categorically not a "company document" was erroneous. Additionally, document drafts fall in the category of "company documents" because they are writings that convey information in the same way as does a document. Reversed and remanded as to this issue.

(2) Yes. Where a state's LLC statute and an LLC operating agreement require that a member will be granted an inspection demand "upon reasonable request," the inquiry as to the reasonableness of the request must weigh the bias in favor of the member's right of inspection against the financial burden a specific request may place upon the LLC. First, under the LLC statute, a manager has the duty to provide members "information" about "all things affecting the members." This means that the manager has a duty to disclose to the member, upon reasonable request, all things affecting the member's financial interest, regardless of whether the information is a record or document. This duty, however, does not limit the types of records and documents that must be disclosed to only those that affect the member's interest. Had the legislature intended to limit the scope of inspection provision to only those "records" that affect a member's membership interest, it would have done so in the text of the inspection provision. The issue then becomes what constitutes a "reasonable request." Kasten (P) argues the reasonableness relates only to the timing and form of the request, whereas Doral Dental (D) argues that it also relates to the breadth of the request, and whether the request is tied to the requester's concerns and the types of records or documents requested, thus attempting to strike a balance between the member's access to information and the company's (D) ability to conduct its business. Rejected, however, is the company's (D) assertion that the reasonableness language should be read to limit the right of inspection to certain kinds of formal records, such as tax returns, financial records and sales tax documents, since under the statute LLC members may inspect any LLC records. Because the statute itself does not address what constitutes reasonableness, it is ambiguous. Appropriate ex-

trinsic sources for its interpretation are other state inspection statutes. Some of those include a "proper purpose" requirement, intended to preclude inspection where the member is improperly motivated. The absence in this state's statute of such a requirement indicates that members do not need to demonstrate, as a threshold matter, that their inspection request is not made for an improper motive. Because the legislature did not intend the inspection statute to threaten the financial well being of the company, "upon reasonable request" pertains to the breadth of an inspection request, as well as the timing and form of the inspection. Therefore, one purpose of the reasonableness language is to protect the company from member inspection requests that impose undue financial burdens on the company. Whether an inspection request is so burdensome as to be unreasonable requires balancing the statute's bias in favor of member access to records against the costs of the inspection to the company. When applying this balancing test, a number of factors may be relevant, including, but not limited to: (1) whether the request is restricted by date or subject matter; (2) the reason given (if any) for the request, and whether the request is related to that reason; (3) the importance of the information to the member's interest in the company; and (4) whether the information may be obtained from another source. Here, these factors must be addressed by the trial court on remand. Reversed and remanded as to this issue.

▶ ANALYSIS

In addition to those jurisdictions that have a reasonableness requirement or a "proper purpose" requirement in their LLC inspection statutes, nine jurisdictions have adopted the Uniform Limited Liability Company Act (ULLCA), which contains a member right to inspect records that includes no language requiring that a request be "reasonable" or made for a "proper purpose." Two states (Nebraska and Wyoming), have LLC statutes that do not include an inspection provision at all.

■=■

Quicknotes

LIMITED LIABILITY COMPANY A business entity combining the features of both a corporation and a general partnership; the LLC provides its shareholders and officers with limited liability, but it is treated as a partnership for taxation purposes.

■=■

Premier Van Schaack Realty, Inc. v. Sieg

Realtor (P) v. Real estate owner (D)

Utah Ct. App., 51 P.3d 24 (2002).

NATURE OF CASE: Appeal from grant of summary judgment to defendant in action to enforce a brokerage fee agreement.

FACT SUMMARY: Premier Van Schaack Realty, Inc. (Premier) (P), a realtor, contended that Sieg's (D) transfer of real property to a limited liability corporation during the term of a listing agreement between the parties constituted a sale or exchange within the meaning of the listing agreement, entitling Premier (P) to a brokerage commission.

🏛 RULE OF LAW

The transfer of property to a limited liability company does not constitute a sale or exchange where the transferor retains essentially the same ownership interest in the property he had prior to the conveyance, and can prevent the record owner from encumbering the property without his permission.

FACTS: Sieg (D) owned real estate and had a listing agreement with Premier Van Schaack Realty, Inc. (Premier) (P), a realtor. During the term of the listing agreement, Premier (P) introduced Sieg (D) to several individuals (collectively, DVJ) who offered to buy the property, but the sale never closed. A few months later, but still during the term of the agreement, DVJ proposed forming an LLC, to be called MJTM, with Sieg (D). The parties signed an operating agreement whereby Sieg (D) would convey his property to MJTM and would receive a 40 percent interest in the LLC and a preferential return of 9 percent on future profits. The agreement also provided that Sieg (D) had a beginning balance of $670,000 in his initial capital contribution account, that MJTM assumed $580,000 of Sieg's (D) debt, that the property was worth $1.3 million, that the other members of MJTM would not to encumber the property without Sieg's (D) approval, and that, "No Member shall be personally liable to any other Member for the return of any part of the Members' Capital Contributions." After Sieg (D) transferred title to the LLC, it borrowed $1.413 million secured by a lien on the property. All of the members of MJTM personally guaranteed the loan, and, with the proceeds from this loan, MJTM paid off a $300,000 loan to Sieg (D) secured by the property. When Premier (P) learned of Sieg's (D) transactions with MJTM, it demanded its commission of 7 percent on $1.3 million, asserting that the transaction constituted a sale or exchange as required by the listing agreement. Sieg (D) refused to pay, claiming that his contribution of the property was an investment, rather than an exchange or sale. Premier (P) brought suit for payment of its commis-

sion, but the trial court granted summary judgment to Sieg (D), finding that the transaction was not a sale or exchange because it lacked consideration. The state's intermediate appellate court granted review.

ISSUE: Does the transfer of property to a limited liability company constitute a sale or exchange where the transferor retains essentially the same ownership interest in the property he had prior to the conveyance, and can prevent the record owner from encumbering the property without his permission?

HOLDING AND DECISION: (Greenwood, J.) No. The transfer of property to a limited liability company does not constitute a sale or exchange where the transferor retains essentially the same ownership interest in the property he had prior to the conveyance, and can prevent the record owner from encumbering the property without his permission. To have either a sale or an exchange, there must be consideration. Sieg (D) argues that his interest in MJTM, including the preferential interest in future profits and an initial capital contribution account balance, cannot serve as consideration because Sieg (D) maintained an ownership interest in the property, and any debt relief fails as consideration because Sieg (D) was personally liable for his personal debt plus the debt of MJTM secured by the property. Here, Sieg (D) is correct that he retained a substantial ownership interest in the property that caused him to assume the risks of an investor instead of the risks of a seller. He is also correct that the debt relief promised in the operating agreement was illusory, since MJTM did not actually relieve Sieg (D) of debt, but rather caused him to personally incur nearly three times more debt than he owed on the property prior to joining MJTM. Regardless of whether MJTM could buy property in its own name separate from its members, the key is whether there was valuable consideration. Because the facts in this case show Sieg (D) continued to have substantially the same ownership interest in the property after the deed to MJTM was executed, and because he could prevent the record owner from encumbering the property without his permission, there was no consideration and a sale or exchange as contemplated in the listing agreement did not occur. Affirmed.

▶ ANALYSIS

In reaching its conclusion, the court emphasizes the investment nature of the transaction, noting that when a person undertakes the risks of an investor, that person

Continued on next page.

assumes the risk that the value of investment will increase or decrease over time, or that the investment may be completely lost. However, as a general rule, once a person sells property, appreciation, depreciation, or total loss of the property is of no concern since the sale severs the seller from any interest in the property. Here, Sieg (D) still retained a significant ownership interest in the property, so that he risked the potential value of its future sale. Moreover, the value of Sieg's (D) interest in MJTM was directly tied to the value of the property because the property was the only asset MJTM owned.

■══■

Quicknotes

CONSIDERATION Value given by one party in exchange for performance, or a promise to perform, by another party.

RECORD OWNER A party who holds title to property as reflected by an official record.

■══■

Pepsi-Cola Bottling Co. v. Handy

Real estate purchaser (P) v. Real estate seller (D)

Del. Ch. Ct., 2000 WL 364199 (2000).

NATURE OF CASE: Action for rescission of contract for the sale of real estate and for damages.

FACT SUMMARY: The Pepsi-Cola Bottling Company of Salisbury, Maryland (Pepsi) (P), which had purchased land from Willow Creek Estates, LLC (Willow Creek) (D) contended that Willow Creek (D) did not shield its members from liability for fraud committed before the LLC was formed.

RULE OF LAW
If an individual makes material misrepresentations to induce a purchaser to purchase a parcel of land at a price far above fair market value, and thereafter forms an LLC to purchase and hold the land, that person later cannot claim that his status as an LLC member protects him from liability to the purchaser.

FACTS: Handy (D), Ginsburg (D) and McKinley (D) were interested in developing a tract of undeveloped land, for which they had a contract of sale. After learning from an environmental study firm that the land had wetlands, which adversely affected the land's value and development potential, they abandoned their development plans, but opted to sell the property after they acquired it. The Pepsi-Cola Bottling Company of Salisbury, Maryland (Pepsi) (P) expressed interest in purchasing the land. Unaware of the existence of wetlands, Pepsi (P) acquired an option to purchase the property from Handy (D), who was acting on his and the other sellers' behalf. During the option period, Handy (D) falsely responded to an environmental investigation questionnaire that there were no wetlands on the land, and he failed to indicate that another environmental study firm had already performed a written preliminary wetlands determination the month before. Moreover, in his response to the question whether any analytical tests or inspections had previously been performed on the property, Handy (D) falsely represented that no "analytical tests or inspections [had] been conducted on the groundwater, surface water, or soil of the Property." Two weeks after Pepsi (P) acquired its option, Handy (D), Ginsburg (D) and McKinley (D) formed Willow Creek Estates, LLC (Willow Creek) (D) for the purpose of selling the property. Willow Creek (D) purchased the property for $174,000 and then sold the property to Pepsi (P) for $455,000 and Willow Creek's (D) members—Handy (D), Ginsberg (D), and McKinley (D)—realized a profit of $281,000 on the sale. After Pepsi (P) learned that the property contained wetlands, it brought an action for rescission and damages, asserting, inter alia, claims of fraud

and unjust enrichment based on the facts that none of the defendants informed Pepsi (P) that the land contained wetlands and that the defendants knew that if Pepsi (P) had been told about the wetlands, Pepsi (P) would not have paid as much as it did. The defendants moved to dismiss, arguing that even if the claims were legally sufficient, no relief could be granted because there could be no recovery against individual members of the LLC in this particular case, as they never individually held legal or equitable title to the land.

ISSUE: If an individual makes material misrepresentations to induce a purchaser to purchase a parcel of land at a price far above fair market value, and thereafter forms an LLC to purchase and hold the land, can that person later claim that his status as an LLC member protects him from liability to the purchaser?

HOLDING AND DECISION: (Jacobs, V. Chan.) No. If an individual makes material misrepresentations to induce a purchaser to purchase a parcel of land at a price far above fair market value, and thereafter forms an LLC to purchase and hold the land, that person later cannot claim that his status as an LLC member protects him from liability to the purchaser. The defendants claim protection under a state statute (DLLCA. § 18-303(a)) that protects members and managers of an LLC against liability for any obligations of the LLC solely by reason of being or acting as LLC members or managers. However, because the facts alleged in the complaint establish that the LLC was not formed (and the property was not acquired by the LLC) until after the allegedly critical wrongful acts had been committed, it follows that the defendants could not have been acting "solely as members of the LLC when they committed those acts." Therefore, the defendants are not shielded from liability by this provision. The defendants next contend that a different statutory provision (DLLCA § 18-607) also protects them. That section prohibits the stripping of corporate assets so as to render an LLC insolvent, and creates a corporate cause of action against LLC members who improperly receive a distribution of those assets. The defendants argue that this is the only provision that allows a third party to recover from an LLC member without piercing the LLC's corporate veil, and that since the complaint did not allege a claim under this provision, the defendants cannot be held liable. However, the defendants read this provision too broadly. Their reading would have the provision shield them from all claims except those brought under the provision itself, but there is nothing in

Continued on next page.

the provision that supports such an interpretation. Moreover, as previously discussed, a third party may recover from an LLC member on claims that do not arise "solely by reason of being" an LLC member or manager. Because all counts of the complaint are based on conduct that occurred before the LLC was formed, and because the LLC statute offers no protection against liability to LLC members who are sued in capacities other than as members of an LLC, those claims are not barred. Motion to dismiss is denied.

▶ *ANALYSIS*

Because the court determined that all the claims were not barred, the court did not need to reach the defendants' alternate argument that the only way personal liability could be imposed on them was by piercing the LLC's corporate veil, whereby the LLC's acts and obligations are legally recognized as those of its constituent members because of the members' great influence over the LLC and such a unity of interest and ownership that the individuality, or separateness, of the members and the LLC has ceased, such that adhering to the fiction of the separate existence of the LLC would, under the circumstances, sanction a fraud or promote injustice.

■══■

Quicknotes

LIMITED LIABILITY COMPANY (LLC) A business entity combining the features of both a corporation and a general partnership; the LLC provides its shareholders and officers with limited liability, but it is treated as a partnership for taxation purposes.

MATERIALITY Importance; the degree of relevance or necessity to the particular matter.

MISREPRESENTATION A statement or conduct by one party to another that constitutes a false representation of fact.

■══■

Kaycee Land and Livestock v. Flahive

Landowner (P) v. Limited liability company (D)

Wyo. Sup. Ct., 46 P.3d 323 (2002).

NATURE OF CASE: Landowner's action for damages against a limited liability company (LLC), alleging that the LLC caused environmental damage to the land when exercising its contractual right to use the surface of the land.

FACT SUMMARY: Kaycee Land and Livestock (Kaycee) (P) contracted with Flahive Oil & Gas LLC allowing the company to use the surface of Kaycee's (P) real property. Roger Flahive (D) was the LLC's managing member. When environmental contamination occurred, Kaycee (P) sued Roger Flahive (D) individually, seeking to pierce the LLC veil and disregard the LLC entity.

🏛 RULE OF LAW
The equitable remedy of piercing the veil is an available remedy under the Limited Liability Company Act.

FACTS: Flahive Oil & Gas (Flahive) was a Wyoming limited liability company (LLC) with no assets at the time of suit. Kaycee Land and Livestock (Kaycee) (P) entered into a contract with Flahive allowing the company to use the surface of Kaycee's (P) real property. Roger Flahive (D) was the managing member of Flahive Oil & Gas at all relevant times. Kaycee (P) brought suit in the district court against Flahive (D) alleging that Flahive (D) caused environmental contamination to its real property. Kaycee (P) sought to pierce the LLC veil, disregard the LLC entity of Flahive Oil & Gas LLC, and hold Roger Flahive (D) individually liable for the contamination. There was no allegation of fraud. The district court certified to the Wyoming Supreme Court the question whether, in the absence of fraud, the entity veil of a limited liability company can be pierced in the same manner as that of a corporation.

ISSUE: Is the equitable remedy of piercing the veil an available remedy under the Limited Liability Company (LLC) Act?

HOLDING AND DECISION: (Kite, J.) Yes. The equitable remedy of piercing the veil is an available remedy under the Limited Liability Company (LLC) Act. While as a general rule a corporation is a separate entity distinct from the individuals comprising it, a corporation's legal entity will be disregarded whenever the recognition of corporate status will lead to injustice. No reason exists in law or equity for treating an LLC differently from a corporation when considering whether to disregard the legal entity. The LLC statute simply states the underlying principle of limited liability for individual members and managers by providing that neither the members of an LLC nor the managers of an LLC managed by a manager are liable for liabilities of the limited liability company. It is difficult to read this statutory provision as precluding courts from disregarding the veil of an improperly used LLC. Lack of explicit statutory language should not indicate the legislature's desire to make LLC members impermeable. Every state that has enacted LLC piercing legislation has chosen to follow corporate law standards and not develop a separate LLC standard. Statutes that create corporations and LLCs have the same basic purpose of limiting individual investor liability while benefiting economic development. Statutes created the legal fiction of the corporation as a separate entity independent from individuals. If the corporation were created and operated in conformance with the statutory requirements, the law would treat it as a separate entity and shelter the individual shareholders from any liability caused by corporate action, thereby encouraging investment. However, courts have consistently recognized that unjust circumstances can arise if immunity from liability shelters those who have failed to operate a corporation as a separate entity. Consequently, when corporations fail to follow statutorily mandated formalities, co-mingle funds, or ignore the restrictions in their articles of incorporation regarding separate treatment of corporate property, the courts disregard the separate identity and do not permit shareholders to be sheltered from liability to third parties for damages caused by the corporations' acts. There is no reason in law or policy to treat LLCs differently, although the factors justifying piercing an LLC veil would not be identical to those in the corporate situation because many organizational formalities applicable to corporations do not apply to LLCs. Certified question answered in the negative.

▶ ANALYSIS

In *Kaycee*, the court noted that among the possible factors to be considered in determining whether the interests of justice require piercing the corporate veil are the following: the commingling of funds and other assets, failure to segregate funds of the separate entities, and unauthorized diversion of corporate funds or assets to other than corporate uses; treatment by an individual of assets of the corporation as his or her own; failure to obtain authority to issue or subscribe to stock; the holding out by an individual that he or she is personally liable for the debts of the corporation; failure to maintain minutes or adequate corporate records and the confusion of the records of the

Continued on next page.

separate entities; identical equitable ownership in the two entities; identification of the directors and officers of the two entities in the responsible supervision and management; failure to adequately capitalize a corporation; absence of corporate assets and undercapitalization; use of a corporation as a mere shell, instrumentality or conduit for a single venture or the business of an individual or another corporation; concealment and misrepresentation of the identity of the responsible ownership, management, and financial interest or concealment of personal business activities; disregard of legal formalities and the failure to maintain arm's-length relationships among related entities; use of corporate entity to procure labor, services, or merchandise for another person or entity; diversion of assets from a corporation by or to a stockholder or other person or entity, to the detriment of creditors, or the manipulation of assets and liabilities between entities so as to concentrate the assets in one and the liabilities in another; contracting with another with intent to avoid performance by use of a corporation as a subterfuge of illegal transactions; and formation and use of a corporation to transfer to it the existing liability of another person or entity.

■━■

Quicknotes

LIMITED LIABILITY An advantage of doing business in the corporate form by safeguarding shareholders from liability for the debts or obligations of the corporation.

LIMITED LIABILITY COMPANY (LLC) A business entity combining the features of both a corporation and a general partnership; the LLC provides its shareholders and officers with limited liability, but it is treated as a partnership for taxation purposes.

■━■

VGS, Inc. v. Castiel

LLC manager/shareholders (D) v. LLC originator/manager/shareholder (P)

Del. Ch. Ct., 2000 WL 1277372 (2000), *aff'd.*, 781 A.2d 696 (2001).

NATURE OF CASE: Equity suit by a manager/shareholder of a limited liability company (LLC) to set aside a reorganization and merger of the LLC by fellow managers.

FACT SUMMARY: David Castiel (P) formed VGS, Inc. (D) as a one-member limited liability company (LLC). The one member was Virtual Geosatellite Holdings. Two other entities, Sahagen Satellite and Ellipso, Inc., later became member/shareholders of the LLC. Castiel named himself and Tom Quinn to the board of managers, and Sahagan named himself as the third member. Sahagen and Quinn subsequently decided to restructure VGS (D) in such a manner that Castiel (P) would become a minority shareholder. They effectuated the restructuring without giving notice to Castiel (P).

🏛 RULE OF LAW
Managers under a limited liability corporation agreement must exercise a duty of loyalty by acting in good faith to one another.

FACTS: VGS, Inc. (D) was controlled by David Castiel (P), a single individual who formed VGS (D) as a one-member limited liability company (LLC). Subsequently, two other entities, Sahagen Satellite and Ellipso, Inc., became members of the LLC. The LLC agreement created a three-member board of managers with sweeping authority to govern the LLC. Castiel (P), the individual owning the original member, had the authority to name and remove, two of the three managers and also acted as CEO. Castiel named himself and Tom Quinn to the board of managers, and Sahagan named himself as the third member. Sahagen and Quinn became disenchanted with Castiel's (P) leadership. Ultimately Sahagen convinced Quinn to join him in a clandestine strategic move to merge the LLC into a Delaware corporation. The appointed manager, Quinn, and the disaffected third member, Sahagen, did not give Castiel (P), still a member of the LLC's board of managers, notice of their strategic move. After the merger, Castiel (P) found himself relegated to a minority position in the surviving corporation. Castiel brought suit in equity to set aside the merger, arguing that, although a majority of the board acted by written consent, if Castiel had received notice beforehand that his appointed manager contemplated action against his interests, he would have promptly attempted to remove him. Castiel (P) contended that because his two fellow managers (Sahagen and Quinn) acted without notice to Castiel (P) under circumstances where they knew that with notice he could have acted to protect

his majority interest, they breached their duty of loyalty to him by failing to act in good faith.

ISSUE: Must the managers under a limited liability corporation agreement exercise a duty of loyalty by acting in good faith to one another?

HOLDING AND DECISION: (Steele, V. Chan.) Yes. The managers under a limited liability corporation (LLC) agreement must exercise a duty of loyalty by acting in good faith to one another. Here, by not giving Castiel (P) notice of their proposed action, Sahagen and Quinn (hence VGS, Inc.) (D) failed to discharge their duty of loyalty to Castiel and exercise their duty of good faith toward him. Section 18-404(d) of the LLC Act states, in part, that the managers of a LLC company may take actions without a vote if a consent in writing, setting forth the action taken, is signed by the managers having not less than the minimum number of votes that would be necessary to authorize such action at a meeting. Therefore, the LLC Act, read literally, did not require notice to Castiel (P) before Sahagen and Quinn could act by written consent. However, this observation does not complete the analysis of Sahagen's and Quinn's actions. Sahagen and Quinn knew what would happen if they notified Castiel (P) of their intention to act by written consent to merge the LLC into VGS, Inc. Castiel (P) would have attempted to remove Quinn and block the planned action. The purpose of permitting action by written consent without notice is to enable LLC managers to take quick, efficient action in situations when a minority of managers could not block or adversely affect the course set by the majority, even if the minority were notified of the proposed action and objected to it. The legislators never intended to enable two managers to deprive, clandestinely and surreptitiously, a third manager representing the majority interest in the LLC of an opportunity to protect that interest by taking an action that the third manager's member would surely have opposed if he had knowledge of it. Equity looks to the intent rather than to the form. Here, in this hopefully unique situation, this application of the maxim requires construction of the statute to allow action without notice only by a constant or fixed majority. It can not apply to an illusory, will-of-the-wisp majority which would implode should notice be given. Nothing in the statute suggests that a court of equity should blind its eyes to a shallow, too clever by half, manipulative attempt to restructure an enterprise through an action taken by a "majority" that existed only so long as

Continued on next page.

it could act in secrecy. Although a majority vote of the LLC's board of managers could properly effect a merger, nevertheless, Sahagen and Quinn failed to discharge their duty of loyalty to Castiel (P) in good faith by failing to give him advance notice of their merger plans under the unique circumstances of this case and the structure of this LLC agreement. Accordingly, the acts taken to merge the LLC into VGS, Inc. were invalid, and the merger is ordered rescinded.

▶ ANALYSIS

In the *VGS* case, Sahagen and Quinn each owed a duty of loyalty to the LLC, its investors, and Castiel (P), their fellow manager. Castiel (P) owned a majority interest in the LLC, and he sat as a member of the board. The majority investor protected his equity interest in the LLC through the mechanism of appointment to the board rather than by the statutorily sanctioned mechanism of approval by members owning a majority of the LLC's equity interests. The agreement allowed the action to merge, dissolve or change to corporate status to be taken by a simple majority vote of the board of managers rather than by reliance upon the default position of the statute which requires a majority vote of the equity interest. Instead, the drafters made the critical assumption that the holder of the majority equity interest had the right to appoint and remove two managers, ostensibly guaranteeing control over a three-member board. When Sahagen and Quinn, fully recognizing that these rights were Castiel's (P) protection against actions adverse to his majority interest, acted in secret and without notice, they failed to discharge their duty of loyalty to him in good faith. The Chancery Court here took the position that the managers owed Castiel (P) a duty to give him prior notice, even if he would have interfered with a plan that they conscientiously believed to be in the best interest of the LLC. Instead, the managers launched a preemptive strike that furtively converted Castiel's (P) controlling interest in the LLC to a minority interest in VGS (D), without affording Castiel (P) a level playing field on which to defend his interest. A traditional maxim of equity holds that equity regards and treats that as done which in good conscience ought to be done. Accordingly, under these circumstances, the court held Sahagen and Quinn should have given Castiel (P) prior notice.

■≡■

Quicknotes

ACTION IN EQUITY Lawsuit in which a plaintiff seeks equitable remedies.

DUTY OF GOOD FAITH AND FAIR DEALING An implied duty in a contract that the parties will deal honestly in the satisfaction of their obligations and without intent to defraud.

DUTY OF LOYALTY A director's duty to refrain from self-dealing or to take a position that is adverse to the corporation's best interests.

EQUITY Fairness; justice; the determination of a matter consistent with principles of fairness and not in strict compliance with rules of law.

LIMITED LIABILITY An advantage of doing business in the corporate form by safeguarding shareholders from liability for the debts or obligations of the corporation.

LIMITED LIABILITY COMPANY (LLC) A business entity combining the features of both a corporation and a general partnership; the LLC provides its shareholders and officers with limited liability, but it is treated as a partnership for taxation purposes.

■≡■

Fisk Ventures, LLC v. Segal

LLC member (P) v. LLC's president (D)

Del. Ch. Ct., 2008 WL 1961156 (2008).

NATURE OF CASE: Motion to dismiss counterclaims and third-party claims in action to dissolve a limited liability company (LLC).

FACT SUMMARY: Fisk Ventures, LLC (Fisk) (P), a member Genitrix, LLC (Genitrix), brought suit to dissolve Genitrix. Segal (D), the founder, president and sole officer of Genitrix, answered the petition and filed counterclaims and third-party claims, asserting various claims for breach of contract and fiduciary duties. The counterclaim and third-party defendants moved to dismiss these claims, asserting that, if at all, their actions constituted the exercise of their contractual rights.

🏛 RULE OF LAW

LLC members do not breach their LLC agreement, the implied covenant of good faith and fair dealing thereunder, or their fiduciary duties by exercising the contractual rights granted to them in the agreement.

FACTS: Segal (D) founded Genitrix, LLC (Genitrix), in which the equity was divided into three classes of membership. Segal (D) held 55 percent of Class A; Fisk Ventures, LLC (Fisk) (P), Johnson (who controlled Fisk (P)), Freund, and Rose held the Class B interests; and the Class C interests were held by passive investors. Genitrix's LLC agreement (LLC Agreement) divided power among the Class A and Class B members, but was drafted in such a way as to require the cooperation of the Class A and B members. Segal (D) appointed two of the board's five members, while the Class B members were able to appoint the remaining three. The Class B members also had a put right, whereby they could, at any time, force the company to purchase any or all of their Class B interests at a price determined by an independent appraisal. If exercised, the put would subrogate what otherwise would be senior claims of new investors. This made it difficult to raise money from new investors, but the Class B members refused to relinquish or suspend their put right. The company had great difficulty raising capital, which caused a Fisk (P) note to convert to Class B equity, thereby diluting the Class A and C interests. Segal (D), who was desperately seeking to raise new money, drafted a Private Placement Memorandum (PPM), but the Class B board representatives refused to consent to it, citing the haste with which Segal (D) was acting. Although the Class B representatives asked to discuss the PPM at a board meeting, no such meeting occurred, as the Class A representatives refused to participate in any meetings. Notwithstanding that Fisk (P) continued to make capital

contributions throughout, the business eventually ran out of operating cash and stalled, and Fisk (P) brought suit to dissolve Genitrix. Segal (D) made counterclaims against Fisk (P) and third-party claims against Johnson, Rose, and Freund. Specifically, Segal (D) contended that the counterclaim/third-party defendants breached the LLC Agreement, breached the implied covenant of good faith and fair dealing implicit in the LLC Agreement, and breached their fiduciary duties to the company—primarily by standing in the way of proposed financing. The counterclaim/third-party defendants moved to dismiss Segal's (D) claims, asserting that he failed to state a claim upon which relief could be granted because his allegations reflected little more than the exercise of their contractual rights.

ISSUE: Do LLC members breach their LLC agreement, the implied covenant of good faith and fair dealing thereunder, or their fiduciary duties by exercising the contractual rights granted to them in the agreement?

HOLDING AND DECISION: (Chandler, Chan.) No. LLC members do not breach their LLC agreement, the implied covenant of good faith and fair dealing thereunder, or their fiduciary duties by exercising the contractual rights granted to them in the agreement. Here, the LLC Agreement did not create duties that the counterclaim/third-party defendants breached. While it may be true, as Segal (D) contends that if only the Class members had acquiesced to his requests, the company would be thriving, but it may also be true that the company would be thriving if Segal (D) had acquiesced to the Class B members' wishes. Regardless of who had the better business judgment, the LLC Agreement did not require either group to acquiesce to the other. Despite Segal's (D) argument to the contrary, the LLC Agreement did not create a code of conduct for its members; to the contrary, the LLC Agreement served to limit or waive liability to the maximum extent permitted by law. Merely because the LLC Agreement limited liability to instances where members acted with gross negligence, fraud, or intentional misconduct, this exculpatory provision did not—and could not—impose an all encompassing and seeming boundless standard of conduct. Even if it did, the court could not enforce such a standard because there would be no limit to its applicability. Finally, even if the LLC Agreement did somehow create a code of conduct for members, Segal (D) has failed to allege facts sufficient to support a reasonable inference that the counterclaim/third-party defendants breached this code; at most, they vigorously championed their own proposals and did not support

Continued on next page.

Segal's (D) plans. Nothing they did was grossly negligent, in bad faith, fraudulent, or willful. As to the breach of the implied covenant of good faith and fair dealing, which is implied in every contract and requires a party to a contract to refrain from acting in such a way as to prevent the other party from receiving the fruits of the bargain, this covenant is not a contractual gap filler. It is intended, instead, to give effect to the spirit of what was actually bargained for. Therefore, it cannot be invoked where the contract itself expressly covers a particular subject. Segal (D) argues that the counterclaim/third-party defendants breached the implied covenant by frustrating or blocking the financing opportunities he proposed. However, neither the LLC Agreement nor any other contract endowed him with the right to unilaterally decide what fundraising or financing opportunities Genitrix should pursue. Moreover, the LLC Agreement did address the subject of financing, specifically requiring the approval of 75 percent of the board. Implicit in such a requirement was the right of the Class B board representatives to disapprove of and therefore block Segal's (D) proposals. In other words, the mere exercise of one's contractual rights, without more, cannot constitute a breach of the implied covenant of good faith and fair dealing. Negotiating forcefully and within the bounds of rights granted by the LLC Agreement does not translate to a breach of the implied covenant on the part of the Class B members. Finally, as to Segal's (D) breach of fiduciary claims, these must also be dismissed because the LLC Agreement restricts or eliminates these to the maximum extent permitted by law and because even if the Class B members had a duty to not act in bad faith or with gross negligence, Segal (D) failed to plead facts that supported a claims that anyone had breached such a hypothetical duty. The motion to dismiss Segal's (D) claims is granted.

▶ *ANALYSIS*

Here, the Genitrix LLC Agreement eliminated fiduciary duties to the maximum extent permitted by law by flatly stating that members had no duties other than those expressly articulated in the Agreement. Because the Agreement did not expressly articulate fiduciary obligations, they were eliminated. This comports with the view that where it is more likely that sophisticated parties have carefully negotiated their governing agreement, as in an LLC agreement, they should be able to eliminate fiduciary duties altogether.

Quicknotes

CONTRACTUAL RIGHT A right or expectation that is created pursuant to a contract.

FIDUCIARY DUTY A legal obligation to act for the benefit of another, including subordinating one's personal interests to that of the other person.

IMPLIED COVENANT OF GOOD FAITH AND FAIR DEALING An implied warranty that the parties will deal honestly in the satisfaction of their obligations and without an intent to defraud.

LIMITED LIABILITY COMPANY (LLC) A business entity combining the features of both a corporation and a general partnership; the LLC provides its shareholders and officers with limited liability, but it is treated as a partnership for taxation purposes.

Anderson v. Wilder

Minority member (P) v. Majority member (D)

Tenn. Ct. App., 2003 WL 22768666 (2003).

NATURE OF CASE: Appeal from summary judgment for defendants in action for breach of fiduciary duties.

FACT SUMMARY: Minority members (P) of FuturePoint Administrative Services, LLC (the "LLC"), a closely held, member-managed LLC, contended that the LLC's majority members (D) breached their fiduciary duties to the minority members (P) by expelling the minority members (P) and, shortly after expulsion, selling the former minority members' (P) units for a price far in excess of the buyout price.

RULE OF LAW

The majority members of a member-managed, closely held LLC owe a fiduciary duty of fair dealing and good faith to the minority members.

FACTS: The minority members (P) of FuturePoint Administrative Services, LLC (the "LLC"), a closely held, member-managed LLC, were expelled by the vote of the majority shareholders (D), who collectively held 53 percent of the LLC. The operating agreement permitted the company to expel a member with or without cause upon a vote or consent of the members who held a majority of the units, and this is what the majority members (D) purported to do. Prior to the expulsion, the members had met to discuss the purchase of ownership units by third parties at $250 per unit. The minority members (P) received $150.00 per ownership unit in the LLC after they were expelled, pursuant to the LLC's operating agreement. Shortly after the expulsion, the majority shareholders (D) sold 499 ownership units, amounting to a 49.9 percent interest in the LLC, to a third party at a price of $250.00 per ownership unit. The minority members (P) filed suit, alleging, inter alia, that the majority shareholders' (D) actions violated their fiduciary duty and duty of good faith and fair dealing to the minority members (P). The majority shareholders (D) moved for summary judgment, arguing that their actions were authorized by the operating agreement and that they acted in good faith in expelling the minority members (P). One reason they gave for the expulsion was that the minority members (P) on the management committee had planned to distribute the company's cash, of around $60,000, to all the members, thereby jeopardizing payroll and operations. The minority members (P) vigorously denied that allegation and claimed it was merely a pretext for buying their units on the cheap and selling the units at a hefty

profit. The trial court granted summary judgment in the majority shareholders' (D) favor, and the state's intermediate appellate court granted review.

ISSUE: Do the majority members of a member-managed, closely held LLC owe a fiduciary duty of fair dealing and good faith to the minority members?

HOLDING AND DECISION: (Goddard, J.) Yes. The majority members of a member-managed, closely held LLC owe a fiduciary duty of fair dealing and good faith to the minority members. Partners in partnerships and shareholders in closely-held corporations owe each other fiduciary duties to act in good faith and integrity in their dealings with one another, so do members of a closely-held, member-managed LLC owe each other similar fiduciary duties. Such a duty is not inconsistent with the state's LLC statute, which, although it does not expressly prescribe a fiduciary duty of majority members to the minority members, does require that each member discharge his or her duties in good faith. Thus, the majority members (D) here owed the minority members (P) the fiduciary duty to act with honesty and good faith toward them. The evidence presented, in the form of conflicting testimony as to why the majority members (D) expelled the minority members, (P) raises a genuine issue of material fact as to whether the majority members were (D) properly motivated or acted in good faith in accordance with their fiduciary duty toward the minority members (P). Therefore, summary judgment was erroneous. Vacated and remanded.

▌ ANALYSIS

The holding in this case arguably is inconsistent with the view that the statute at issue defines the fiduciary duty of members of a closely-held, member-managed LLC as one owing to the LLC, not to the individual members. However, the holding can be seen as carving out an exception to that general rule in the case of duties owed by majority members to minority members, so as to avoid minority oppression. In any event, on remand, the majority members (D) were found to have breached their fiduciary duties to the minority members (P) (*see Anderson v. Wilder*, 2007 Tenn. App. LEXIS 582).

■=■

Continued on next page.

Quicknotes

BREACH OF FIDUCIARY DUTY The failure of a fiduciary to observe the standard of care exercised by professionals of similar education and experience.

DUTY OF GOOD FAITH OF FAIR DEALINGS An implied duty in a contract that the parties will deal honestly in the satisfaction of their obligations and without intent to defraud.

■▬■

Achaian, Inc. v. Leemon Family LLC

LLC member (P) v. LLC member (D)

Del. Ch. Ct., 25 A.3d 800 (2011).

NATURE OF CASE: Action for dissolution of a limited liability company (LLC) seeking a declaratory judgment as to the apportionment of membership interests.

FACT SUMMARY: Achaian, Inc. (P), initially a 20 percent member of Omniglow, LLC, contended that the transfer and assignment to it by the Randye M. Holland and Stanley M. Holland Trust (Holland) of Holland's 30 percent interest, rendered Achaian (P) a 50 percent member under Omniglow's LLC Agreement, notwithstanding that the other 50 percent owner, Leemon Family LLC (Leemon) (D), had not given its approval for that transfer and assignment.

🏛 RULE OF LAW
One member of an LLC may assign its entire membership interest, including that interest's voting rights, to another existing member, notwithstanding the fact that the limited liability company agreement requires the affirmative consent of all of the members upon the admission of a new member, where the agreement, when read as a whole, allows an existing member to transfer its entire membership interest, including voting rights, to another existing member without obtaining the other members' consent.

FACTS: Omniglow, LLC had three members, with interests as follows: (i) 50 percent was owned by the Leemon Family LLC (Leemon) (D); (ii) 30 percent was owned by the Randye M. Holland and Stanley M. Holland Trust (Holland); and (iii) 20 percent was owned by Achaian, Inc. (P). Holland and Leemon (D) initially managed Omniglow's business with Achaian (P) taking a passive role as an investor. Then, however, Leemon (D) allegedly took sole control of Omniglow over the objection of both Achaian (P) and Holland, and in contravention of Omniglow's "LLC agreement" that vested managerial authority in the members in proportion to their respective interests. Holland, fed up with controversy, purported to transfer and assign its entire 30 percent interest to Achaian (P), which then filed suit in Delaware Chancery Court, claiming that it and Leemon (D) were deadlocked, 50/50, as to the management of Omniglow. Achaian (P) sought an order of dissolution on the grounds that it was no longer reasonably practicable to carry on Omniglow's business in conformity with Omniglow's LLC agreement. Leemon (D) moved to dismiss the complaint, arguing that Holland's assignment was only effective to give Achaian (P) an additional 30 percent economic interest in Omniglow. Specifically, Leemon (D) argued that for Achaian (P) to have received a 30 percent

membership interest in Omniglow, the LLC agreement required Leemon's (D) consent to the assignment because, in its view, Achaian (P) was in effect being readmitted as a member with respect to its newly acquired 30 percent interest. Achaian (P) sought a declaratory judgment that it was now a 50 percent owner. The parties relied on provisions of the LLC agreement in making their arguments. First, the agreement defined a "Member's Interest" as meaning "the entire ownership interest of the Member." Two related sections of the LLC agreement then dealt specifically with the transfer of interests. The first, § 7.1, allowed a member to transfer all or part of its interest to any person or entity at any time. This permissive grant of free transferability, however, was subject to the express restriction contained in § 7.2, which prohibited the admission of a new member without the written consent of existing members.

ISSUE: May one member of an LLC assign its entire membership interest, including that interest's voting rights, to another existing member, notwithstanding the fact that the limited liability company agreement requires the affirmative consent of all of the members upon the admission of a new member, where the agreement, when read as a whole, allows an existing member to transfer its entire membership interest, including voting rights, to another existing member without obtaining the other members' consent?

HOLDING AND DECISION: (Strine, Chan.) Yes. One member of an LLC may assign its entire membership interest, including that interest's voting rights, to another existing member, notwithstanding the fact that the limited liability company agreement requires the affirmative consent of all of the members upon the admission of a new member, where the agreement, when read as a whole, allows an existing member to transfer its entire membership interest, including voting rights, to another existing member without obtaining the other members' consent. When the LLC agreement is viewed as a whole in conjunction with the state's LLC statute, it permits an existing member to transfer its entire membership interest, including voting rights, to another existing member without obtaining the other members' consent. In reaching this conclusion, it is clear that the default rule under the Delaware LLC Act is that an assignment of an LLC interest, by itself, does not entitle the assignee to become a member of the LLC; rather, an assignee only receives the assigning member's economic interest in the LLC to the extent

Continued on next page.

assigned. It is equally clear, however, that the default rule may be displaced by the provisions of an LLC agreement itself, and that in the event of a conflict, the LLC agreement prevails. Here, the LLC agreement's provisions dealing with member interests and their transferability permitted the free transfer by one member of "the entire ownership interest of the Member" to another member. Such an ownership interest includes voting rights, not just economic rights. This interpretation rests on a plain language interpretation of the term "entire," as well as on the second sentence of § 7.1, which makes it clear that the broad definition of "Interest" includes all aspects of membership, including managerial voting rights. That sentence provides that if a transfer results in Omniglow having more than one member, the LLC agreement will be amended to reflect that the company will be treated as a partnership for tax purposes. This makes clear that a "Member's Interest"—i.e., its "entire ownership interest"—includes every aspect of a Member's Interest, including the portion that confers the status of member, in whom, under the LLC agreement, managerial authority is vested. If it were otherwise, and an interest in Omniglow represented only a member's economic interest, the second sentence of § 7.1 would seem to be unnecessary because in that case, an existing member could not transfer or assign the voting rights included in its interest to another person or entity such that as a result of such transfer or assignment, that person or entity could become a member. Read in complete context, the LLC agreement made interests in Omniglow freely transferable subject only to the limited proviso in § 7.2 that required the written consent of the existing members in order for a transfer to confer membership status on a person or entity not already a member at the time of transfer. Accordingly, because Achaian (P) was already a member at the time of the purchase agreement and nothing in the LLC agreement required that it be readmitted as a member with respect to each additional interest it acquired in Omniglow, it was entitled to receive the "entire ownership interest" owned by Holland, including that interest's corresponding voting rights. In summing up this conclusion, a Commodore's song, titled "Three Times a Lady," is apt. The key verse of that song is "You're once, twice, three times a lady/And I love you . . . ." "The problem for Leemon is that nothing in the LLC Agreement supports Leemon's reading of it that would require an already admitted Member, like Achaian, to be become once, twice (or even three times) a Member each and every time that Member acquires an additional block of Interests." By its plain terms, § 7.2 is directed at, and applies only to, a "Person" (which term encompasses entities) who is not yet "admitted as a Member." Because Achaian (P) was already admitted as a member at the time of Holland's transfer, § 7.2 has no application. Therefore, Achaian (P) is entitled to the declaratory judgment it seeks, namely that Omniglow had two members—Leemon (D) and Achaian (P)—each holding an identical 50 percent membership interest. Judgment for Achaian (P).

ANALYSIS

Under 6 Del. C. § 18-702, the default LLC Act rule, "[a] limited liability company interest is assignable in whole or in part except as provided in a limited liability company agreement. The assignee of a member's limited liability company interest shall have no right to participate in the management of the business and affairs of a limited liability company except as provided in a limited liability company agreement . . . . Unless otherwise provided in a limited liability company agreement, [a]n assignment of a limited liability company interest does not entitle the assignee to become or to exercise any rights or powers of a member [and instead only] entitles the assignee to share in such profits and losses, to receive such distribution or distributions, and to receive such allocation of income, gain, loss, deduction, or credit or similar item to which the assignor was entitled, to the extent assigned." One motivation for this default rule is tax related, and came out of states' early attempts to create an entity that, as a matter of tax law, was classified as a partnership with each owner treated as a partner, but whose owners were shielded by state law from automatic personal liability. This aspect of the default rules has now been rendered largely unnecessary after the United States Treasury Department adopted the "check-the-box" federal income tax classification regime in 1997, under which an unincorporated entity, like a limited liability company, is taxed as a partnership if it has two or more owners, or is disregarded for income tax purposes if it has one owner, unless it elects to be taxed as a corporation by "checking the box." A second reason for the default rules in the Act regarding the transferability of interests may rest on the notion that one generally is entitled to select her own business associates in a closely held enterprise, like an LLC.

Quicknotes

DECLARATORY JUDGMENT A judgment of the court establishing the rights of the parties.

Lieberman v. Wyoming.com LLC

Disassociated LLC member (D) v. LLC (P)

Wyo. Sup. Ct., 82 P.3d 274 (2004).

NATURE OF CASE: Appeal from summary judgment, on remand, for plaintiff in declaratory judgment action to determine the financial consequences of the withdrawal of an LLC member.

FACT SUMMARY: After Lieberman (D) withdrew from Wyoming.com LLC (P), the LLC (P) brought a declaratory judgment action to determine the financial consequences of his withdrawal, asserting that the LLC (P) was obligated to pay to Lieberman (D), after repayment of his capital contribution, only the value of his capital account (which had a negative value), rather than, as Lieberman (D) asserted, the fair market value of his equity interest (which he claimed was worth $400,000).

🏛 **RULE OF LAW**
Where neither a state's LLC statute nor an LLC's operating agreement address the financial consequences of a member's dissociation from the LLC, a withdrawing member continues as an equity owner who is under no obligation to sell his equity interest but who cannot force the LLC to buy his equity interest.

FACTS: Lieberman (D) was a member of Wyoming.com LLC (P), credited with a 40 percent equity interest and a $20,000 capital contribution. After he was terminated as an employee, Lieberman (D) tendered his withdrawal from the LLC (P), which the remaining members accepted. The remaining members also determined to continue, rather than dissolve, the LLC (P). Lieberman (D) then demanded the immediate return of "his share of the current value of the company," estimating the value of his share at $ 400,000, "based on a recent offer from the Majority Shareholder." The LLC (P) offered Lieberman (D) his stated capital contribution of $20,000, but he declined to accept this, claiming he was entitled to more. The LLC (P) then brought a declaratory judgment action, and the trial court ruled that Lieberman (D) had the right to demand the return of only his stated capital contribution, $20,000, which the court ordered to be paid in cash. The court also ruled that the LLC (P) was not in a state of dissolution. Lieberman (D) appealed, and the state's highest court, in *Lieberman I*, 11 P.3d 353 (Wyo. 2000), affirmed the trial court on its dissolution ruling, but held that because the state's LLC statute did not address the financial consequences of the withdrawal of a member, but only the only the withdrawal of a member's capital contribution, Lieberman (D) was entitled to the return of his capital contribution, regardless of his status as a member of Wyoming.com (P). Since Lieberman (D) expected more,

however, the court remanded the case "because it is unclear what, became of Lieberman's ownership or equity interest (as represented by a membership certificate)" requiring further proceedings "for a full declaration of the parties' rights." On remand, the trial court and the parties operated under the assumption that Lieberman (D) had withdrawn as an equity owner and that his equity interest needed to be valued and returned to him. The LLC (P) maintained that under Wyoming.com's (P) operating agreement, it owed Lieberman (D) only the value of his capital account on the date of his withdrawal, which, at the time of withdrawal, had a negative value. The trial court agreed, and granted summary judgment to Wyoming.com (P), ordering the liquidation of Lieberman's (D) equity interest. The state's highest court granted review.

ISSUE: Where, neither a state's LLC statute nor an LLC's operating agreement address the financial consequences of a member's dissociation from the LLC, does a withdrawing member continue as an equity owner who is under no obligation to sell his equity interest but who cannot force the LLC to buy his equity interest?

HOLDING AND DECISION: (Golden, J.) Yes. Where neither a state's LLC statute nor an LLC's operating agreement address the financial consequences of a member's dissociation from the LLC, a withdrawing member continues as an equity owner who is under no obligation to sell his equity interest but who cannot force the LLC to buy his equity interest. The state LLC statute contains no provision relating to the fate of a member's equity interest upon the member's dissociation. Thus, it was entirely up to the members of Wyoming.com (P) to contractually provide for terms of dissociation. Upon careful review of all the agreements entered into by the parties regarding Wyoming.com (P), it is clear that the agreements contain no provision regarding the equity interest of a dissociating member. The provision relied on by the trial court only provides a method for distributing capital upon liquidation. It contains no indication of when liquidation can or must occur, nor does it mandate a buyout or a liquidation of a member's equity interest. As such, it has no application to the immediate issue, and the trial court's reliance upon it was misplaced. Since no provision mandates a different result, Lieberman (D) retains his equity interest. A member's interest in an LLC consists of economic and non-economic interests. These interests are distinct, and it is clear from Lieberman's (D) notice of withdrawal that he had no intention of forfeiting his economic, or equity,

Continued on next page.

interest in the company. Lieberman's (D) withdrawal regarded his non-economic membership interest only. His withdrawal notice did not terminate his equity interest, and he has not voluntarily forfeited his equity interest. No evidence was presented that his membership certificate has been canceled or forfeited. Moreover, the operating agreements clearly anticipate a situation where a person could be an equity owner in Wyoming.com (P) but not a member. Because Lieberman (D) retains his equity interest, he is under no obligation to sell his equity interest, but correspondingly, Wyoming.com (P) is under no obligation to buy his equity interest. The parties essentially admit this in their respective briefs: Lieberman (D) argues that there is nothing in the agreements allowing Wyoming.com (P) to acquire his ownership interest at less than fair market value, while Wyoming.com (P) argues that there is nothing in the agreements requiring Wyoming.com (P) to pay fair market value for Lieberman's (D) ownership interest. Both arguments are correct. There simply is no contractual agreement that any party must buy or sell an ownership interest for any amount, and the parties are left at status quo—the court will not write a buyout provision for them. The question of valuation is, therefore, moot. The decision of the trial court liquidating Lieberman's (D) equity interest is reversed, and the case is remanded to the trial court for a declaration of the parties' rights consistent with this opinion. Reversed and remanded.

DISSENT: (Lehman, J.) While the majority is correct that there is no express provision in the operating agreements dealing with a dissociated member's equity interest, this does not mean that the operating agreements by implication do not provide guidance as to what the parties intended upon a member's withdrawal. Because the agreements contemplate a member's ability to terminate his or her membership and the remaining members' ability to continue the business, by implication the parties must have contemplated some sort of buyout. In addition, the LLC statutory scheme implies that, absent other agreement, a member has a right to terminate his continued membership in the LLC and be compensated for this interest. The typical LLC statutes choose to utilize partnership principles, rather than corporate principles, for exiting members, and partnership exit rules ordinarily allow for any partner to dissolve the firm at any time and demand liquidation and accordingly be paid for his equity interest. Because the legislature recognized this partnership rule as the norm applying in the LLC context, the resulting implication is a member may terminate his membership in an LLC and must be paid for this interest unless otherwise provided. The majority also erred in concluding that Lieberman's (D) withdrawal regarded his non-economic membership interest only; the reality is that a withdrawing member does not envision that his withdrawal will result in this split in his interest. Even though the parties themselves proceeded under the assumption that Lieberman (D) had withdrawn as a member and an equity owner, and that he was entitled

to be bought out, the majority refuses to provide relief for this situation. Because the majority's analysis could equally be applied where a member has been expelled, the majority creates the potential for minority oppression, whereby some of the members could expel a member and then refuse to negotiate for a buyout. Therefore, a remedy should be provided. That remedy should be the valuation of the departing member's interest as though the company were being dissolved. In other words, the withdrawing member's interest, absent a provision in the operating agreement to the contrary, should be valued at what he would have received had the business been dissolved on the day he terminated his membership in the LLC. Fair market value would be a reasonable alternative estimate of the departing member's share. However, because the remaining members have elected to continue the company, some consideration must be given to the duties and hardship the company may encounter as a result of paying the departing member's equity interest—such as payment over time. Furthermore, until the member is paid in full, that member should still receive any distributions to which his interest is entitled, much like a transferee without the right to participate in the management of the business.

▶ *ANALYSIS*

The court's decision arguably has created a situation where the remaining members may be in a position of power to dictate the terms of any negotiations for a buyout, since they are now conceivably in a position to retain earnings and avoid distributions, but, as an equity owner with no say in the business, Lieberman (D) would still be required to pay taxes on those earnings. Additionally, Lieberman (D), with not control over his equity interest in any manner, may be forced to take a lower buyout to avoid such negative consequences.

━■━

Quicknotes

CONTRACTUAL RIGHT A right or expectation that is created pursuant to a contract.

DECLARATORY JUDGMENT A judgment of the court establishing the rights of the parties.

LIMITED LIABILITY COMPANY A business entity combining the features of both a corporation and a general partnership; the LLC provides its shareholders and officers with limited liability, but it is treated as a partnership for taxation purposes.

━■━

Dunbar Group, LLC v. Tignor

Co-equal member (P) v. Co-equal member (D)

Va. Sup. Ct., 593 S.E.2d 216 (2004).

NATURE OF CASE: Appeal from order dissolving a limited liability company.

FACT SUMMARY: Dunbar Group, LLC (Dunbar) (P), a co-equal member and manager with Tignor (D) in XpertCTI, LLC (Xpert), contended that Xpert should not be dissolved after Tignor's (D) expulsion therefrom because there was insufficient evidence showing that it would not be reasonably practicable to carry on Xpert's business even after Tignor's (D) expulsion.

🏛 RULE OF LAW
An LLC will not be judicially dissolved where there has not been a showing that it will not be reasonably practicable to carry on the LLC's business.

FACTS: Dunbar Group, LLC (Dunbar) (P) was a co-equal member and manager with Tignor (D) in XpertCTI, LLC (Xpert). Dunbar Group (P) was controlled by its sole owner, Robertson (P), and Tignor (D) was a 50 percent owner of X-tel, Inc. Dunbar's (P) role in Xpert was to provide software, and Tignor's (D) role was to provide access to business contacts. Xpert's operating agreement provided a procedure for a member to assert a breach of the agreement by another member, where, if the breach was not timely cured by the defaulting member, the complaining member had the "right to petition a court of competent jurisdiction for dissolution of the Company." The agreement also stated that the "dissolution of a member or occurrence of any other event that terminates the continued membership of a member in the Company shall not cause the dissolution of the Company." Xpert had a 36-month contract with one of its key clients, Samsung, which was to renew annually unless terminated by either party. Eventually, disagreements arose between Robertson (P) and Tignor (D) about the management and distribution of company assets. Dunbar, Robertson (P) and Xpert (collectively "Dunbar") (P) filed suit seeking Tignor's (D) expulsion, asserting numerous allegations of Tignor's (D) misconduct, including Tignor's (D) commingling of Xpert's funds with those of X-tel. Tignor (D), in turn, sought judicial dissolution of Xpert, asserting that it was not reasonably practicable to carry on Xpert's business in conformity with its articles and operating agreement because the company was deadlocked in its ability to conduct its business affairs. The actions were consolidated, and the trial court found that Tignor (D) had indeed commingled Xpert's funds with X-tel's; had authorized a change in the status of Xpert's checking account without informing Robertson (P); restricted Robertson's (P) access to equipment that impacted Xpert's ability to timely fulfill orders

and impacted the quality of the company's products; terminated Robertson's access to his Xpert email account; and had committed other misconduct that was contrary to Xpert's best interest and adversely affected its ability to carry on its business. Determining that Tignor's (D) conduct warranted immediate expulsion under the state's LLC statute, the trial court order Tignor's (D) expulsion. In addition, however, the court ordered that Xpert be dissolved after its contract with Samsung terminated. In doing so, the trial court did not consider the evidence in light of the fact that Tignor (D) was being expelled. Dunbar (P) appealed the portion of the court's order dissolving Xpert. The state's highest court granted review.

ISSUE: Will an LLC be judicially dissolved where there has not been a showing that it will not be reasonably practicable to carry on the LLC's business?

HOLDING AND DECISION: (Keenan, J.) No. An LLC will not be judicially dissolved where there has not been a showing that it will not be reasonably practicable to carry on the LLC's business. As per the state's LLC statute, judicial dissolution may be decreed only "if it is not reasonably practicable to carry on the business in conformity with the articles of organization and any operating agreement." This statutory language is unambiguous, so its plain meaning will be applied. Here, the trial court did not evaluate the evidence in light of the fact that Tignor (D) would be expelled as a member and manager. Because Tignor's (D) conduct had created numerous problems in Xpert's management, his being relegated to a more passive role of mere investor could ameliorate those problems, and there was no showing that it would not be reasonably practicable for Xpert to carry on its business pursuant to its operating authority. Moreover, even the trial court's order shows that the trial court believed Xpert could continue to operate for an extended period of time, since dissolution was to follow the termination of the Samsung contract—which ostensibly could have gone on for years. Accordingly, the evidence was insufficient to support such a judicial dissolution. Affirmed as to Tignor's (D) expulsion. Reversed as to dissolution of Xpert. Final judgment entered.

▶ ANALYSIS

The statutory standard for dissolution of an LLC is a strict one, reflecting legislative deference to the parties' contractual agreement. While a board or management deadlock that prevents an LLC from operating or from furthering its

Continued on next page.

stated business will usually be held to mean that it is not reasonably practicable for the company to carry on its business, here, the court implies that the expulsion of Tignor (D) from management will prevent any such deadlock going forward.

■■■

Quicknotes

COMMINGLED ASSETS The combining of money or property into a joint account or asset.

DISSOLUTION Annulment or termination of a formal or legal bond, tie or contract.

LIMITED LIABILITY COMPANY A business entity combining the features of both a corporation and a general partnership; the LLC provides its shareholders and officers with limited liability, but it is treated as a partnership for taxation purposes.

■■■

Poore v. Fox Hollow Enterprises

[Parties not identified.]

Del. Super. Ct., 1994 WL 150872 (1994).

NATURE OF CASE: Motion to strike answering brief.

FACT SUMMARY: Poore (P) attempted to strike Fox Hollow's (D) answering brief on the basis that a limited liability company could not appear in a Delaware court without representation by counsel.

🏛 RULE OF LAW
The formation of a limited liability company creates a separate legal entity that must be represented by legal counsel in court.

FACTS: Poore (P) filed a motion to strike Fox Hollow's (D) answering brief on the basis that Fox Hollow (D) failed to properly file an answer to her complaint. Campbell, who appeared in court to represent Fox Hollow (D) and drafted the answering brief, admitted that he was not licensed to practice law in Delaware. However, he claimed that because of Fox Hollow's (D) status as a limited liability company, representation by a licensed attorney was not required.

ISSUE: Does the formation of a limited liability company create a separate legal entity that must be represented by legal counsel in court?

HOLDING AND DECISION: (Steele, J.) Yes. The formation of a limited liability company creates a separate legal entity that must be represented by legal counsel in court. Under Delaware law, the general rule is that a corporation cannot appear in court without appropriate representation. The rationale for this rule is that a corporation is an artificial entity, and not a natural person, which must act through its agents. Thus, the corporation cannot avail itself of the same right that a natural person has to represent himself in court though he may not be a licensed attorney. The limited liability company is a business enterprise created to combine the most advantageous features of both a partnership and a corporation. The limited liability company enjoys the tax benefits of a partnership as well as the limited liability of a corporation. However, the limited liability company conducts its operations as a distinct legal entity. It demonstrates the features of centralized management, and its members are analogous to shareholders in their limited liability to the corporation up to the amount of their investment. Due to these similarities, the legislature did not contemplate that a limited liability company would appear in court without representation of counsel. Motion granted.

▶ ANALYSIS

The limited liability company (LLC) is an alternative business enterprise that combines the most advantageous features of both a general partnership and a corporation. It enjoys the corporation's advantage of limited liability while its members also enjoy the favorable tax treatment of a partnership. The LLC provides great flexibility of form so that its owners may choose to structure the entity as either a general partnership, with its members participating equally, or as a corporation, with centralized management and limited participation of its members.

■═■

Quicknotes

LIMITED LIABILITY COMPANY A business entity combining the features of both a corporation and a general partnership; the LLC provides its shareholders and officers with limited liability, but it is treated as a partnership for taxation purposes.

■═■

Glossary

Common Latin Words and Phrases Encountered in the Law

A FORTIORI: Because one fact exists or has been proven, therefore a second fact that is related to the first fact must also exist.

A PRIORI: From the cause to the effect. A term of logic used to denote that when one generally accepted truth is shown to be a cause, another particular effect must necessarily follow.

AB INITIO: From the beginning; a condition which has existed throughout, as in a marriage which was void ab initio.

ACTUS REUS: The wrongful act; in criminal law, such action sufficient to trigger criminal liability.

AD VALOREM: According to value; an ad valorem tax is imposed upon an item located within the taxing jurisdiction calculated by the value of such item.

AMICUS CURIAE: Friend of the court. Its most common usage takes the form of an amicus curiae brief, filed by a person who is not a party to an action but is nonetheless allowed to offer an argument supporting his legal interests.

ARGUENDO: In arguing. A statement, possibly hypothetical, made for the purpose of argument, is one made arguendo.

BILL QUIA TIMET: A bill to quiet title (establish ownership) to real property.

BONA FIDE: True, honest, or genuine. May refer to a person's legal position based on good faith or lacking notice of fraud (such as a bona fide purchaser for value) or to the authenticity of a particular document (such as a bona fide last will and testament).

CAUSA MORTIS: With approaching death in mind. A gift causa mortis is a gift given by a party who feels certain that death is imminent.

CAVEAT EMPTOR: Let the buyer beware. This maxim is reflected in the rule of law that a buyer purchases at his own risk because it is his responsibility to examine, judge, test, and otherwise inspect what he is buying.

CERTIORARI: A writ of review. Petitions for review of a case by the United States Supreme Court are most often done by means of a writ of certiorari.

CONTRA: On the other hand. Opposite. Contrary to.

CORAM NOBIS: Before us; writs of error directed to the court that originally rendered the judgment.

CORAM VOBIS: Before you; writs of error directed by an appellate court to a lower court to correct a factual error.

CORPUS DELICTI: The body of the crime; the requisite elements of a crime amounting to objective proof that a crime has been committed.

CUM TESTAMENTO ANNEXO, ADMINISTRATOR (ADMINISTRATOR C.T.A.): With will annexed; an administrator c.t.a. settles an estate pursuant to a will in which he is not appointed.

DE BONIS NON, ADMINISTRATOR (ADMINISTRATOR D.B.N.): Of goods not administered; an administrator d.b.n. settles a partially settled estate.

DE FACTO: In fact; in reality; actually. Existing in fact but not officially approved or engendered.

DE JURE: By right; lawful. Describes a condition that is legitimate "as a matter of law," in contrast to the term "de facto," which connotes something existing in fact but not legally sanctioned or authorized. For example, de facto segregation refers to segregation brought about by housing patterns, etc., whereas de jure segregation refers to segregation created by law.

DE MINIMIS: Of minimal importance; insignificant; a trifle; not worth bothering about.

DE NOVO: Anew; a second time; afresh. A trial de novo is a new trial held at the appellate level as if the case originated there and the trial at a lower level had not taken place.

DICTA: Generally used as an abbreviated form of obiter dicta, a term describing those portions of a judicial opinion incidental or not necessary to resolution of the specific question before the court. Such nonessential statements and remarks are not considered to be binding precedent.

DUCES TECUM: Refers to a particular type of writ or subpoena requesting a party or organization to produce certain documents in their possession.

EN BANC: Full bench. Where a court sits with all justices present rather than the usual quorum.

EX PARTE: For one side or one party only. An ex parte proceeding is one undertaken for the benefit of only one party, without notice to, or an appearance by, an adverse party.

EX POST FACTO: After the fact. An ex post facto law is a law that retroactively changes the consequences of a prior act.

EX REL.: Abbreviated form of the term "ex relatione," meaning upon relation or information. When the state brings an action in which it has no interest against an individual at the instigation of one who has a private interest in the matter.

FORUM NON CONVENIENS: Inconvenient forum. Although a court may have jurisdiction over the case, the action should be tried in a more conveniently located court, one to which parties and witnesses may more easily travel, for example.

GUARDIAN AD LITEM: A guardian of an infant as to litigation, appointed to represent the infant and pursue his/her rights.

HABEAS CORPUS: You have the body. The modern writ of habeas corpus is a writ directing that a person (body) being detained (such as a prisoner) be brought before the court so that the legality of his detention can be judicially ascertained.

IN CAMERA: In private, in chambers. When a hearing is held before a judge in his chambers or when all spectators are excluded from the courtroom.

IN FORMA PAUPERIS: In the manner of a pauper. A party who proceeds in forma pauperis because of his poverty is one who is allowed to bring suit without liability for costs.

INFRA: Below, under. A word referring the reader to a later part of a book. (The opposite of supra.)

IN LOCO PARENTIS: In the place of a parent.

IN PARI DELICTO: Equally wrong; a court of equity will not grant requested relief to an applicant who is in pari delicto, or as much at fault in the transactions giving rise to the controversy as is the opponent of the applicant.

IN PARI MATERIA: On like subject matter or upon the same matter. Statutes relating to the same person or things are said to be in pari materia. It is a general rule of statutory construction that such statutes should be construed together, i.e., looked at as if they together constituted one law.

IN PERSONAM: Against the person. Jurisdiction over the person of an individual.

IN RE: In the matter of. Used to designate a proceeding involving an estate or other property.

IN REM: A term that signifies an action against the res, or thing. An action in rem is basically one that is taken directly against property, as distinguished from an action in personam, i.e., against the person.

INTER ALIA: Among other things. Used to show that the whole of a statement, pleading, list, statute, etc., has not been set forth in its entirety.

INTER PARTES: Between the parties. May refer to contracts, conveyances or other transactions having legal significance.

INTER VIVOS: Between the living. An inter vivos gift is a gift made by a living grantor, as distinguished from bequests contained in a will, which pass upon the death of the testator.

IPSO FACTO: By the mere fact itself.

JUS: Law or the entire body of law.

LEX LOCI: The law of the place; the notion that the rights of parties to a legal proceeding are governed by the law of the place where those rights arose.

MALUM IN SE: Evil or wrong in and of itself; inherently wrong. This term describes an act that is wrong by its very nature, as opposed to one which would not be wrong but for the fact that there is a specific legal prohibition against it (malum prohibitum).

MALUM PROHIBITUM: Wrong because prohibited, but not inherently evil. Used to describe something that is wrong because it is expressly forbidden by law but that is not in and of itself evil, e.g., speeding.

MANDAMUS: We command. A writ directing an official to take a certain action.

MENS REA: A guilty mind; a criminal intent. A term used to signify the mental state that accompanies a crime or other prohibited act. Some crimes require only a general mens rea (general intent to do the prohibited act), but others, like assault with intent to murder, require the existence of a specific mens rea.

MODUS OPERANDI: Method of operating; generally refers to the manner or style of a criminal in committing crimes, admissible in appropriate cases as evidence of the identity of a defendant.

NEXUS: A connection to.

NISI PRIUS: A court of first impression. A nisi prius court is one where issues of fact are tried before a judge or jury.

N.O.V. (NON OBSTANTE VEREDICTO): Notwithstanding the verdict. A judgment n.o.v. is a judgment given in favor of one party despite the fact that a verdict was returned in favor of the other party, the justification being that the verdict either had no reasonable support in fact or was contrary to law.

NUNC PRO TUNC: Now for then. This phrase refers to actions that may be taken and will then have full retroactive effect.

PENDENTE LITE: Pending the suit; pending litigation under way.

PER CAPITA: By head; beneficiaries of an estate, if they take in equal shares, take per capita.

PER CURIAM: By the court; signifies an opinion ostensibly written "by the whole court" and with no identified author.

PER SE: By itself, in itself; inherently.

PER STIRPES: By representation. Used primarily in the law of wills to describe the method of distribution where a person, generally because of death, is unable to take that which is left to him by the will of another, and therefore his heirs divide such property between them rather than take under the will individually.

PRIMA FACIE: On its face, at first sight. A prima facie case is one that is sufficient on its face, meaning that the evidence supporting it is adequate to establish the case until contradicted or overcome by other evidence.

PRO TANTO: For so much; as far as it goes. Often used in eminent domain cases when a property owner receives partial payment for his land without prejudice to his right to bring suit for the full amount he claims his land to be worth.

QUANTUM MERUIT: As much as he deserves. Refers to recovery based on the doctrine of unjust enrichment in those cases in which a party has rendered valuable services or furnished materials that were accepted and enjoyed by another under circumstances that would reasonably notify the recipient that the rendering party expected to be paid. In essence, the law implies a contract to pay the reasonable value of the services or materials furnished.

QUASI: Almost like; as if; nearly. This term is essentially used to signify that one subject or thing is almost analogous to another but that material differences between them do exist. For example, a quasi-criminal proceeding is one that is not strictly criminal but shares enough of the same characteristics to require some of the same safeguards (e.g., procedural due process must be followed in a parole hearing).

QUID PRO QUO: Something for something. In contract law, the consideration, something of value, passed between the parties to render the contract binding.

RES GESTAE: Things done; in evidence law, this principle justifies the admission of a statement that would otherwise be hearsay when it is made so closely to the event in question as to be said to be a part of it, or with such spontaneity as not to have the possibility of falsehood.

RES IPSA LOQUITUR: The thing speaks for itself. This doctrine gives rise to a rebuttable presumption of negligence when the instrumentality causing the injury was within the exclusive control of the defendant, and the injury was one that does not normally occur unless a person has been negligent.

RES JUDICATA: A matter adjudged. Doctrine which provides that once a court of competent jurisdiction has rendered a final judgment or decree on the merits, that judgment or decree is conclusive upon the parties to the case and prevents them from engaging in any other litigation on the points and issues determined therein.

RESPONDEAT SUPERIOR: Let the master reply. This doctrine holds the master liable for the wrongful acts of his servant (or the principal for his agent) in those cases in which the servant (or agent) was acting within the scope of his authority at the time of the injury.

STARE DECISIS: To stand by or adhere to that which has been decided. The common law doctrine of stare decisis attempts to give security and certainty to the law by following the policy that once a principle of law as applicable to a certain set of facts has been set forth in a decision, it forms a precedent which will subsequently be followed, even though a different decision might be made were it the first time the question had arisen. Of course, stare decisis is not an inviolable principle and is departed from in instances where there is good cause (e.g., considerations of public policy led the Supreme Court to disregard prior decisions sanctioning segregation).

SUPRA: Above. A word referring a reader to an earlier part of a book.

ULTRA VIRES: Beyond the power. This phrase is most commonly used to refer to actions taken by a corporation that are beyond the power or legal authority of the corporation.

Addendum of French Derivatives

IN PAIS: Not pursuant to legal proceedings.

CHATTEL: Tangible personal property.

CY PRES: Doctrine permitting courts to apply trust funds to purposes not expressed in the trust but necessary to carry out the settlor's intent.

PER AUTRE VIE: For another's life; during another's life. In property law, an estate may be granted that will terminate upon the death of someone other than the grantee.

PROFIT A PRENDRE: A license to remove minerals or other produce from land.

VOIR DIRE: Process of questioning jurors as to their predispositions about the case or parties to a proceeding in order to identify those jurors displaying bias or prejudice.